"In the new *When the Soul Remembers Itself*, th
Ancient Greece, Modern Psyche, Singer and co-au
dreams and parallel Olympian worlds from beyond the ancient looking glass.
Never before as well presented and discussed, the work is a brilliant collection of
Jungian reflections upon our modern condition."

> **– Peter and Ileana Nomikos, The Petros M. Nomikos
> Conference Centre, Santorini, Greece**

"Filtered through their classical scholarship and training in Analytical Psychology,
the authors of *When the Soul Remembers Itself* articulate the mystery of how and
why the world of ancient Greece *still* offers a meaningful way for modern men and
women to make sense of the concerns, fears and ponderings about our common
human condition and our place in the cosmos. This outstanding and unique volume is both timely and timeless in exploring the imaginal world shared by ancient
Greece and modern psyche."

> **– Baruch Gould, Emeritus Director of External
> Education, C. G. Jung Institute of
> San Francisco, USA**

"I danced with these authors in a collective 'rhythmo.' This is a wonderful work
for the many people curious about the continuum between ancient Greece
and modern psyche. Greek myth shows us what the soul has always yearned
for. Today's fragmented and uprooted Greek society can find rebalancing and
reparation from its classical era. The book demonstrates that the transgenerational crimes with which mythology is preoccupied also play out in today's
suffering world and nature."

> **– Sissy Lykou, lecturer in psychotherapy, Regents University,
> and dance movement psychotherapist, UK**

WHEN THE SOUL REMEMBERS ITSELF

Do the ancient Greek poets, playwrights, philosophers and mythologies have anything to say to modern human beings? Is their time finished, or do their insights have as much relevance to the human condition as they did 2,500 years ago? *When the Soul Remembers Itself* continues the exploration of the connections between ancient and modern psyche with a resounding affirmation of its ongoing relevance.

Uniquely combining poetry, drama and storytelling in a pioneering collection, an international selection of contributors each explore a character, myth or theme from ancient Greece in the context of its relevance to the modern psyche. Each author enters an imaginative dialogue that pieces and bridges together fragments of the past with the present, exploring themes such as initiation, war, love, paranoia, tragedy and the soul's journey through the vicissitudes of life on earth, through characters such as Ajax, Persephone, Orpheus, Electra, the Apostle Paul, Perpetua and Jocasta. Understanding myth is crucial in Jungian analysis, and by connecting the modern person with the age-old questions of life and death, the contributors bring truly archetypal narratives to life and speak to the human condition throughout the ages.

When the Soul Remembers Itself will be of great interest to academics and students of Jungian and post-Jungian studies, classics, ancient religion, archetypal studies and mythology. As the contributors' conclusions apply to both contemporary theory and clinical practice, it will also appeal to Jungian analysts and psychotherapists in practice and training.

Thomas Singer is a psychiatrist and Jungian psychoanalyst with interests in symbolic imagery, cultural studies and the relationships between ancient Greece and modern psyche. He has written and edited many books and articles with most recent emphasis on the relationship between politics, the collective psyche and mythology. He is co-editor of *Ancient Greece, Modern Psyche: Archetypes Evolving* (Routledge).

Jules Cashford is a Jungian analyst and the author of previous books on Greek mythology, including a translation of *The Homeric Hymns*.

Craig San Roque is an analytical psychologist who has lived in remote Central Australia for over twenty-five years. He writes on complex cultural matters and indigenous Australian affairs.

WHEN THE SOUL REMEMBERS ITSELF

Ancient Greece, Modern Psyche

Edited by Thomas Singer, Jules Cashford and Craig San Roque

Routledge
Taylor & Francis Group

LONDON AND NEW YORK

First published 2019
by Routledge
2 Park Square, Milton Park, Abingdon, Oxon OX14 4RN

and by Routledge
52 Vanderbilt Avenue, New York, NY 10017

Routledge is an imprint of the Taylor & Francis Group, an informa business

British Library Cataloguing-in-Publication Data
A catalogue record for this book is available from the British Library

Library of Congress Cataloging-in-Publication Data
A catalog record has been requested for this book

ISBN: 978-1-138-31072-8 (hbk)
ISBN: 978-1-138-31075-9 (pbk)
ISBN: 978-0-429-45925-2 (ebk)

Typeset in Bembo
by Swales & Willis Ltd, Exeter, Devon, UK

CONTENTS

SYNOPSIS

A young artist says, "We don't need those old myths; we make up our own."

True – and the sung poetry of the world, what of that?

"We speak Digital . . ."

And the sagas of Iceland, Africa, ancient Greece, these will you forget?

"We have outrun them."

And the knowledge of human behavior; the cause of war, the birth of paranoia, the mother hanging above the bed in Thebes, the folly of men, the women silenced . . . the making of the mind, the songs of beauty . . . Would you remember this?

"True," she says, "Some things seem eternal. Some things are worth remembering."

And here is the point of this book –

Do the ancient Greek poets, playwrights, philosophers and mythologies have anything to say to modern human beings? Is their time finished, or do their insights have as much relevance to the human condition as they did 2,500 years ago?

This third volume in the Ancient Greece, Modern Psyche series continues the exploration of the connections between ancient and modern psyche – with a resounding affirmation of ongoing relevance.

Minoan art, Plato's Cave, Orpheus, Ajax, Jocasta, Dionysos, Persephone, Electra, Aeschylus and the present state of Greece, all gathered up in a net for you – and as a special treat – ninety images and film clips digitally linked to the Archive for Research in Archetypal Symbolism for your consideration.

"Cool," she says.

To Baruch Gould

The secret and magical ingredient to every success we have had in the three Ancient Greece, Modern Psyche conferences is BARUCH GOULD. Unflappable, endlessly gracious and seamlessly competent, Baruch has been responsible for all the details of organization and problem solving that go into arranging an international conference. Baruch is not only incredibly efficient, he is also kind. He performs his work in the background with good humor and wisdom. For all these reasons and many more, we dedicate this book to Baruch Gould.

To Virginia Beane Rutter

Virginia transformed many lives through her joyous and generous love. She shared that same love in her dedication to realizing the Ancient Greece, Modern Psyche series.

FIGURES

EDITORS

Thomas Singer, MD, is a Jungian analyst and psychiatrist who narrated his mythological tale of building a house on a Greek island at the first Ancient Greece, Modern Psyche conference and moderated the second conference. He continued his storytelling and moderating at the third conference. After studying religion and European literature at Princeton University, he graduated from Yale Medical School and later trained at Dartmouth Medical Center and the C. G. Jung Institute of San Francisco. His writing includes articles on Jungian theory, politics and psychology, and his recent books include *The Vision Thing: Myth, Politics and Psyche in the World* (2000); *The Cultural Complex: Contemporary Jungian Perspectives on Psyche and Society* (2004), with Samuel L. Kimbles; *Initiation: The Living Reality of an Archetype* (2007), with Thomas Kirsch and Virginia Beane Rutter; *Psyche and the City: A Soul's Guide to the Modern Metropolis* (2010); *Ancient Greece, Modern Psyche: Archetypes in the Making* (2011), with Virginia Beane Rutter; and *Ancient Greece, Modern Psyche: Archetypes Evolving* (2015), also with Virginia Beane Rutter. His newest books, *Placing Psyche: Exploring the Cultural Complexes of Australia* (2011), *Listening to Latin America* (2012) and *Europe's Many Souls* (2016), explore cultural complexes.

Jules Cashford, MA, studied philosophy at St. Andrews and graduate literature at Cambridge, where she was a supervisor on tragedy for some years. She then trained as a Jungian analyst with the Association of Jungian Analysts in London. At the last Santorini conference in 2012 she gave a talk on "*The Homeric Hymn to Hermes*: How Hermes and Apollo came to love each other." Her books include *The Myth of the Goddess: Evolution of an Image* (1993), with Anne Baring; *The Moon: Symbol of Transformation* (2003, 2016); *The Homeric Hymns: A Translation* (2003); *The Mysteries of Osiris* (2010); *Gaia: From Story of Origin to Universe Story* (2012); and many booklets on myth and symbolism. She contributed to *Europe's Many Souls*, edited by Tom Singer and Joerg Rasche, and has made two films on Jan van Eyck, the Early Northern Renaissance painter – *The Mystery of Jan van Eyck* and *The Mystic Lamb* – and described the making of the films in the Archive for Research in Archetypal Symbolism (March 2013). She now writes and lectures on mythology, and has long had a fascination with the culture and tradition of Greek and Egyptian mysteries and how their insights may inform our understanding of the psyche.

Craig San Roque, PhD, is a Jungian analyst living in Central Australia, where he works as a community psychologist in Aboriginal affairs. At the 2012 Ancient Greece, Modern Psyche conference he presented *Kore Story/Persephone's Dog*, a version of the Demeter/Persephone narrative influenced by an Australian sense of place and Greek mythopoetics. Over thirty years, Craig has facilitated a spectrum of theatre performances and workshops exploring classical mythological heritage. His publications on psychological and cultural themes include contributions to four books edited by Thomas Singer and others on complex psychocultural themes: *The Vision Thing: Myth, Politics and Psyche in the World* (2000); *The Cultural Complex: Contemporary Jungian Perspectives on Psyche and Society* (2004); *Psyche and the City* (2010); and *Placing Psyche: Exploring the Cultural Complexes of Australia*, which he also co-edited (2011). He is co-creator with Josh Santospirito of the evocative graphic novel *The Long Weekend in Alice Springs*.

CONTRIBUTORS

Eve Jackson, MA, is a semiretired training analyst and member of the Independent Group of Analytical Psychologists. She worked for many years in private practice in London and has taught regularly in the Independent Group of Analytical Psychologists (IGAP) Studies Program for more than twenty years, as well as lecturing throughout the United Kingdom and at the C. G. Jung Institute Zurich. She has also given Jungian seminars in Athens, Greece. She has published three books – two on astrology and one on Jungian psychology, *Food and Transformation: Imagery and Symbolism of Eating* (1996) – and *Eating and Communion*, a pamphlet produced by the Guild of Pastoral Psychology, London, as well as a number of articles and book reviews in *Harvest*, the journal of the C. G. Jung Analytical Psychology Club, London. She is also a teacher of taiji and qigong, which she took up soon after starting analysis – the embodiment of psyche is consequently a long-term preoccupation. Her connections with Greece go back more than fifty years, beginning with an unforgettable summer visit at the age of nineteen. Some years later she completed a postgraduate thesis in comparative literature at Oxford University, which involved studying twentieth-century Greek poetry in Athens.

Tamar Kron, PhD, is a clinical psychologist and Jungian analyst. She studied clinical psychology at the Hebrew University of Jerusalem, where she also taught for many years. She is a training analyst with the Israeli Institute for Jungian Psychology and is Professor Emeritus of the Hebrew University. She initiated a research project on the dreams of people living in a state of continuous stress from rocket attacks. Tamar is the author of seven books, including *Women in Pink: The Motherhood Wound in Postpartum Depression* (1989) and *The Archetypal Couple* (2012), as well as two books on supervision. She has also published three novels. Her many articles include "Can dreams during pregnancy predict postpartum depression?" with A. Brosh, in *Dreaming*, 2003, 13(2); "Psychotherapists' dreams about their patients," with N. Avni, in *The Journal of Analytical Psychology*, 2003, 48(3); and "Helpless heroes: The dreams of men in the shadow of continuous life-threatening missile attacks," with O. Hareven, in *Montreal 2010 Proceedings, Facing Multiplicity: Psyche, Nature, Culture*, 2012. Her chapter "Dreaming under fire" is included in *Research in Analytical Psychology*, edited by Christian Roesler and Joe Cambray, *Vol. I: Empirical Research* (edited by Christian Roesler), in press with Routledge.

Joerg Rasche, psychiatrist, Jungian analyst and sandplay therapist (ISST), studied in Berlin and Zurich with Dora Kalff. He is a president of the German Jungian Association (DGAP) and the German Society for Sandplay Therapy (DGST) and was vice president of the International Association of Analytical Psychology (IAAP). He is also a trained musician. His interests are in mythology, culture and politics. He has published many articles and books, such as *The Song of the Green Lion: Music as a Mirror of the Soul* (in German) and, with Thomas Singer, *Europe's Many Souls: Exploring Cultural Complexes and Identities* (2016). He is engaged in Jungian training in Eastern European countries and lives in Berlin, is married and has three adult children.

Virginia Beane Rutter, MA, MS, was a Jungian analyst who passed away in March 2016. She trained at the C. G. Jung Institutes of Zurich and San Francisco. Her first master's degree in art history, taken at the University of California, Berkeley, together with an early sustaining love of Greece, developed into a passion for studying ancient myths and rites of passage through art, archaeology and psychology. These studies grew out of her clinical practice and coalesced around archetypal themes of initiation as they manifest in the unconscious material of women and men today. She is the author of three books, including *Woman Changing Woman: Feminine Psychology Re-Conceived Through Myth and Experience* (1993, 2009). Her most recent work includes "The archetypal paradox of feminine initiation in analytic work," in *Initiation: The Living Reality of An Archetype* (2007); "Saffron blessings and blood sacrifice: Transformation mysteries in Jungian analysis," in *Ancient Greece, Modern Psyche: Archetypes in the Making* (2011); and "The hero who would not die: Warrior and goddess in ancient Greek and modern men," in *Ancient Greece, Modern Psyche: Archetypes Evolving* (2014).

Craig E. Stephenson, PhD, is a graduate of the C. G. Jung Institute Zurich, the Institut für Psychodrama auf der Grundlage der Jungschen Psychologie, Zumikon and the Centre for Psychoanalytic Studies, University of Essex. His books include *Possession: Jung's Comparative Anatomy of the Psyche* (2009/2016), *Anteros: A Forgotten Myth* (2011), *Jung and Moreno: Essays on the Theatre of Human Nature* (2013) and *Ages of Anxiety* (2015). For the Philemon Foundation, he edited *On Psychological and Visionary Art: Notes from C. G. Jung's Lecture on Gérard de Nerval's Aurélia* (2015). He is director of training at the Jungian Psychoanalytic Association (JPA) and has a private practice as a licensed psychoanalyst (LP) in New York City.

Evangelos Tsempelis is an analyst who lives and practices in Zurich. He is a cofounder of Stillpoint Spaces (www.stillpointspaces.com). He has a background in history and international relations and is particularly interested in integrating psy-choanalytic theory and practice in his personal quest to better understand our time and the suffering associated with it.

Luigi Zoja, PhD, is a former training analyst of the C. G. Jung Institute Zurich, and past president of the Centro Italiano di Psicologia Analitica (CIPA). He is also the former president of the International Association of Analytical Psychology (IAAP). He has taught at the School of Psychiatry of the Faculty of Medicine, State University of Palermo, and at the University of Insubria, and was a visiting professor at the Beijing Normal University and at the University of Macao. His clinical practice began in Zurich, followed by a private practice in Milan, then in New York, and, at present, again in Milan. He holds a Diploma in Analytical Psychology from the C. G. Jung Institute Zurich. He is the author of several books in English, including *Drugs, Addiction and Initiation* (1989, 2000); *Growth and Guilt* (1995); *The Father* (2001), which also won the Gradiva Award in 2001; *The Global Nightmare: Jungian Perspectives on September 11* (2002); *Cultivating the Soul* (2005); *Ethics and Analysis* (2007), which also won the Gradiva Award in 2008; and *Violence in History, Culture and the Psyche* (2009).

ACKNOWLEDGMENTS

Peter Nomikos and family

Peter Nomikos and his family have opened the doors of their magnificent Nomikos Conference Centre at the edge of the Santorini caldera to the three Ancient Greece, Modern Psyche conferences. The spaces are both intimate and grand; the views of the Aegean and the town of Thera are incomparable. The Nomikos καλοσύνη (kindness) and φιλοξενία (love of strangers or foreigners) are deep and genuine. Without their generosity, neither the three conferences, nor the three books that grew out of the conferences, would exist. We are immensely grateful.

LeeAnn Pickrell

We are deeply indebted to LeeAnn Pickrell whose skills include and go well beyond copy-editing. It is no easy task to track the work of multiple authors and editors. Managing the flow of communications between authors and editors, exercising impeccable taste and good judgement in what works and doesn't, and pulling the whole project together to send off to the publisher requires a discipline and attention to detail that few in today's world seem to cultivate. LeeAnn is simply the best!

Academic acknowledgments

Material in Chapter 2 from "The Mysteries" (VI) by H.D. (Hilda Doolittle), from *Collected Poems*, 1912–1944, copyright © 1982 by The Estate of Hilda Doolittle. Reprinted by permission of New Directions Publishing Corp.

Chapter 3, "The madness of Ajax," was originally published in *Paranoia: The Madness that Makes History* by Luigi Zoja, pp. 1-8 (Routledge, 2017) and appears here by permission of Taylor & Francis.

INTRODUCTION

Thomas Singer, Jules Cashford, and
Craig San Roque

Thomas Singer: origins

In the early 1970s I traveled to a much different Santorini than one finds today. It had not yet become an international tourist destination that now feels a bit like a futuristic space station from another galaxy. I especially remember waiting at a windswept, barren bus stop in the middle of nowhere, reading Doris Lessing's *Briefing for a Descent into Hell*, a magnificent tale of the soul's preparation for bodily incarnation and then its descent into earthly existence in which it forgets itself. Coupled with that memory is that of the only lines of poetry that I ever seem to be able to recall, which I first read in Greece in 1964. They are the first lines of George Seferis's "Argonauts" in which he quotes from Plato's *Alcibiades*:

> And if the soul
> is to know itself
> it must look
> into a soul

The title of this book, *When the Soul Remember Itself: Ancient Greece, Modern Psyche*, has its origins in these two highly specific memories, both of which connect the soul's journey with Greece. It is no accident that this volume of essays, based on the 2017 Ancient Greece, Modern Psyche conference held in Santorini at the glorious Nomikos Conference Centre, focuses on the soul's forgetting and remembering itself in both ancient and modern Greece. The ancient Greeks knew well and modern citizens know well the experience of forgetting the soul, of losing the soul, of the fragmentation of soul, of the dismemberment of soul. And both have felt the urgent need to remember, to gather together the soul's scattered and fragmented pieces. This book is a small effort in that remembering and gathering together of the fragmented pieces that litter our landscape. Each author enters into an imaginative dialogue between what the meaning of the ancient myth might have been and its relations to our modern psyches. Santorini, too, as one of the sacred places of the world, must also wrestle with forgetting and remembering its soul.

Craig San Roque: on cultural recognition

Being human is a venture in relationships. The practice of psychotherapy is also a venture in relationships. Those relationships include the connection of ourselves with the human cultural and sociopolitical genealogies in which we float – or in which many of our ancestors have drowned. And burned.

The cultural patterns of Europe and the European colonies have been signifi-cantly influenced by what has gone on within the Mediterranean region since the days of the Neanderthal and Cro-Magnon peoples – perhaps 40,000 or more years ago. The Mediterranean peoples who settled, fought, built, loved, and died within those regions have formed part of the social, emotional, and mental heritage of the European peoples. The Mediterranean Sea has been the trading pool of Europe, Africa, and Asia. It has been the mixing bowl of civilizations and continues thus. Among those first peoples are those who have, in a simplistic generalization, been named as "the Greeks" – but what is a Greek? This question hovers over every line in Evangelos Tsempelis's chapter and threads its way through each of the chapters, as the writers contemplate how ancient Greece influences his or her "modern psy-che." The debt to Greece is huge.

And yes, there is justified criticism to be made of writers who romance the Greeks or strain to adapt myth to clinical circumstances, as though it were part of a bigger project to prove "ancient myth" equals "primal patterns" equals "keys to therapy." A critique of such simplistic pattern matching could well be taken up here, but I prefer to recognize the positive usefulness of the narrative rep-ertoire of humanity. In particular, for this book, we recognize the repertoire of the Mediterranean peoples as it has come down to us through the languages and iconographies of the Minoans, the Mycenaeans, the Hellenic Greeks, with all their fertile predecessors and successors – acknowledging the influences from north, south, east, and west that came to form the great story net of Grecian civilization.

A recognition of cultural perspective and a working knowledge of the reper-toire of cultural stories of the world are essential for the education of therapists and all citizens (I would say). This recognition acknowledges the multicultural diver-sity that is now a part of our shifting contemporary civilizations. Many schools and universities encourage the understanding of diverse myth in order to encour-age tolerance and understanding of the way different peoples think and imagine. Facility with mythic thinking may also open up "right-brain" intuitive capacities and encourage skill in handling contradiction. A flexible neuroplastic brain is a useful brain to cultivate. Mental flexibility is a handy skill for a modern psyche to acquire.

It is notable that much contemporary practice (in so many fields) is dictated by one-sided rationalistic methodologies and a Euro/American conceptual orientation, as though the cultural perceptions of the rest of the world – including the indigenous past and present – have no value. Being an Australian, embedded in Australian Aboriginal affairs, I am witness to how rapidly the indigenous cultural stories and practices that sustained life and relationships in our country are being eroded and subsumed into a dominant (and invasive) Anglo/American language and sensibility. I presume similar situations of mental domination are in train elsewhere and that "psychic cultural invasion" is one of the causes of mental distress and disorder among many peoples who are compelled to move into and adapt to a contemporary urban way of life. The modern psyche is under a lot of pressure.

I see this book series, the Santorini conferences, and the Archive for Research in Archetypal Symbolism (ARAS) as part of a gracious and serious project that acknowledges human history; that acknowledges the spirit, intelligence, illusions, and the perceptions of our predecessors. These were people who wrapped their thinking into intensely dramatic mythopoetic narratives – narratives that exist in the present in a timeless way.

Although it is true that "Hollywood" exploits mythic heroes or mythic themes to make big movies full of sound, fury, and world salvation, the Ancient Greece, Modern Psyche project is more intimate and more intricate and works within the complexities of our (mostly) Mediterranean heritage. There are other tales to tell, but Greece has been our focus. So far.

The Ancient Greece, Modern Psyche series is a cultural recognition project.

Jules Cashford: pilgrims to Ithaca

We hope we come not as trespassers but as pilgrims to ancient and modern Greece, bearing our gifts of gratitude for the journey, accepting what the soul sets up in front of us.

Perhaps one of the special delights of meeting in the magical courtyard of the Nomikos Centre, with the wine-dark sea far below, is the community of souls drawn together from distant places around the Earth, gathering to explore our shared inheritance, which we, unknowing, live, as it must live through us, mingling the generations before and after and to come.

Whether we encounter Jocasta or Ajax, Proteus or Plato, Dionysos or Orpheus, and whether we are spellbound in the underworld with Persephone or rooting for Electra, dancing in the Minoan labyrinth, imprisoned in the Cave of Fools, or honoring Paul and the martyr Perpetua singing her hymns in the arena of death, we are rapt in the timeless dream that is myth, which speaks to us of who we are or may be or could become. On awakening, we may mourn the loss of myth in our time – until we remember our nightly dreams when bitter-sweet myths come back to claim us as their own, lest we forget they never really went away.

Let us begin, then, with thanking all the companions of our odyssey.

In the words of C. P. Cavafy in his poem "Ithaka":

> . . . Ithaka gave you the marvelous journey.
> Without her you would not have set out.
> She has nothing left to give you now.
>
> And if you find her poor, Ithaka won't have fooled you.
> Wise as you will have become, so full of experience,
> you will have understood by then what these Ithakas mean.[1]

Dear reader

Because there is a limitation on the number of color images that can be included in a print text, we have created a special arrangement with ARAS (the Archive for Research in Archetypal Symbolism) that permits us to link the reader to many more color images and even film clips that add greatly to the written text. ARAS has graciously set up a special place on their website for the reader to access these images and film clips, which can be reached simply by visiting the URL link indicated at the appropriate places in the text (https://aras. org/ancient-greece-modern-psyche). Once the reader arrives at the ARAS page hosting this feature, he or she will be able to view the specific image or film clip according to chapter location.

FIGURE 0.1 Vimeo link: Ancient Greece, Modern Psyche Speakers, Fiona Walsh (https://aras.org/ancient-greece-modern-psyche)

Note

1 *Collected Poems* by Constantine Cavafy. Reproduced with permission of Princeton University Press in the format book via Copyright Clearance Center.

THE INVOCATIONS

Jules Cashford and Craig San Roque

Calling out/calling in

> *I hear a voice singing my death.*

For a very long time there has been a custom among many peoples that applies when approaching a sacred site or crossing a threshold into a numinous location. Throughout Eurasia, Africa, and the world there are stones, wells, springs, caves, and mountains associated with the presence of holy events, or with beings of mythic history, or with locations of folktale or "divine" intervention – the cave of Orpheus in Thrace; the Hill of Tara in County Meath, Ireland; La Sainte-Baume, a cave above Marseilles dedicated to Mary Magdalene; a place near Thebes where three roads meet; the Dome of the Rock, the Western Wall in Jerusalem . . .

In Australia this threshold custom is also a living practice. Indigenous Australians, on approaching a special site, a valley, a cave, a water source, a towering rock . . . call out the name of whoever or whatever dwells there, reassuring that "phenomenon" that we enter with respect and care. Such respect of presence-in-locality seems so eroded in our present time.

In a similar way (as you might see in the *Homeric Hymns*), no poet would begin a story without first acknowledging and "calling in" the divinity or muse or presence associated with that tale. It is not a good thing to begin to recite as though you yourself were the important one.

There is some wisdom in careful attunement to a site. It is said that hippocampal memory (that seahorse in the brain) aids navigation and memory. Perhaps intimate whispers at the threshold of spatial locations attune the human to who and what might dwell there – attune for danger or for sustainment. And, having crossed a threshold, the receptive brain prepares itself to feel the story and emanations associated with that place. A site can be a link in a network that might sustain a wandering, ungathered modern soul. It is respectful, then, from our place in being and time, to begin this book by acknowledging ancient custodial sites and characters of culture whom you will encounter herein.

This then is an invocation, an acknowledgment of the places, themes, figures of mythic and mental activity who featured in the Nomikos Conference presentations.[1] They are all there and we have taken some care to call out to them, to acknowledge them and their independence.

The volcanic island of Santorini/Thera/Akrotiri has inspired awe for many people for a long time, even though now the place is overwrought with the rattle of suitcase wheels along the streets. We begin in the present with the island and with a line from the Greek poet Odysseas Elytis: "A single flash is man, and who sees, sees."[2]

Thera, Akrotiri (location of volcanic history)

Thera, it was you whose mountain erupted,
you who covered this sky with smoke and ash,
you who unsettled the sea,
disturbed the island people;
you who brought down Knossos
and all the beauty.

You and your history speak.
We catch your words as the sun sets upon us
A net.
Traveler, you love this fragile place?
Take care that you do not destroy it.

FIGURE I.1 The view of the caldera of Santorini from Nomikos Centre

Eumenides (after Aeschylus so long ago)

Daughters of Black Night,
may we call upon you in your homes beneath the Earth,
buried in the brains of humans who call you "Furious?"
You hold the memory of evil, the mind of the past,
that a man might know fear of the law of blood,
that the killing of family is a crime of horror.

Come, Eumenides, be kindly to us in these terrible times,
all of us are guilty, all of us cry out to you,
cast your web upon the Earth,
so gentle winds may wash over the soil,
seeds sprout and blossom, flocks fatten,
and fruit fall when it is due.
Hold back the barren sickness that creeps from the mouths of men.
Let this bloodshed for bloodshed become grace for grace,
for only with your consent, the Mothers' consent,
shall families be happy and prosper,
and Love be the common will.[3]

Sphinx (Thebes)

It was you who sat outside Thebes, you who let Oedipus pass through and into his
fate. It was you who knew his mother would hang above the bed. And it was you
who set going the idea in the mind of Sigmund Freud that fragment of Oedipus's
story that became a claustrum. A dead-end guide to the nature of relations of men
and women and children, that, for a while, informed us, then constricted our love.
It was you who saw it and knew it and you who did nothing to liberate the city.

It was you who cursed us all.

Jocasta (Thebes)

Jocasta, it wasn't you.
It could have been any of us.
A stranger comes with dust on his feet
and a look in his eye that says, "I know you."
What can you do?

How can you tell this sphinx of a man
that only love
can unriddle the myth of himself,
and if it does then the gods
will close round us both?
How can you tell him
what you know?

Dionysos (Thebes)

Dionysos, it was you who descended to Aidos, looking for Semele, she, your second mother. It was you who brought her ashes home to your hometown – it was you who negotiated with your family and gained for her that respectful recognition and her eternal place as that raging constellation, Thyone – a sign of a woman and mother who was incinerated, yet rose again, rose well above the cruelty of women to women. Of Hera to Semele. It was you, Semele, whose trial by fire gave Dionysos unquenchable life.

Orpheus (Thrace)

> *I hear a voice singing my death*
> Orphee, it was you who descended
> looking for Euridice;
> and you, bringing her home,
> at the exit
> slipped and fell.

> And it was you who those maenads,
> that pack of unrequited women,
> in rage, tore limb from limb.

> And it was Dionysos,
> in grief at your loss, Orphee,
> who set going your Mysteries,
> so that your resurrecting music would never ever die.

> *Though I hear always a voice singing my death*

Persephone (Eleusis)

And it was you, Persephone, who descended to Aidos's arms, and it was you who at last brought compassion to the dark places of the earth. And you, Persephone, who restored your mother to a fullness of life that we now so carelessly neglect. And you, Persephone, may you come again and again to confront the folly of men in high towers who would destroy your mother's beautiful life-giving . . . on and on . . . or perhaps it was the Nazarene who consulted with you after his trial and after Golgotha and agreed to rise again and carry on your compassion, even though so many holy men on the road to Damascus would have you spurned or burned, leaving smoking tyres black on the road to warn your mother, Demeter, to keep out of the way.

Ajax (Troy)

It was you, the hero caught up in that endless war where you lost your mind, slaughtered the wrong creatures, fell in pain, set going the paranoia that continues to bleed out the milk of the world. The curse of war. It was you who fell into nothing. Nil, Nix. And it was you who set going the world's suicide. Damascus upon Damascus. City after city. Electra after Electra. *In Perpetua* . . .

Ariadne in the dark again

And it is we now who acknowledge you all, though we are hopeless, and yet with that Kazantzakis Cretan gaze that accepts death and life at the same instant, we might, with good humor, leap through the horns, trace a way through this and that dilemma of Europe, find a thread through this strange maze that engulfs us. And we acknowledge the dystonic meditation of Evangelos on the present state of Greece. And any unknown thing or uninvited guest who cares to appear . . . And not to forget you, Snakes who are dreamed and dreaming, Snakes suckling blood, Snakes wreathed in tangles, robbing the Furies, and Snakes at peace in the home, musing on leaping and dancing satyrs and endlessly shifting shapes, settling slowly into strange patterns of truth . . .

> Above all, forgive us our (daily) Folly – our huge, cinematic, big-screen hubris –
> for we can see, here on the edge of this volcano, that we are ever on the brink . . .
> *And, finally, we remember with gratitude the signs and steps of Minoa, labyrinth, shell, fish tail, moon, and bull that flowed through all these islands so long ago.*
> May such beauty turn and return and gather us, whenever we are able, into blue enfolding light and the "smiling knowledge of eternity."[4]

Gaia

> Gaia, Mother of All, the Oldest One,
> the Foundation, I shall sing to Earth.
> She feeds everyone in the world.
>
> Whoever you are,
> whether you walk upon her sacred ground
> or move through the paths of the sea,
> you who fly,
> She it is who nourishes you
> from her treasure-store.
>
> Queen of Earth, through you
> beautiful children, beautiful harvests, come.
> You give life and you take life away.

Blessed are those you honor with a willing heart.
Those who have this have everything ...

Farewell, Mother of the Gods,
bride of starry Heaven.
For my song, life allow me,
one my heart loves.
And now, and in all other songs,
I will remember you.[5]

FIGURE I.2 Vimeo link: Ancient Greece, Modern Psyche Opening
(https://aras.org/ancient-greece-modern-psyche)

Notes

1 These versions are adapted from original texts or conference presentations and are composed by Jules Cashford and Craig San Roque.
2 Line from Odysseas Elytas is from "As the Oyster So Its Pearl," in *Eros, Eros, Eros, Selected and Late Poems*, trans. Olga Broumas, Port Townsend, WA: Copper Canyon Press, 1998.
3 Eumenides lines adapted from Aeschylus's *Eumenides*.
4 The German novelist Thomas Mann, in his address on the occasion of Freud's 80th birthday, spoke of myth as offering a "smiling knowledge of eternity." Cited in Jules Cashford, "The Myth of the Messenger," *ARAS Connections*, 2011, no. 3. Available online: https://aras.org/documents/myth-messenger.
5 Retranslated 2017 by Jules Cashford from the original Greek Homeric Hymn to Gaia, c. 500 BCE. For an alternative version see *The Homeric Hymns*, trans. Jules Cashford, London: Penguin Classics, 2003, p. 140.

1

A FOOL'S GUIDE TO FOLLY

Thomas Singer

Part one: introduction – personal experiences with folly

> A man must be a little mad if he does not want to be even more stupid.
>
> *(Michel de Montaigne, Book III, chapter XI)*[1]

I begin with a drawing I produced in medical school in the late 1960s (Figure 1.1). Hold it in mind as I take you on my "Fool's Guide to Folly" that starts with a few rec-ollections of folly in my personal life. (All the images and film clips referenced in this chapter are at the Archive for Research in Archetypal Symbolism (ARAS), https:// aras.org/ancient-greece-modern-psyche. At each point where an image or film clip is discussed, the link to ARAS appears in bold.) This particular drawing reflects how I have often felt in my life. It shames me a bit while also warming my heart. It depicts through the body a particular state of mind and feeling that I want to convey – the legs are disjointed, in a somewhat awkward but simultaneously nimble dance. The middle part of the body is tied up obsessively in conflicting tendencies, and the head has a surprisingly radiant, even illuminated quality about it. This drawing can be seen as the self-portrait of the fool in the midst of "dancing the folly of life."

Perhaps less glowing but equally foolish is Durer's 1511 version of the *Goose Fool* (Figure 1.2), which I only recently stumbled upon in writing this essay – but he has the same knock-kneed instability and even a hat with a couple of doodads that bear a resemblance to the heady balls of my more radiantly ambiguous figure – all of which reminds me of a conversation I had with a Greek cab driver on arriving in Athens on one of many journeys to Greece over the decades. My pidgin Greek allowed me to engage in a simple exchange with him. He asked me what I did and where I lived. I told him I was a psychiatrist from the United States. He responded – with something of his own foolish wisdom – that he was a Greek cab driver and that his mind was much like the Aegean Sea, mostly full of watery emptiness with a few rocky islands interspersed. He had a sense of folly.

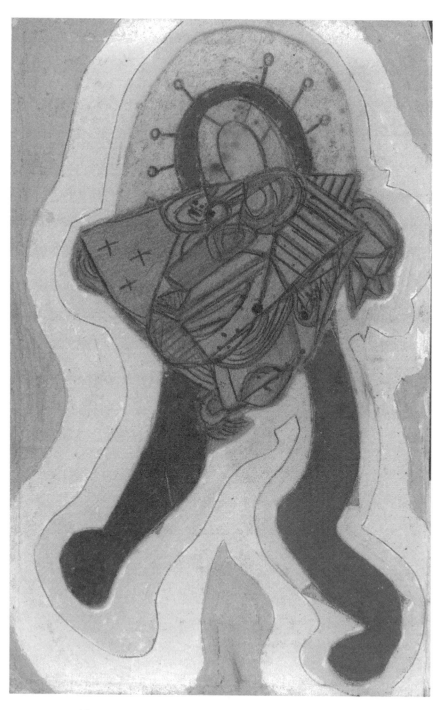

FIGURE 1.1 Self-portrait from medical school

(https://aras.org/ancient-greece-modern-psyche)

FIGURE 1.2   Albert Durer, *Goose Fool*, woodcut, 1511 (from www.spaight woodgalleries.com/Pages/Durer_Fools_1.html)

(https://aras.org/ancient-greece-modern-psyche)

Here is a dictionary definition of folly:[2]

1:   lack of good sense or normal prudence and foresight. *His folly in thinking he could not be caught.*

2a: criminally or tragically foolish actions or conduct **b:** *obsolete:* evil, wickedness; *especially:* lewd behavior.

3:   a foolish act or idea. *The prank was a youthful folly.*

4:   an excessively costly or unprofitable undertaking. *Paying so much for that land was folly, since it was all rocks and scrub trees.*

5:   an often extravagant picturesque building erected to suit a fanciful taste.

But I maintain that this definition of folly is lacking in the more positive and inspired variety of folly, which is generative of creativity in life. So there is folly and there is folly – for the source, content, and outcome of folly can often shift before one's eyes in an instant. There is the folly that can lead one into the joyful, almost ecstatic delight in life that takes one on totally unexpected and essential paths, and there is the folly that makes a mess of life or even destroys it. Sometimes these two experiences of folly are indistinguishable; sometimes one leads to the other; and sometimes they are not linked at all. On the one hand, a sense of folly can lead to the ability to laugh at our human foolishness, allowing us to plunge into life with abandon, enjoying the folly of being human that occasionally joins hands with divine folly and the creative madness that it can inspire. And a sense of folly can allow us to tolerate and even laugh at what is otherwise both unbearable and ridiculous – a challenge that faces many of us today, both in the United States and in the rest of the world on a daily basis. As Jung said, "Do you believe, man of this time, that laughter is lower than worship? Where is your measure, false measurer? The sum of life decides in laughter and in worship, not your judgement."[3]

There is also that kind of absurdly blind folly that can launch major powers into reckless wars that achieve nothing but the destruction of countless lives and unending animosities and trauma that pass from generation to generation. This essay, then, foolishly presents itself as a Fool's Guide to Folly, exploring both the creative and destructive sides of folly – that which is humanly or divinely inspired and that which is blindly stupid. And there are many shades of folly in between these extremes – from the sublime to the horrific, from the comic to the tragic, from the life-affirming to the death-dealing. Folly includes everything from play to murder. Folly can be a truth teller, and folly can be a deceiver. Folly can lead us forward, and folly can take us backward. Sometimes which roles the fool and folly are playing get all mixed up with one another and we find ourselves in a stew of folly, revealing and hiding the truth of folly leading us forward and backward in human and social development. For instance, in 1867, U.S. Secretary of State William H. Seward negotiated a treaty with Russia for the purchase of Alaska for $7 million. Despite the bargain price of roughly two cents an acre, the Alaskan purchase was ridiculed in Congress and in the press as "Seward's folly." After a slow start in U.S. settlement, the discovery of gold in 1898 brought a rapid influx of people to the territory, and Alaska, rich in natural resources, has contributed to American prosperity ever since.

Perhaps we come to know folly best through the emotions she (following Erasmus who identifies her as feminine) evokes in us, which range from joy and delight, to horror and disgust, to shame and humiliation, and finally from incredulity and disbelief to their opposites, credibility and belief. Folly is polymorphous indeed.

A landmark date in my personal discovery of folly was in the summer of 1963 when I spent my first day ever in Greece by buying a copy of the newly published English version of Nikos Kazantzakis's *Zorba the Greek* and climbing Mt. Lykabettos in the heart of Athens. After the steep climb, the blinding sun, and the magic of reading *Zorba the Greek* for hours atop Lykabettos, I was never quite the same. *Zorba the Greek* is the story of a young English writer named Basil who has come to Greece to inspect an abandoned mine in Crete owned by his father. He invites Zorba to join him on his trip and "folly strikes." In many ways, Zorba himself can be seen as the very incarnation of divinely inspired human folly, as can be seen in "The Full Catastrophe," a scene in which Zorba tells Basil, "Am I not a man? And is a man not stupid? I'm a man, so I married. Wife, children, house, everything. The full catastrophe" (Figure 1.3).[4]

FIGURE 1.3 Film clip: *Zorba the Greek*, "The Full Catastrophe"
(https://aras.org/ancient-greece-modern-psyche)

Perhaps the height of Zorba's folly – and his message of folly to the Boss (Basil) – comes in the wonderful misadventure of a lumbering scheme that includes building a contraption to carry logs from a mountaintop to the sea (Figure 1.4).

FIGURE 1.4 Film clip: *Zorba the Greek*, "The Collapse of the Structure"
(https://aras.org/ancient-greece-modern-psyche)

This is the kind of inspired folly that ends in literal collapse and disaster, but not in the breaking of the human spirit. Throwing oneself into life with a sense of folly can be liberating and affirming of the human (and perhaps the divine) spirit. It is the affirmation of plunging into life itself, not unlike Joseph Conrad's advice, spoken by the German Stein, in *Lord Jim*:

> The shadow prowling amongst the graves of butterflies laughed boisterously.
> "Yes! Very funny this terrible thing is. A man that is born falls into a dream like a man who falls into the sea. If he tries to climb out into the air

as inexperienced people endeavour to do, he drowns – *nicht wahr?* . . . No! I tell you! The way is to the destructive element submit yourself, and with the exertions of your hands and feet in the water make the deep, deep sea keep you up. So if you ask me – how to be?"

His voice leaped up extraordinarily strong, as though away there in the dusk he had been inspired by some whisper of knowledge. "I will tell you! For that, too, there is only one way."

With a hasty swish of his slippers he loomed up in the ring of faint light, and suddenly appeared in the bright circle of the lamp. His extended hand aimed at my breast like a pistol; his deep-set eyes seemed to pierce through me, but his twitching lips uttered no word, and the austere exaltation of a certitude seen in the dusk vanished from his face. The hand that had been pointing at my breast fell, and by-and-by, coming a step nearer, he laid it gently on my shoulder. There were things, he said mournfully, that perhaps could never be told, only he had lived so much alone that sometimes he forgot – he forgot. The light had destroyed the assurance which had inspired him in the distant shadows. He sat down and, with both elbows on the desk, rubbed his forehead. "And yet it is true it is true. In the destructive element immerse." . . . He spoke in a subdued tone, without looking at me, one hand on each side of his face. "That was the way. To follow the dream, and again to follow the dream – and so – *ewig-usque ad finem* . . ." The whisper of his conviction seemed to open before me a vast and uncertain expanse, as of a crepuscular horizon on a plain at dawn – or was it, perchance, at the coming of the night?[5]

I remember reading and studying *Lord Jim* as an adolescent and, just as Zorba's "full catastrophe" took up permanent residence in my soul, so did the phrase: "In the destructive element immerse."

This is the positive notion of folly into which the Zorbatic spirit initiated me. Feeling much like the bookish narrator, I began my own dance with Zorba and his joyful embrace of folly, of setting reason aside for a different kind of logic that can affirm the nonrational as a source of life. Retrospectively, I have come to think of this kind of folly as a sort of inspired madness that just a few years later allowed me to jump into a crazy project with some friends and plant our little flag on a remote, empty bay named Klima some ten miles from Santorini where we, in time, built three houses. The Klima folly has continued for almost fifty years, although we are running out of juice and inspiration.

FIGURE 1.5   The dock that lasted twenty-four hours at Klima
(https://aras.org/ancient-greece-modern-psyche)

In the spirit of Zorba's doomed construction project (Figure 1.5), our most glorious failure at Klima (other than starting the project at all and not knowing what to do about it now as we age) was building a 30,000-pound cement dock that lasted less than twenty-four hours. The cement had not hardened when a huge spring storm swept the entire baby dock into the Aegean. It was our own moment of the Zorbatic falling apart of the grand scheme.

I remember another moment of being possessed by the spirit of folly that has long been a source of embarrassment about how crazy I was in medical school but which, in retrospect, had its own wisdom. I was attending medical school in New Haven in the late 1960s. As one can glean from Robert Rauschenberg's *Signs*, it was, among other things, a time of great political and cultural upheaval, of overwhelming and highly charged folly – all mixed up in a psychic stew that one swam in, sometimes just hoping not to drown, other times delighting in its thrilling and unexpected highs, and ultimately witnessing the devastation that flowed from its folly (Figure 1.6).

FIGURE 1.6   Robert Rauschenberg, *Signs*, 1970 silkscreen
(https://aras.org/ancient-greece-modern-psyche)

I vividly remember the violent outbreak of riots in New Haven in 1970 when I found myself literally in the middle of it as a volunteer first-aid and crowd-control person. Bobby Seale, a famous leader of the Black Panthers, was on trial in New Haven for murdering an informant. It was a chaotic and disorienting time with black rage flaring at home and the war in Vietnam raging abroad. One day while on a pediatric clerkship, I showed up for rounds with a child's holster strapped around my head like a hippie bandana with the toy guns hanging over each of my ears. When asked what in heaven's name I was doing appearing on the ward like that, I answered, "I can't hear you. I have guns in my ears." I'm very lucky they didn't throw me out of medical school and commit me to the psychiatric wards. I was quite mad, but in some ways I was acting out a frightening truth for all of us.

To introduce the tour through this history of the different kinds of folly and fools that have captured the human imagination and spirit over time, I have included a link to a three-second film image from Fellini's *Satyricon* of visitors being shuttled through a museum. Perhaps we can metaphorically think of ourselves as being like these tourists in *Satyricon* who roll by in the background of this scene as we take a brief tour of the ancient, medieval, and contemporary museum of folly (Figure 1.7).[6]

FIGURE 1.7   Film clip: museum tour in *Satyricon*
(https://aras.org/ancient-greece-modern-psyche)

Part two: Plato's Cave

> There is no wish more natural than the wish to know.
>
> *(Michel de Montaigne, Book III, chapter XIII)*

What better place to start our Fool's Guide to Folly than in Plato's Cave, which appears in Plato's *The Republic*, written somewhere between 380 and 360 BCE in the Classical Age of Greece.

The Cave marks a beginning of the awakening in the history of the Western psyche of a split between the real and the illusory. What we take to be real in the everyday world may, at best, be a shadowy illusion of reality, which in fact is truly known only in the realm of ideal forms, of which Jung's archetypes would be an expression.

Here is a wonderful image of the Cave that orients us to the central features of Plato's allegory (Figure 1.8).[7]

Imprisonment in the Cave

Human beings, known as "prisoners," are lined up facing a wall on which they see shadows dancing before their eyes. Puppeteers carry objects on a roadway behind the backs of the prisoners. Behind the roadway is a fire. The fire's light casts shadows of the puppeteer's objects onto the wall that the prisoners are facing. What we see as mortals, according to Plato, are the shadows of objects, not the real thing. And even the objects themselves do not reflect reality. To perceive the true forms of reality, one needs to leave the Cave altogether and emerge into the light of the "real world" embodied in the "sunlight" (which was a bit like how I felt when I climbed Lykabettos as a young man and began to read *Zorba the Greek* in the full, dazzling light of the Greek summer sun).

Departure from the Cave

Plato asks us to imagine that a prisoner is freed to turn around and is blinded by the light of the fire that is actually the source of light casting the reflected shadowy

Plato's Cave

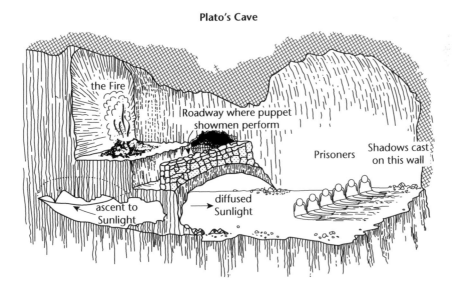

FIGURE 1.8 Plato's Cave

(https://aras.org/ancient-greece-modern-psyche)

images onto the walls at which the prisoners gaze. The prisoner would have to decide what is real and what is shadow, and Plato imagines that the freed prisoner would turn away and run back to what he is accustomed to (that is, the shadows of the objects). Plato writes, "it would hurt his eyes, and he would escape by turning away to the things which he was able to look at, and these he would believe to be clearer than what was being shown to him."[8]

Plato continues his narrative:

> Suppose . . . that someone should drag him . . . by force, up the rough ascent, the steep way up, and never stop until he could drag him out into the light of the sun. The prisoner would be angry and in pain, and this would only worsen when the radiant light of the sun overwhelms his eyes and blinds him.

Slowly, his eyes adjust to the light of the sun. First he can only see shadows. Gradually he can see the reflections of people and things in water and then later see the people and things themselves. Eventually, he is able to look at the stars and moon at night until finally he can look upon the sun itself (516a). Only after he can look straight at the sun "is he able to reason about it" and what it is (516b).[9]

Return to the Cave

Plato imagines that the freed prisoner would think that the world outside the Cave was superior to the world he experienced in the Cave; "he would bless himself for the change, and pity [the other prisoners]" and would want to bring his fellow Cave dwellers out of the Cave and into the sunlight (516c).[10]

The returning prisoner, whose eyes have become accustomed to the sunlight, would be blind when he reenters the Cave, just as he was when he was first exposed to the sun (516e).[11] The prisoners, according to Plato, would infer from the returning man's blindness that the journey out of the Cave had harmed him and that they should not undertake a similar journey. Socrates concludes that the prisoners, if they were able, would therefore reach out and kill anyone who attempted to drag them out of the Cave (517a).[12]

If we accept Plato's allegory of the Cave as accurately reflecting something about the human condition, we can begin to imagine the various places in the Cave, or stages in the unfolding of the story, in which both the fool and folly might take up permanent but shape-shifting residence and play a role in the story's evolution. Here are folly's potential places or roles in the Cave that I have imagined; the reader may come up with more.

- *Folly of everyday life*, otherwise known as stupidity, can be quite destructive in its refusal to see anything other than the reflected images on the wall as being real. This is the fate of most "prisoners." And, if we imagine folly as a god or goddess (which we will see Erasmus doing almost 2,000 years after Plato), there is ample room for her to play huge tricks on us with the objects she parades in front of the fire to reflect on the wall as shadowy images – including images of ourselves.

- An enormous human *creative* (perhaps divinely inspired) *folly* is needed to step outside the Cave in the first place, even if the prisoner is initially dragged out.
- The prisoner who has stepped outside the Cave needs *divine folly* to compassionately reenter the Cave in an effort to awaken the prisoners who will laugh at the fool who stepped outside, doubt his story of what exists outside the Cave, and perhaps, as Plato tells the story, kill the fool for presenting another view of reality that throws their own illusory view of what's real into doubt.

We might think of these follies as a tripartite or quadrated theory of folly that emerges out of Plato's primal split of the Western psyche into an illusory world of everyday reality and the real world of ideal forms:

- The totally ignorant, stupid form of folly in which we are unable to see anything but shadowy reflections of objects floating in front of us that we take to be absolutely real.
- A divinely inspired human madness form of folly that allows us to step out of the Cave in the first place and glimpse the world of Pure Forms, what Jungians have come to know as archetypes – which can be just as deceiving if taken too literally as concrete reality.
- A compassionate form of folly that would lead us back into the Cave with the misguided notion that the prisoners inhabiting it would want to be awakened from their illusory world.
- A tricksterish form of folly that would insert herself in the role of puppeteer, showing the prisoners images that would simply reflect back to them the way in which they would like to see themselves and the world (Erasmus will have more to teach us about this incarnation of folly).

I hope in the course of this chapter to show you the many forms that folly can take as I have extrapolated them from an imaginal excursion into Plato's Cave with both the fool and folly as my guide. But should we take Plato too seriously, Aristophanes was already on the scene in his play *The Clouds*, referring to Socrates and his school as the "Thinkery," where the folly of fools was being pursued in such important questions as the origin of the humming sound of gnats:

> Our Chaerephon was asking [Socrates'] opinion / on whether gnats produce their humming sound / by blowing through the mouth or through the rump.

> *(ll. 156–158)*

[Socrates] said the gnat has a very narrow gut, / and, since the gut's so tiny, the air comes through / quite violently on its way to the little rump; / then, being an orifice attached to a narrow tube, / the asshole makes a blast from the force of air.

(ll. 160–164)[13]

Part three: Erasmus's *The Praise of Folly*

Whoever will be cured of ignorance, let him confess it.

(Michel de Montaigne)[14]

Plato wrote his allegory of the Cave between 380 and 360 BCE. Some 1,800 years later, in 1509, Erasmus conceived of *The Praise of Folly* while riding over the Alps on a horse. The book was printed in 1511.

But Erasmus was not as distant from Plato in his thought as he was in time. Plato's Cave provided Erasmus and Western humans with the template of an archetypal split between illusion (our natural condition) and reality, of mistaking shadowy reflections for what is truly *real*. This split creates fertile soil in which folly can romp. Folly loves the split between illusion and reality. It is her natural play-ground in which one minute the fool and folly are a source of staggering stupidity, hypocrisy, and corruption. And in the very next minute, as occurs in Erasmus's book, folly can be a way to wisdom. In one moment folly cruelly caters to self-serving and destructive interests, and in the next she points to redemption.

As I mentioned earlier, if we put ourselves in Plato's Cave and imagine where Erasmus's folly would be working her magic, she would most likely spend much of her time on the "roadway where puppet showmen perform" (as labeled in Figure 1.8). Indeed, she may be the star "puppet showman" on that stage in which objects destined to become shadowy reflections on the wall of the Cave are paraded in front of the fire. In Erasmus's *The Praise of Folly*, folly reveals herself to be the progenitor and sustainer of the illusions that shield us from the painful truths about ourselves, others, and the world as a whole. She allows us to live in illusion, even as in *The Praise of Folly* she unveils her "trickery" to us as if she is encouraging us to leave the Cave. In other words, living in Plato's Cave can be thought of as akin to living in the embrace of Erasmus's folly. What has folly kept hidden from us in the Cave? Listen to her own voice as she reveals her sorcery to an assembly of the learned:

what part of life is not sad, unpleasant, graceless, flat,

and burdensome, unless you have pleasure added to it,

that is, a seasoning of folly.[15]

In the first part of *The Praise of Folly*, folly takes a developmental approach to her role in the lifecycle:

• About the newborn and childhood, Erasmus says through folly:

> "Who does not know that the earliest period of a man's life is by far the
> happiest for him and by far the most pleasant for all about him? What
> is it in children that we should kiss them the way we do, and cuddle
> them, and fondle them – so that even an enemy would give aid to one
> of that age – except this enchantment of folly, which prudent nature
> carefully bestows on the newly born; so that by this pleasure, as a sort
> of prepayment, they win the favor of their nurses and parents and make
> these forget the pains of bringing them up."[16]

• About youth after childhood, Erasmus continues through folly:

> "After childhood, comes youth. How welcome it is in every home!
> How well everyone wishes it! How studiously does everyone promote
> it, how officiously they lend it the helping hand! But, I ask, whence
> comes this grace of youth? Whence but from me (Folly), by whose
> favor the young know so little – and how lightly worn is that little!
> And presently when lads grown larger begin, through experience and
> discipline, to have some smack of manhood [aside: Erasmus did not give
> much thought to girls and women], I am a liar if by the same token the
> brightness of their beauty does not fade, their quickness diminish, their
> wit lose its edge, their vigor slacken. The farther one gets from me, then
> the less and less he lives, until *molesta senectus* (that is, irksome old age)
> arrives, hateful to others, to be sure, but also and more so to itself."[17]

• And about old age, folly proclaims:

> "Old age would not be tolerable to any mortal at all, were it not that
> I, out of pity for its troubles, stand once more at its right hand; and just
> as the gods of the poets customarily save, by some metamorphosis or
> other, those who are dying, in like manner, I bring those who have one
> foot in the grave back to their infancy again, for as long as possible; so
> that the folk are not far off in speaking of them as 'in their second child-
> hood'" (Figure 1.9).[18]

FIGURE 1.9 David Hockney, *Ann at a Mirror Combing*, 1979 (www.pinterest.com/
pin/242420392418506876)

(https://aras.org/ancient-greece-modern-psyche)

"If anyone would like to know the method of bringing about this alteration, I shall not conceal it. I lead them to my spring of Lethe – for that

stream rises in the Fortunate Isles, and only a little rivulet of it flows in the underworld – so that then and there they may drink draughts of forgetfulness. With their cares of mind purged away, by gentle stages they become young again. But now, you say, they merely dote, and play the fool. Yes, quite so. But precisely this it is to renew one's infancy. Is to be childish anything other than to dote and play the fool? As if in that age the greatest joy were not this, that one knows nothing!!!!"[19]

Folly is the one thing that makes fleeting youth linger and keeps ugly old age away.[20]

For Erasmus, folly, then, is the source of illusions and only illusions make life bearable. Folly tricks everyone into seeing nonexistent good qualities in themselves and others. Her magic enables husbands to tolerate wives, wives to tolerate husbands, and teachers to tolerate students and vice versa. Without folly, no one could bear his or her companions, to say nothing of him- or herself . . .

Folly especially turns on those who supposedly embody wisdom and piety. In the second section of *The Praise of Folly*, she turns her sardonic wit on and exposes the hollowness of most humans – especially merchants and those who make claims to authority or wisdom. This includes grammarians, poets, rhetoricians, authors, lawyers, logicians, theologians, scientists, monks, priests, kings, courtiers, bishops, cardinals, popes, and all those who make claim to wisdom. I'm afraid a modern version of these professions would likely include myself and most of my dear readers. Erasmus's contemporary, Sebastian Brant, enumerated some 112 different kinds of fools in his 1494 book, *Ship of Fools*, which, interestingly enough, also originated in an allegory from Plato's *The Republic* (Figure 1.10).

FIGURE 1.10   Albrecht Dürer in *Stultifera navis* (*Ship of Fools*) by Sebastian Brant, published by Johann Bergmann von Olpe (de) in Basel in 1498

(https://aras.org/ancient-greece-modern-psyche)

In the third part of *The Praise of Folly*, the role of folly dramatically shifts and takes on a far more positively transformative aspect in Erasmus's cosmology. In this section, Erasmus, a devout Christian, although highly critical of the Christianity of his time, praises the folly that leads man to a true Christian life. Here is how Anthony Grafton writes about this folly in his Foreword to the Princeton classic edition:

In the third and shortest part of her speech, Folly pivots again – this time to the teaching of Christianity and philosophy. What looks to humans like wisdom, she argues, is really madness . . . True Christianity, Folly argues, yields none of the things that ordinary, prudent men and women seek: not wealth, not power, not fame. Instead, it offers "the foolishness of the cross" by which Jesus brought healing to sinful humanity . . . True Philosophy, Folly argues, is not a pursuit of useless knowledge or sophisticated logical tricks, but a "study of death," in Plato's words, "because it leads the mind away from visible and bodily things, and certainly death does the same." True Christianity and true philosophy converge. Both teach those who embrace them to be fools to this world, "rapt away in the contemplation of things unseen."[21]

As you can see, with Erasmus we find ourselves once again in Plato's Cave out of which folly is encouraging us to emerge into the light. What a Fool's Guide to Folly both Plato and Erasmus offer us!

Part four: the Wise Fool in Shakespeare's *King Lear*

By Jules Cashford

The Wise Fool has two virtues: the gift of seeing through appearances to the reality within them; and the ability to *play* the fool, to show the real folly its "form and pressure."

In Plato's terms, perhaps the Wise Fool, embodying divine folly, might be seen as the one who has been freed from the Cave but returns out of compassion to free the other prisoners. His wisdom is to understand that the "real folly" is the blindness of those in the Cave, which means they will not be able to accept the truth presented to them as fact until they have let go of their conviction that what they see is real. Thus, the Wise Fool has to play with the ideas of those still imprisoned, so that they might begin to laugh at, and then call into question, what they are seeing – even though it is all they can see, strapped as they are to their seats before the screen. This form of *divine* folly is designed to prevent human folly from making sense and so eventually to free the prisoners from illusion. This prison is ultimately Plato's symbol of the "unexamined life."

Shakespeare's response to this in his play *King Lear* is to show, through the fates of Lear and Gloucester, that we cannot see truly unless we "see feelingly," which is to see with our whole being. From the moment the play begins, it is clear there is division in the kingdom and, ultimately, within the King himself because he sees people without feeling – only as reflections of himself. Lear proposes to give his kingdom to his three daughters in equal parts, but asks instead for them to give something to him – to earn their portion of his "gift" by telling him how much they love him, and even, in an elision of love and land, to compete for territory with flattery:

> Which of you shall we say doth love us most,
> That we our largest bounty may extend
> Where nature doth with merit challenge?
>
> *(Act I, scene i, ll. 31–33)*

The two elder sisters, Goneril and Regan, reply in kind. Lear turns to his favorite, his "joy":

> What can you say to draw
> A third more opulent than your sisters?

Cordelia: Nothing, my Lord.
Lear: Nothing?
Cordelia: Nothing.
Lear: Nothing will come of nothing. Speak again.
Cordelia: Unhappy that I am, I cannot heave
              My heart into my mouth. I love your majesty
              According to my bond. No more nor less.

(I, i, 86–93)

Lear: So young and so untender?
Cordelia: So young, my lord, and true.

(I, i, 107–108)

The play explores the essential conflict of values between them. Lear's first response is to banish her:

Lear: Hence and avoid my sight!

(I, i, 124)

But later, still not getting his own way, he disowns her:

Lear: We have no such daughter, nor shall ever see
              that face of hers again . . .

(I, i, 264–265)

Lear does not know he is a fool in the sense of *Ate*, the Greek goddess of Folly and Ruin, daughter of *Eris*, Strife – often called a "blind fool." The underlying metaphor in *King Lear* is one of vision and moral blindness.

But his Fool is always with him in his folly: *Lear:* "Where's my Fool? Ho, I think the whole world's asleep" (I, iv, 47). The Fool, very much awake, offers Lear a compassionately bitter wit, issuing elliptically, in allusion, analogy, and epigram, which breaks through into Lear's consciousness where reasoned argument would fail. The Fool continually taunts Lear with his judgment, to force him to grasp that he has a false notion of himself. As the Fool puts it: "Truth's a dog must to kennel" (I, iv, 120). By teasing and parodying him, the Fool prevents him from forgetting what he has done and inexorably presses him to see he was wrong: "Why, this fellow has banished two on's daughters, and did the third a blessing against his will" (I, iv, 101–104). We learn that the Fool "hath much pined away" since Cordelia went to France, and he carries Lear's deeply buried conscience as intuitive knowledge until Lear is reconciled with Cordelia – his heart, the *Cor* of Cordelia.

The Fool plays with the terms already present in Lear's mind, like a thought that will not go away, but twists them to mean the opposite of what Lear would have them mean. The fateful "nothing" always comes up:

Fool: Can you make no use of nothing, nuncle?
Lear: Why, no, boy. Nothing can be made out of nothing.

Fool: Prithee tell him; so much the rent of his land comes to.
         He will not believe a fool . . .
Lear: Dost thou call me fool, boy?
Fool: All other titles thou hast given away; that thou wast born with.

(I, iv, 146–147)

Then he tries it from another angle:

Fool: Prithee, Nuncle, keep a schoolmaster that can teach thy fool to lie.
Lear: And you lie, sirrah, we'll have you whipped.
Fool: I marvel what kin thou and thy daughters are. They'll have me whipped
         for speaking true; thou'lt have me whipped for lying; and sometimes I am
         whipped for holding my peace. I had rather be any kind of thing than a
         fool. And yet I would not be thee, nuncle. Thou hast pared thy wit o'both
         sides and left nothing i'the middle.

(I, iv, 178–184)

As Lear is watchful of Goneril's frown, the Fool concludes:

. . . Now thou art an O without a figure. I am better than thou art now;
I am a fool; thou art nothing.

(I, iv, 189–190)

And when Lear, raging at Goneril's censure of him, cries:
Does any here know me? This is not Lear.
Does Lear walk thus, speak thus? Where are his eyes? . . .
Who is it that can tell me who I am?
"Lear's shadow," The Fool replies.

(I, iv, 222–227)

So crucial is the Fool to the finding of Lear's humanity that he leads Lear to his
first moment of compassion, first toward himself and then to all dispossessed people.
"O Fool, I shall go mad!" (II, iv, 281). The turning point comes when Lear
hurls himself into the storm onto the heath at night – "Blow, winds, and crack
your cheeks!" (III, ii, 1) – and has to confront what he later calls the "tempest
in my mind" (III, iv, 12): Only the Fool is with him, who, we hear, "labours to
out-jest / His heart struck injuries" (III, i, 15–16).
When Kent, in disguise, finds a hovel for them, Lear shows his first moment of
concern for another person, significantly for his Fool:

Come on, my boy. How dost my boy? Art cold?
I am cold myself. Where is this straw, my fellow?
The art of our necessities is strange
And can make vile things precious. Come, your hovel.
Poor fool and knave, I have one part in my heart
That's sorry yet for thee.

(III, ii, 68–73)

Lear makes the Fool go into the hovel before him: "In boy; go first. – You houseless poverty" (III, iv, 27). This act of feeling moves his heart beyond self-pity to genuine pity for others, who, now like himself, have nothing to shield them from the storm:

> Poor naked wretches, whereso'er you are,
> That bide the pelting of this pitiless storm,
> How shall your houseless heads and unfed sides,
> Your loop'd and window'd raggedness, defend you
> From seasons such as these? O! I have ta'en
> Too little care of this. Take physic, Pomp;
> Expose thyself to feel what wretches feel . . .
>
> *(III, iv, 28–34)*

Once Lear is on his way to Cordelia at Dover, the Fool disappears – as though Lear has absorbed his wisdom in his own heart. At the end, holding Cordelia's body, Lear says: "And my poor fool is hanged," bringing the Fool together with Cordelia in death.

We see this when, just before Cordelia awakens him, Lear says to the blind Gloucester:

> If thou wilt weep my fortunes, take my eyes.
> I know thee well enough; thy name is Gloucester.
> Thou must be patient; we came crying hither.
> Thou knowest the first time that we smell the air
> We wawl and cry. I will preach to thee – Mark! . . .
> When we are born we cry that we are come
> To this great stage of fools.
>
> *(IV, vi, 177–184)*

Lear has found his conscience and compassion, showing us the meaning of Plato's phrase: "To know you are a fool is the beginning of wisdom."

Part five: folly in modern times – Fellini and Lapham

> We are all blockheads.
>
> *(Michel de Montaigne)*[22]

Following Plato's and Erasmus's lead over the past 2,500 years of human history, what do our polymorphous fool and folly look like in the modern world? (Perhaps the reader should take a break now and go throw up.) As I was imagining this section and since we live in an era of images, I kept coming back to scenes from Fellini's films, and it occurred to me that it might work to shift from word to image and let Fellini pick up where he left off in the museum of *Satyricon* and resume as our tour guide through the modern museum of folly. I think Fellini must have been married to folly because she is truly the guiding and enlivening Spirit of so many of his films.

Let's start with the folly of everyday life – at the family dinner table in *Amarcord*, a semi-autobiographical film about a young boy growing up in an eccentric town in Fascist Italy.[23] In the clip (Figure 1.11), hilarious slapstick prevails as the folly of husband and wife plays itself out while the grandfather excuses himself to fart in another room.

FIGURE 1.11 Film clip: dinner in *Amarcord*
(https://aras.org/ancient-greece-modern-psyche)

And, along with Erasmus, let's look at youthful folly as it encounters the folly of established traditions in the ritual of Catholic confession (Figure 1.12).

FIGURE 1.12 Film clip: *Amarcord*, "youthful confession"
(https://aras.org/ancient-greece-modern-psyche)

And then there is the folly of madness itself and even its insane wisdom in another scene from *Amarcord*, in which the family takes Uncle Teo, confined to an insane asylum, out to the country for the day (Figure 1.13). Teo climbs a tree, shouting, "I want a woman!" and throwing rocks at anyone who tries to get him down. When the midget nun from the asylum finally gets Teo to come down, the doctor pronounces, "Some days he's normal; some days he's not, just like the rest of us."

FIGURE 1.13 Film clip: *Amarcord*, "I want a woman"
(https://aras.org/ancient-greece-modern-psyche)

Just as a youth suffers the folly of institutionalized religion in the "youthful confession" scene in *Amarcord*, Fellini shows us that another version of folly can also lead us out of the "caves" of religious dogma in which we are prisoners, even martyrs, into another realm of being and perhaps even joyful delight, in his film *Juliet of the Spirits*. The grandfather as Wise Fool liberates Juliet from the cruel martyrdom of her youthful Catholicism (Figure 1.14).

FIGURE 1.14 Film clip: *Juliet of the Spirits*, "release from the cross"
(https://aras.org/ancient-greece-modern-psyche)

And later in the film, the grandfather appears once again as an almost divine incarnation of that form of folly that is on the side of life as he leads Juliet and the beautiful Circus Queen in a joyful flight that soars away from and above the conventional attitude of the vengeful and naysaying clergyman (Figure 1.15).

FIGURE 1.15 Film clip: *Juliet of the Spirits*, "the magical flight of folly"
(https://aras.org/ancient-greece-modern-psyche)

If Fellini's folly-filled visions bring such joyful delight to us, other visions of modern folly are far darker. Lewis Lapham, a distinguished American essayist, recently published a book about our contemporary world entitled *Age of Folly*. Here he describes one of the many follies of our times, which gained momentum after the fall of the Berlin Wall and the breakup of the Soviet Union when the United States was riding high:

> Reinforced by the fortunes accruing to . . . Silicon Valley . . . and by the . . . speculation floating the Dow Jones Industrial Average across the frontier of a new millennium, the delusions of omnipotent omniscience bubbled upward to so condescending a height that in March 2001, six months before the destruction of the World Trade Center, *Time Magazine* gave voice to what . . . had become a matter of simple truth and common knowledge:
>
> America is no mere international citizen. It is the dominant Power in the world, more dominant than any since Rome . . .
>
> The old Greeks . . . had a word, hubris, for the unbridled vanity that goeth before a fall, men tempted to play at being gods and drawn to the flame of their destruction on the wings of braggart moths. Thus President George W. Bush . . . on May 1, 2003, six weeks after launching a second American invasion of Iraq, stepping aboard the aircraft carrier U.S.S. *Abraham Lincoln* . . . stationed close inshore the coast of California to pose for the news cameras under a banner headlined MISSION ACCOMPLISHED.
>
> . . . Boy wonder as deus ex machina in *Top Gun* navy fighter pilot costume. But what was the mission to which the banner headlined referred? . . .The accomplishment was the dramatic significance of the invasion as prime-time television spectacle. Frivolity unbound. An act of folly more glorious than any since the Athenians in 415 BC sent a costly fleet of gilded ships to its destruction in Sicily, and by so doing lost both the Peloponnesian war and the life of their democracy.[24]

George Bush's declaration of "mission accomplished" aboard the U.S.S. *Abraham Lincoln* might remind us of Dürer's image of the *Ship of Fools* (Figure 1.16).

FIGURE 1.16 Albrecht Dürer in *Ship of Fools* by Sebastian Brant (https://aras.org/ancient-greece-modern-psyche)

So Lapham, too, has an eye for that side of folly that leads us blindly to destruction. From Lapham's *Age of Folly*, portraying the fools of our age pursuing policies for their own self-advancement or simply out of misguided patriotism, we easily progress in our Fool's Guide to Folly to the end result of this kind of folly in a scene from the film *The Fifth Element*, in which a beautiful woman from another planet embodies PEACE and LOVE (Figure 1.17).[25] Perhaps her planet is the realm of Plato's Pure Forms or Jung's archetypes. She is totally innocent of the extent to which humans will go to destroy one another in the name of some grand ideal behind which lurk far more sinister ambitions. In this scene, she gets a quick "download" lesson in the destructive folly of man.

FIGURE 1.17   Film clip: *The Fifth Element*

(**https://aras.org/ancient-greece-modern-psyche**)

And there is a wonderfully foolish contemporary combined portrait of Kim Jong Un and Donald Trump showing how our world leaders bamboozle us in their obsession with pursuing world domination for their own self-aggrandizement that will inexorably lead us into war (Figure 1.18).[26]

FIGURE 1.18   Trump and Kim Jong Un face swap from Google

(**https://aras.org/ancient-greece-modern-psyche**)

This is, of course, a photo-shopped image created in the spirit of creative folly to demonstrate the monstrousness of folly. In the modern confusion and fusion of images in our collective psyche, we witness how two apparently antagonistic world leaders have become one and the same thing. As mirror images of one another that blend into one another, they create a most dangerous paranoid "axis of evil" – two loose-cannon madmen quite capable of triggering the most horrific folly.

Part six: conclusion

> Every other knowledge is harmful to him who does not have knowledge of goodness.
>
> *(Michel de Montaigne, Book I, chapter 25)*[27]

It has been the goal of this Fool's Guide to Folly to give a perspective on how to hold folly in one's heart, mind, and spirit as a guide to what is real and what is important. I believe that a sense of folly is essential for embracing life to the fullest, just as I believe that folly may well lead to the destruction of life on earth. There is the spirit of folly that makes a person vital, and there is the possession by folly that can kill civilizations. I leave you with the following questions: How can we live inside and outside of Plato's Cave? How can we live in praise of folly and in terror of our age of folly? How can we walk hand in hand with folly at our sides (or even inside us) in a way that may actually help us keep our wits, perspective, and sense of humor in a time when folly could devour everything? I end with folly's wink from Fellini's *Juliet of the Spirits*, a tiny glimpse of an attitude that I hope each of you carries forth both inside you and into the world from our Fool's Guide to Folly (Figure 1.19).[28]

FIGURE 1.19   Film clip: *Juliet of the Spirits*, "the wink"

(**https://aras.org/ancient-greece-modern-psyche**)

Notes

1 Michel de Montaigne, *The Essays of Montaigne*, trans. Charles Cotton, first published 1686, Book III, chapter XI.
2 By permission. From Merriam-Webster.com © 2018 by Merriam-Webster, Inc. www.merriam-webster.com/dictionary/folly.
3 C. G. Jung, *The Red Book: A Reader's Edition*, ed. Sonu Shamdasani, New York: W. W. Norton & Co., p. 122.
4 Nikos Kazantzakis, *Zorba the Greek*, New York, Simon and Schuster, 1952. The film of the same name was directed by Michael Cacoyannis who also wrote the screenplay. The film was released on December 17, 1964.
5 Joseph Conrad, *The Project Gutenberg eBook of Lord Jim*, available at www.gutenberg.org/files/5658/5658-h/5658-h.htm (last update September 10, 2016).
6 *The Satyricon*, directed by Federico Fellini, screenplay by Federico Fellini, Bernardino Zapponi, and Brunello Rondi, released March 11, 1970.
7 Eric H. Warmington and Philip G. Rouse (eds.), *Great Dialogues of Plato*, trans. W. H. D. Rouse, New York: Signet Classics, 1999, p. 316.
8 Plato, *The Republic Book VII*, ed. W. H. D. Rouse, New York: Penguin Group, Inc., 1951, pp. 365–401.
9 Ibid., sections 516a–b. See also "Plato's Analogy of the Sun," which occurs near the end of Plato's *The Republic*, Book VI, ed. Benjamin Jowett, New York: The Modern Library, 1941.
10 Ibid.
11 Ibid.
12 Ibid.
13 Aristophanes, *Three Comedies*, Indianapolis, IN: Focus Publishing (an imprint of Hackett Publishing), 1992, lines 155–165.
14 Michel de Montaigne, quotes and images from the works of Michel de Montaigne, Project Gutenberg, www.gutenberg.org/ebooks/7551?msg=welcome_stranger.
15 All quotes from Desiderius Erasmus, *The Praise of Folly*, trans. Hoyt Hopewell Hudson with a foreword by Anthony Grafton, Princeton, NJ: Princeton University Press, 2015, p. 16.
16 Ibid.
17 Ibid., pp. 16–17.
18 Ibid., p. 17.
19 Ibid.
20 Ibid., p. 19.
21 Ibid., pp. x–xi.
22 Michel de Montaigne, quotes and images from the works of Michel de Montaigne, Project Gutenberg.
23 *Amarcord*, directed by Federico Fellini, screenplay by Federico Fellini and Tonino Guerra, released December 18, 1974.
24 Lewis H. Lapham, *Age of Folly: American Abandons Its Democracy*, London and New York: Verso, 2016, pp. xii and xiii.
25 *The Fifth Element*, directed by Luc Besson, screenplay by Luc Besson and Robert Mark Kamen, released May 9, 1997.
26 Available via Google search, www.google.com/search?q=trump+and+kim+jong+un+face+swap&tbm=isch&tbo=u&source=univ&sa=X&ved=0ahUKEwjvw7qk9KPaAhVP4VQKHU-tBqQQ7AkINA&biw=1118&bih=623#imgrc=npWG8c2UTsqaOM.
27 Michel de Montaigne, "On schoolmasters' learning," in *Essays*, trans. M. Screech, New York: Penguin, 1991, Book I, chapter 25, p. 159.
28 *Juliet of the Spirits*, directed by Federico Fellini, screenplay by Federico Fellini, Tullio Pinelli, Ennio Flaiano, and Brunello Rondi, released November 3, 1965.

2

THE MYSTERY OF DIONYSOS

Cultivating the vine of life

Virginia Beane Rutter

> I keep the law,
> I hold the mysteries true,
> I am the vine,
> the branches, you
> and you.

> *(H.D. [Hilda Doolittle, 1886–1961])*[1]

The ancient Greeks made a distinction between *Zoe* – infinite, enduring life – and *Bios* – characterized or individual life. Twice-born Dionysos is the archetype of *Zoe*, indestructible life. Dismembered and reconstituted, surrounded by women, he is the giver of wine, a healer who also causes madness, an ecstatic lover, and "eater of raw flesh." Psychologically, what does it mean to honor this god of paradox?

When the archetype of Dionysos erupts in the psyche of a woman or a man, the individual's fate is deeply impacted by the encounter that ensues. In this chapter, I discuss examples of initiation into the Dionysian mysteries in Greece and in Roman Pompeii to amplify clinical material and to bring the archetype alive through images.

Pictures will be described where they occur in the argument, along with a link to the actual image, in the Archive for Research in Archetypal Symbolism (ARAS), at https://aras.org/ancient-greece-modern-psyche.

Dionysos: possession and healing

Inside this cup is an image of Dionysos – extravagantly bearded, wreathed with ivy, ecstatically singing and strumming his lyre – entirely possessed, lost to anything but the song and the dance (Figure 2.1). Two young satyrs with fluffy tails gambol around him, keeping the rhythm with the clappers in one hand while holding up a

FIGURE 2.1 Dionysos and Satyrs. Brygos Painter. Interior of attic red-figured ceramic cup. c. 480 BCE. Cabinet des Medailles. Louvre

(Wikicommons images)

grapevine with the other. The satyr dancing on the right is draped in a dead animal, showing the bestial nature of the god and of the humans who carry his image in their heart. Even Dionysos has a shadow.

To introduce the archetype of Dionysos, I have to discuss him briefly in relation to his complementary opposite, Apollo.

In an engraving on the back of a mirror from the archaic period, Apollo and Dionysos stand face to face. Apollo wears a *chlamys* and holds his laurel spray, and Dionysos wears a long *chiton*. Jane Harrison, in her book *Themis*, writes that both are calendar gods, while the sun, a disk with the head of a young man, "shines impartially between them." But, with a great vine on either side of the bases on which they stand and the panther prowling above, the place seems to belong to Dionysos, though Apollo, as *Delphinios*, may claim the dolphins (Figure 2.2).

FIGURE 2.2   Apollo and Dionysos depicted as young men, *Kouroi.* Engraving on the
metal back of a mirror. Greek archaic period

(From Harrison, *Themis*, p. 442. **https://aras.org/ancient-greece-modern-psyche**)

She continues:

> There came then to Delphi, tradition tells us, two Kouroi, the greatest
> Kouroi the world has ever seen, Apollo and Dionysos. Were they, who seem
> so disparate, really the same? So far as they are Kouroi and Year-Gods, yes.
> But they are Kouroi and Year-Gods caught and in part crystallized at differ-
> ent stages of development. Apollo has more in him of the Sun and the day,
> of order and light and reason, Dionysos more of the Earth and the Moon, of
> the divinity of Night and Dreams. Moreover, Apollo is of man's life, sepa-
> rate from the rest of nature, a purely human accomplishment; Dionysos is of
> man's life as one with nature, a communion not a segregation.[2]

Dionysos and Apollo shared the Delphic year together. Dionysos was there in the
winter solstice when his particular song, the *dithyramb*, was sung. Dionysos' grave,
or omphalos, is in Delphi, and there he is also ritually awakened as a child from the
cradle, reborn. He is called *Liknites* – "he of the winnowing fan."

Jung, in *Psychological Types*, volume 6 of his *Collected Works*, in his chapter on
"The Apollonian and the Dionysian," speaks of Nietzsche's obsession with this
pair, describing Apollonian as dreaming, the inner world of fantasy and individuation; as images of beauty, of measure, of controlled proportioned feeling, the
state of introspection, contemplation, healing, light, intellectualized, civilized.
Dionysian, by contrast, is intoxication, impulse, liberation of unbounded instinct,
extraverted feeling, sensate, pure affect, the bodily sphere.[3]

Culturally, the two may have reflected the civilized Greek and his own bar-
barian nature. The mirror discussed as Figure 2.2 may have been a gift given
to a young man for an initiation ceremony. It is a moment of recognition
between the two gods, perhaps symbolizing the young man's own coming to
terms with himself.

Zoe and Bios

Where an individual psyche or a culture puts too one-sided an emphasis on the
rational light side, the dark Dionysian side will emerge in destructive ways. On a
cultural level, we have only to call up September 11, and the chaotic, impassioned,
bloody state of world affairs that has ensued, to see the truth of Jung's statement
written in 1935:

> Dionysos is the abyss of impassioned dissolution where all human dis-
> tinctions are merged in the animal divinity of the primordial psyche – a
> blissful and terrible experience. Humanity, huddling behind the walls of

its culture, believes it has escaped this experience, until it succeeds in letting loose another orgy of bloodshed. All well-meaning people are amazed
when this happens and blame high finance, the armaments industry, the
Jews, or the Freemasons.[4]

Another reflection of Jung's, made after America dropped the bomb on
Hiroshima, has haunted me in recent years after September 11. He said: "The
world hangs by a thread, and that thread is the psyche of man."[5] He also insisted
in many places throughout his work that the only possibility for saving the world
is for each man and woman to hold the tension between the opposites in his or
her individual psyche.

So my task here is psychologically to hold these opposites, as I delve into the
mysteries of the dark, bloody god Dionysos, who must take his place next to his
bright, light brother Apollo, in my psyche. To that end, I invite you to open
yourself to finding where the archetype of Dionysos relates to your individual psyche. What does it mean to be called to a confrontation with Dionysos? What has
become sterile and needs fertilizing by the stream of ongoing life?

Dionysos and the mask

In parallel to the ancient material, I will look at some examples of modern
Dionysian dilemmas and the psychological ways to work with this archetype, so
that an encounter with "possession or madness" can eventually be enlivening and
healing, not annihilating.

Dionysos's life has been depicted in three stages – infant, boy/young man, and
a bearded older man. In a sixth-century mask he has long, hanging, snaky hair,
and wears a crown of ivy leaves, alternately black and purple. The mask is both
his symbol and his incarnation. The mask itself – painted on the vessel – *is* the god
(Figure 2.3).

FIGURE 2.3 Mask of bearded Dionysos in his older manifestation, no longer a young
man. Black-figure amphora. From Tarquinia, Attica, 530–520 BCE

(https://aras.org/ancient-greece-modern-psyche)

There is also a sixth-century vessel that becomes a mask when you raise it
to your lips to drink (Figure 2.4). It has *apotropaic* eyes (literally, "turning away
evil"). Dionysos is seated on the left with a satyr dancing before him. Vines are
falling everywhere. The use of a mask in ritual had a particular potency when
turned toward the observer – as when drinking to the health and good fortune
of one's friends.

FIGURE 2.4 Cup-like kylix. Chalkidian black-figure eye-cup, c. 530 BCE. Staatliche
Antikensammlungen, Munich

(https://aras.org/ancient-greece-modern-psyche)

On a more somber level, these great eyes looking directly out at us show us a god of confrontation.[6] In Euripides' play *The Bacchae*, the worshipper says: "He saw me, I saw him," and Dionysos himself says to Pentheus: "it is the god you see . . . You see what you could not when you were blind."[7] The experience of the believer involves the reciprocal vision of the Bacchant and his god. His worship or acknowledgment required participation, not just sacrifice. The appearance of Dionysos causes a psychological confrontation with the self of dramatic proportions. The eye of the ego meets the eye of the self – in Jung's sense of the dimension of the psyche where the divine reaches us – an encounter that forces us to reckon with a new reality, to "face the truth." The mask is then both the symbol of the confrontation and the ritual container of the Dionysian energy. Jung says:

> The Dionysian element has to do with emotions and affects which have found no suitable religious outlets in the predominantly Apollonian cult and ethos of Christianity. The medieval carnivals and *jeux de paume* in the Church were abolished relatively early; consequently the carnival became secularized and with it divine intoxication vanished from the sacred precincts. Mourning, earnestness, severity, and well-tempered spiritual joy remained. But intoxication, that most direct and dangerous form of possession, turned away from the gods and enveloped the human world with its exuberance and pathos. The pagan religions met this danger by giving drunken ecstasy a place within their cult . . . to exorcise the danger. Our solution, however, has served to throw the gates of hell wide open.[8]

The central theme in the ancient Dionysian mysteries is the necessity for participation in the release of these energies. If one did not recognize him – spurned his mysteries – he took vengeance: whether it was on the women who were too righteous as wives and mothers, or the men who dismissed him as an intruder.

But beyond punishment, there was then an encounter with absolute reality, the confrontation.[9] And why should this be so? Because, psychologically, such avoidance is a refusal to incorporate the wisdom of the feared energies, and that wisdom is needed for wholeness.

So when and where Dionysos was denied his rites, madness ensued – at its most extreme this took the form of killing one's own children. This punishment is Dionysos at his darkest – violent, debased, possessed – seen in Euripides' *The Bacchae*, where mother and son, Argoe and Pentheus, both turn away from Dionysos and are destroyed by the compulsion of the god. Pentheus, the son, becomes a fool, dresses like a woman, and is led to doom at his own mother's hands. Argoe, his mother, becomes the destroyer – the shadow side of the maternal feminine arises – and she kills and dismembers her own child.

So what does it mean when such a primitive, unconscious tendency appears in our psyches or our lives? How can we entertain, or even acknowledge, such a potentially destructive god? The answer is that, in Dionysos's dark realm, renewal lies, all that the too-one-sided ego needs for its revitalizing expansion.

Here are some of the ways in which we may see the masked god, the stranger, and hear a different call in ourselves, asking to be recognized:

- *Violence* – anger, rage; good violence, creative, lifegiving, vital, as distinguished from bad or criminal violence
- *Eros* – possession or obsession with a loved one or with erotic images
- *Addiction* – to drugs, alcohol, to ecstatic states, to work, to seduction
- *An abandoned call* – to adventure, to war
- *Manic or other emotional state* – especially those that manifest in movement
- *Initiatory dreams* – in which Dionysos or his symbolic attributes appear

Dionysos is most often imagined dancing. In a red-figure amphora, Dionysos, dressed in long robes, holds his *kantharos* of wine in one hand and grasps his vine above his head in the other hand, participating in a ritual dance. He is facing toward a wand or staff of giant fennel covered with ivy vines and leaves. This is his *thyrsus*, often wound with a narrow band or ribbon and always topped with a pine cone, the source of spiritual fire and erotic fertility (Figure 2.5).

FIGURE 2.5   Dionysos dancing with satyrs and maenads, holding a kantharos, draped with a leopard skin, vines hanging over him. Red-figure amphora by the Kleophades Painter. Antiker Museum, Munich

(https://aras.org/ancient-greece-modern-psyche)

Dionysos in clinical practice

The following are a few clinical vignettes of predicaments with a Dionysian appearance.

One man, a 45-year-old wealthy lawyer with an excellent mind, rational, logical, thorough, his life under control, married with four young children, a stellar leader in his community and his church, finds himself madly in love with a 22-year-old paralegal in his firm, after struggling in vain to put her aside and out of his mind. He comes to therapy in desperation. Previously he thought therapy was a waste of time and people who sought it weak. He appears in shock, disbelieving, that something he morally abhors has overtaken him, without his consent. "Because," he says, "I have never before encountered a dilemma I could not solve." And now he can not only *not* stop himself from thinking about the young woman, but also he is unable to stop feeling tormented, desiring her. This becomes a life crisis in which he struggles to come back each week to face the most difficult problem of his life – that of his own conflicted self. He deeply loves his wife and children, but he also truly loves the other woman.

A second man – a 39-year-old real-estate agent who is affable, outgoing, successful, married, with two children – agreeably seeks therapy at his wife's request. She is having a positive experience in her therapy and thinks their marriage and parenting can improve if he looks at some of his own history. He tells me early on that his father had been an alcoholic and that often, from a very young age, he had been sent by his mother to fetch his father out of bars. He had felt threatened both by his father's inebriation and by the atmosphere in the bars; repulsed by his father's drunkenness, he had vowed to never touch alcohol, and he has lived by that self-imposed rule, but, in the course of our work, he begins to go to parties where people offer him cocaine – synchronistically. Again, suddenly and uncharacteristically, some fascination seizes him and he begins to dabble, then spin out of control, becoming addicted to cocaine and increasingly addicted to therapy to try to get to the root of his compulsion.

A 35-year-old woman, an obstetrician, a well-respected expert in her field, obsessively committed to her patients, at every hour of the day or night, has a baby herself and begins to feel out of control. She only comes to therapy because her infant son has developed "failure to thrive" syndrome and is in mortal danger. It emerges that she has become so intoxicated with the "ecstasy" of delivering babies and with her own drive for success that she resents her own child for interfering with her own drive. She barely has time for therapy, but in her hours she begins to see the split she is living and to fall into an extremely dark place emotionally.

A 56-year-old woman, a conventional librarian, who never married, was content with her books, with being a distant aunt to her brother's children and participating in a local charity, seeks therapy when she suddenly becomes obsessed with a long-haired, wild teenage boy in her neighborhood and begins to stalk him. She is possessed and distraught by the power of her attraction and the deviance from who she has known herself to be. She feels lost and helpless: "How can I be doing this? Who am I?" she asks herself.

A timid woman in her mid-70s, physically weakened by a congestive heart problem, who has been in therapy for many years, looking at her dreams and working on consciousness, and who is still in a lifelong marriage, with children grown, suddenly begins to dream of bullfights and bullfighters – many of the dreams bring her face to face with the bull – then she awakens, frightened but thrilled. Her deeply fearful nature contrasts dramatically with these powerful images, and as we begin to explore how this energy will manifest, we see the danger as well as the numinosity in this challenge. Overcoming her deeply ingrained fears in order to fulfill this call will be truly awesome. But what will this mean in terms of her outer life? What will it ask of her at this stage of her life? Will she have the strength, the longevity, and the determination to endure such a violent transformation?

These conflicts, representative of Dionysian seizure, are characterized by suddenness, a sense of being wholly possessed, and are emotionally experienced in the body. And, finally, such a conflict threatens the established life of the man or woman called to the confrontation.

The more repressed or split-off an aspect of the instinctual Dionysian nature becomes, the more violent and explosive are the results of its release. Looked at clinically and archetypally, we can say that the Dionysian archetype brings fluidity to what is rigid, determined, and controlled; breaks down useless attitudinal barriers; and dissolves outlived collective values.

But this does not do justice to the *living* of such a crisis that is painful, overwhelming, and violent, and here there is no map to follow. Each individual has to discover, through suffering the problem, what exactly has been outlived. Which deeply held truths *are* the "useless attitudinal barriers or collective values"?

Of course, there are some glib or unsatisfactory collective answers floating around; for example, in the case of a triangle: "Don't live in a marriage that doesn't fulfill you." But if the person is really searching for the truth, he or she will ask: "How did I get here? What has gone before? And what *is* fulfillment, or happiness, or love?" "Is it remaining loyal and finding an inner solution? Or, while being as kind and loving to my wife, or husband, and children as possible, is it creating a new outer life where the passion is? And what will be the consequences of that?"

It is only by struggling with these questions that some integration of the personality will eventually come. Acting out a solution will only repress the other side. This is a precarious edge, this process of trying to figure out what is outlived, what is correct, what is the right thing to do for oneself and others, instead of throwing out the precious center of one's being and flipping to the other side in identifying with the overwhelming rush of sensation, ecstasy, or possession, which is dissolving the ego. What is necessary is to hold tight and try to maintain one's balance while some transformation happens.

In addiction, as the body becomes dependent on the substance, the ego becomes attached to the high, the chaos, the dissolution, the dismemberment, and stays stuck there, repeating the orgiastic godlike participation. The man who is becoming enthralled by cocaine is fighting not to go there.

Transformation involves a slow process of differentiation. There is nothing fast about transformation. Both the intrusion of the god, and enlightenment, are lightning-like, but transformation lies in the slow fermentation of a problem. So how do we hold the tension between the ego and the self and between inner and outer – the opposites in ourselves – when confronted with these dramatic, spontaneous eruptions that threaten to carry us away?

Let us turn back to Dionysos – his story, his myth, and his rites – and see how and why he also embodies hope for these transformations that we need psychologically.

Birth of Dionysos

There are two stories of the birth of Dionysos. In the most familiar one, Zeus united with Semele, daughter of Cadmus; but Semele, tricked by Hera, begged Zeus to show himself to her as he truly was, and she was consumed by lightning. The baby in her womb was rescued and sewn into the thigh of Zeus until he was ready to be born. Zeus gave the baby to Hermes to give to the nymphs of Nysa. So Dionysos, whose name means "Son of Zeus," was born of fire, and his song, *dithyrambos*, derives from "he who entered life by a double door."

In the Cretan version, this Dionysos (sometimes called Zagreus) was the son of
Zeus and Persephone. Hera, still jealous, sends the Titans to slay the baby while he
is playing with his toys – a cone, knuckle bone, a mirror among them. They tore
him limb from limb, and some say they cooked him in a cauldron and ate him,
but his heart was saved by Athena and either sewn again into Zeus's thigh or else
his body was reconstituted from the heart by his grandmother, Rhea, one of the
Titans born to Gaia and Uranus. A black-figure painting on a terracotta vessel from
the sixth century BCE dramatizes Dionysos being reborn from the cauldron of his
own death, with vines shooting out from his right arm and shoulder. Two women
sit facing the cauldron, one on either side; they may be Semele and Persephone
(Figure 2.6).

FIGURE 2.6 *The Child in the Cauldron.* Black figure, terracotta vessel, Attica, 520–500 BCE
(https://aras.org/ancient-greece-modern-psyche)

In his orgies, worshippers often tore wild animals to pieces or, as in Argoe's
case, a mother tore her child to pieces, paradoxically, in order to reintegrate his
dismembered spirit. Jung said: "The breaking loose of the unbridled dynamism of
animal and divine nature dissolves the individual into the collective instincts . . . it
is an explosion of the isolated ego through the world . . . in the Dionysian orgy . . .
individuation is entirely obliterated."[10] So in order to individuate, we have to dissolve back into the collective, into a symbolic death, periodically, and sometimes
in dramatic ways, then reemerge. It occurs always in momentous transitions, like
puberty, acts of sex, childbirth, or nursing a baby, because death and the powers of
the underworld are present at life's central moments and festivities.[11]

Dionysos, in his own dismemberment, suffers the horror that he later commits –
a destructive frenzy that tears a living creature limb from limb – he is called *Omistis*,
eater of raw flesh. The bloodthirstiness of the maenads, the female worshippers
who follow him, is that of the god himself. But what is divine madness? The rapture and terror of life are so profound because they are intoxicated with death. An
extreme example of a bloody Dionysian ritual acted out would lie in the violence
of those groups whose actions result in a drunken frenzy or death. For instance,
suicide bombers, terrorists – in the name of religion – show a modern way of dismembering, with bombs.

Psychologically, if we are dismembered – disintegrated from within or without –
our task is to re-collect the scattered parts of ourselves. A child may be subjected
very early in life to a dismembering and devouring and only be able to reassemble
himself or herself much later with the help of a mother archetype, a containing
analyst or therapist, whether male or female. Jung says:

> The integration or humanization of the self is initiated from the conscious
> side by our making ourselves aware of our selfish aims; we examine our
> motives and try to form as complete and objective a picture as possible
> of our own nature. It is an act of self-recollection, a gathering together

of what is scattered, of all the things in us that have never been properly related, and a coming to terms with oneself with a view to achieving full consciousness.[12]

So a visitation from Dionysos brings us up against our own divided selves. Jung continues:

> Self-recollection . . . is about the hardest and most repellant thing there is for a man, who is predominantly unconscious. Human nature has an invincible dread of becoming more conscious of itself. What . . . drives us to it is the self, which demands sacrifice . . . Conscious realization or the bringing together of the scattered parts is in one sense an act of the ego's will, but in another sense it is a spontaneous manifestation of the self, which was always there.[13]

The Dionysian archetype offers the chance that, after the dismemberment, there will be both a reconstitution, a putting back together of the dismembered parts, and also a rebirth – a reintegration of the psyche in a new, more alive, healthier form.

On the front face of a Roman sarcophagus is a relief of a *liknon* – a word that means both cradle and winnowing fan – which shows a triumphal procession of Bacchos. At one of the ends, two men – one bearded, nude with a cloak; one youthful, clothed in animal skin – carry the infant god in the *liknon* by its handles, having emerged from behind a curtain draped between two trees. Both men hold up a curtain and flaming torches that point to a mystery scene enacted by night. A *liknon* was a shovel-shaped basket, used for the carrying of fruits and the winnowing of the grain in order to separate the chaff, and the winnowing fan was one of the implements used in the Mysteries. Two lions are seated above the scene, on either side of a vase of grapes (Figure 2.7).[14]

FIGURE 2.7   *Liknon* (a word that means both cradle and winnowing fan) containing a naked baby. Sarcophagus relief. Roman period. Fitzwilliam Museum, Cambridge

(Diagram in Harrison, p. 524, fig. 150. **https://aras.org/ancient-greece-modern-psyche**)

Zeus gave the "twice-born" baby to Hermes, who gave him to Silenus and the nymphs to raise on Mount Nysa. Silenus tended the baby in a cave and fed him with honey. It was in Crete that he found the vine and invented wine. Dionysos's fate as a baby offers itself as an *Epiphany*. He becomes the god who vanishes and reappears; he is present and absent; he dies and is reborn (Figure 2.8).

FIGURE 2.8   Hermes delivering baby Dionysos to Silenus and the nymphs of Nysa. Athenian red–figure kalyx krater, c. fifth century BCE. Gregorian Etruscan Museum, Vatican Museums

(**https://aras.org/ancient-greece-modern-psyche**)

Dionysos Mainomenos – "the mad one"

Hera does not give up her persecution. She recognizes Dionysos as a young man and induces madness, *mania*, in him. He appears at times of cultural transitions as well as individual transitions. So, culturally, Hera's act of driving the god mad could reflect the conservative opposition to the ritual use of wine, as well as the extravagant maenad fashion that was coming into vogue in Greece at the time. Once again, Dionysos is cured of his madness by Rhea, Zeus's mother, his grandmother, who purifies him. As he recovers his wits, he learns his own ceremonies, his *teletai*. Rhea gives him his Bacchants' costume, his *stole*, thyrsus, ivy, long robe, and fawnskin.

In a fifth-century terracotta kylix, *Dionysos Mainomenos* is dancing, wreathed in vine leaves, maybe a snake, dressed in pleated chiton, a leopard skin over his shoulders (Figure 2.9). This is the savage brutal side of the god. He is holding a fawn he has torn in half. Mock deaths became substitutes for human sacrifice in initiation ceremonies. Here it is the animal, the fawn, in place of the initiand. He is called "womanish" in this garb, an allusion to an androgynous/ hermaphroditic state, which may refer to the liminal space that occurs in transitional periods in culture or at critical thresholds in life. These liminal spaces are expressed in the process of analysis as "I don't know who I am any more . . . I'm not who I used to be . . . I don't have my old stability, but I don't know what the new one is yet," or, often, "Why can't I just go back to being unconscious?"

FIGURE 2.9 *Dionysos Mainomenos*, with goat, leopard skin, and boots. Terracotta kylix red figure, c. 490 BCE

(https://aras.org/ancient-greece-modern-psyche)

Dionysos Dithyrambos

Dithyrambos means literally "twice-born" – but it really means being reborn over and over. Because of his own narrative, the madness Dionysos inflicts always calls for *catharsis*, the cleansing of the impurity of frenzied violence that needs purification and healing. Psychologically, this depends on the power and capacity of the ego to hold fast in the frenzy. We cannot underestimate the power of *catharsis*, the "getting it all out" function in therapy. This is the purification.

Dionysos Katharsios

Dionysos's purification takes place in trance – he is called *Dionysos Katharsios*, the god who purifies, or *Dionysos Lysios*; literally, the loosener, the god who unties the knots, who releases into madness. His is the madness that attends life – in music and dance. He is also a prophet. In the art of prophecy, madness is represented as secret knowledge.

He is often depicted wearing boots, which refers to him being both the hunter and the hunted. Psychologically, it is the ego hunting for knowledge of itself and other, hunting for our illusions, rigidities, integrities, or grandiose fantasies, the solutions to the conflict, all the different light and shadow sides of ourselves – these are all prey. But, going deeper, the self is the hunter, and in the process of the hunt, or analysis, the eye of the hunter and the eye of the prey meet; and, paradoxically, the self is also prey because it holds what we need to incorporate in order to be reborn.

In a black-figure amphora of 500 BCE, Dionysos, snaky and vine-crowned, sits on a white-horned bull, as a symbol of fertility. He holds a vine branch with grapes in his left hand, while he pours wine back into the Earth from the *kantharos* he holds in his right hand. Dionysos is represented here as the bull himself, as well as the flowing bowl whose wine falls back into the earth. The bull was a sacrificial animal, reminiscent of the Minoan/Mycenaean Cretan Bull, all images of death and rebirth in nature (Figure 2.10).

FIGURE 2.10 Dionysos on his bull. Terracotta amphora black figure, 500 BCE
(https://aras.org/ancient-greece-modern-psyche)

Dionysos Diomorphos

Dionysos was also called *Diomorphos* – god of many forms. On one side, the lion, panther, leopard, and lynx, embodying the bloodthirsty desire to kill; but also, on the other side, the bull, goat, and ass (herbivorous animals), suggesting fertility and sexual desire.

In a Hellenistic sculpture from Rome in the Greco-Roman era, two maenads are engaged in a wild dance around Dionysos, who takes the form of a massive bull with his head lowered – a symbol of instinctual vitality and the life force, like a primitive nature god (Figure 2.11). Dreams of bulls often come to women, like the one in my example, who need to relate to their own instincts and were never given permission to get down into them. Bullfighting probably originated as a dance with the bull, as in the 1500 BCE Minoan fresco of the bull-dancers in ancient Crete. Then, later in classical Greece, this dance became the killing and eating of the bull, receiving the *mana/spirit* of the god.

FIGURE 2.11 Two maenads with a bull. Hellenistic sculpture. Rome. Greco-Roman era
(https://aras.org/ancient-greece-modern-psyche)

The goat was another fertility and sacrificial animal in the Dionysian Mysteries. In another escapade, when Dionysos was an infant, Zeus turned him into a kid to get him out of Hera's grasp. The sacrifice of the animal is symbolically the sacrifice of our animal nature, reminding us we have both to sacrifice it and yet also stay in touch with it (Figure 2.12).[15]

FIGURE 2.12 Mask with goats, glyptic seal. Crete
(https://aras.org/ancient-greece-modern-psyche)

Greek tragedy arose out of this essentially religious ceremony: the term *trag-edy* is a synthesis of *tragos*, "goat," and *oidos*, "song." Imaginal violence provides the *catharsis* for the troubled soul. Ritual/theatre/religion is an arena for dealing with violent energies, especially those that develop from the individual psyche. Historically, drama gave this aspect of the Greeks a cultural container for Dionysos' energy. In Athens the plays were performed in the theatre of Dionysos in the precinct of the god, where his image was present: the chorus danced around his altar, while his priest sat in the front row and took the central seat of the spectators. The god was there as the daimon of death and resurrection, of reincarnation, the rebirth of spring, of the spring of humans as well as Nature's spring.

Dionysos and his followers

Dionysos has, for his companions, the satyrs and, in particular, the horse-tailed, earth-born, and bearded satyr, Silenus, who is older and wiser than other *sileni*. Silenus is frequently drunk and is often called Dionysos's tutor. In one vase, Dionysos, crowned with ivy, holds the *kantharos* and vine stock above the head of a lion who sits upright at his feet looking up at him with his mouth open and his tongue ready to catch the drops (Figure 2.13). On his right, Silenus is playing his pipes to the horse who is dancing in tune.

FIGURE 2.13 Dionysos with lion and Silenus. Black-figured vase. c. 530–500 BCE
(https://aras.org/ancient-greece-modern-psyche)

Dionysos had epiphanies as Serpent, Lion, and Bull, because these were the calendar emblems of the tripartite year – born in winter as a serpent (hence his serpent crown), became a lion in the spring, and killed and devoured as a bull, goat, or stag at midsummer. Clement of Alexandria, an early Greek Christian writer and presbyter who flourished in Alexandria in the late second century CE, commented: "The bull is father of the snake, and the snake is father of the bull."[16] Jung says:

> This atavistic identification with human and animal ancestors can be interpreted psychologically as an integration of the unconscious, a veritable bath of renewal in the life-source where one is once again a fish, unconscious as in sleep, intoxication, and death. Hence the sleep of incubation, the Dionysian orgy, and the ritual death in initiation. Naturally, the proceedings always take place in some hallowed spot.[17]

The other followers of Dionysos were the groups of women called maenads. In one terracotta vessel from 540 BCE, two maenads present a small stag to Dionysos;

a hare hangs down from one maenad's waist as though forming a part of her dress (Figure 2.14). The women, unusually calm, dance sedately toward him, their arms around each other's necks. Dionysos, wearing the leopard skin, with an ivy branch falling from it, holds the *kantharos*, and his outstretched hand accepts the gift of the tiny stag. His epiphany brings madness, pandemonium, the din: he is called "loud-roaring" – *Erivromos* – "the joyous one." There were typically drums, flutes, and cymbals, first a wild uproar and then a numbed silence. A melancholy silence becomes the sign of women who are possessed by Dionysos.[18] Psychologically, this is the frenzied or catatonic or frozen state of madness. It can also be a kind of stillness and calm, such as in the analytic hour, which is characteristic of liminal states and can, paradoxically, be quite productive.

FIGURE 2.14   Two maenads presenting a small stag to Dionysos, with a hare hanging down from the maenad's waist, as though a part of her dress. Black-figure painting on terracotta vessel. Attica c. 540 BCE. Cabinet des Medailles, Paris

(https://aras.org/ancient-greece-modern-psyche)

The gift of the vine

In another black-figure amphora from 530 BCE, a gray-bearded Silenus, on the left of the painting, is pouring water from a hydria into a large earthenware vessel (Figure 2.15). Behind him, another silen is playing upon a double flute. A large silen at the back treads the grapes that another silen to the left of him is placing in the basket. On the far right, a further silen picks grapes from the overhanging vine. In the frieze above, five sileni and four maenads are dancing around Dionysos who is seated with a drinking horn in his hand. This is Dionysos as a nature god. Aeschylus called wine "the Wild Mother."[19]

FIGURE 2.15   Silenus in a wine harvest scene. Amphora, black figure, c. 530 BCE

(https://aras.org/ancient-greece-modern-psyche)

The gift of wine was on occasion so precious that in certain cities it became a drug – *pharmakon* – and was to be administered in its pure state to the elderly, to whom it would bring "initiation and recreation" – *telete* and *paidia*. The coming together of friends was not intended in classical Greece to lead to drunken abandon. Rather, the purpose of the wine was to free the mind to speak more eloquently and with greater insight. The amazing miracle of "one-day vines" – *efemeree ampelee* – took place when the vines flowered and bore fruit in the course of a few hours during the festivals of the epiphany of the god. This was understood as a genuine sign of his presence. Compare the ear of grain that miraculously grows and is cut off and presented to the participants in the Eleusinian Mysteries as the culmination of the Mystery Night.

Wine also brings *the ecstatic* – the being "beside oneself" – with anxiety, astonishment, fear, or passion, transported in rapture. The refuse of wine was also used to paint the faces in the Dionysian festivals that were the beginning of theatre, first tragedy, then later comedy.

Dionysos is the one who tames the wine, mixes it with water in a krater, celebrates the first *symposium*, and institutes the etiquette of wine-drinking. Wine carries the wonders and secrets, the boundless wild nature of the god. It brings forgetfulness to the sorrows of humans. Wine not only reveals the truth but also, in the growing intensity of its effects, changes its nature, moving from well-being, love, desire, and sleep, to wantonness, cries, deeds of violence, and finally madness.

The vine plant requires many stages: the vine to be planted, the technique of vine-growing, the maturation of the fruit, followed by the trampling of the grape and the fermentation of the wine. Wine is called the "Blood of the Earth." The juice of grapes ferments rapidly. It works, cooks by itself, begins to boil, transforms the juice of the grapes in the huge wine vats into wine spirits. This parallels the process within an individual – a similarly mysterious process – once alive and bubbling, it alters this natural raw material into spirit. This cooking is what happens in analysis when an individual is willing to steep himself or herself in the work. It is the stage of fermentation in alchemy.

Dionysos Orthios – the "upright one"

In this aspect of himself the god is upright – a civilizing god, when the wine is mixed as a remedy. It was even said that "by drinking properly-mixed wine, men ceased to stand in a bent posture" – strangely similar to Demeter's story in which barley and cereal plants gave humans the strength to stand erect, to cease to behave as tetrapods.[20] From wheat to bread and vine to wine, this process was an image of the "cultivated" life.

Dionysos Hugiates – the "dispenser of health"

As well as the vine and ivy, other plants were associated with Dionysos, such as the pine tree and pine cones, the myrtle, and the phallic fig tree.

In festivals of Dionysos the mask of the god was often hung on a pillar or a tree. Dionysos was too powerful a god for participants to imagine they could become him themselves, so participants never wore the mask and, when the rite was over, they put the mask away and returned, renewed, to the tasks of everyday life. One of these figures, a fifth-century BCE red-figured terracotta from Naples, has been adorned, dressed in a chiton (what the Romans later called a *tunic*) and an over-garment with ivy twigs; an ornamental wreath hangs from his belt (Figure 2.16). Round ritual cakes have been placed on either side of the god's mask. On the left, a maenad, wearing an ivy wreath, ladles wine. There is a dancing maenad opposite her, suggesting this was a wine festival to consecrate the new wine. Plutarch, in the second century CE, writes that in early festivals, "the wine jar came first, then a vine stock, a he-goat, a basket of figs, and finally the phallus."[21]

FIGURE 2.16   Festival of Dionysos. Red-figured terracotta from Naples. Early Greek classical vessel/stamnoi, 425–400 BCE

(https://aras.org/ancient-greece-modern-psyche)

The dancing maenads are here in a state of mystical communion with their god, in the throes of an ecstatic deliverance, standing outside or beyond themselves (Figure 2.17). Semele herself during pregnancy was supposedly seized by an irrepressible desire to dance, and the child in her womb danced too.[22] She was already filled with divine spirit and so too were the women who touched her blessed body. What is known as the "bacchic step" is a leaping force that invades the body and takes control of it, carrying it irresistibly along. Dionysos jumps and leaps, or capers like a goat, the Dionysiac trance beginning with the foot, the leaping.

FIGURE 2.17   Detail. Procession of maenads, playing pipes and tambourine with the young god and a leopard following. Villa Quintiliana, Appian Way. Roman, 100 CE. British Museum

(https://aras.org/ancient-greece-modern-psyche)

This god always appears in a surge of natural energy, spontaneously, whether it is the vine that grows up "in the blink of an eye," or the leaping to the feet and running out the door, leaping, boiling, spurting. He is a god of paradox with many names: "the friendly god who lavishes blessings" or else he is "the bestial and wild one."[23]

Dionysos and Ariadne

For a god who, archetypally, brings such disruption and causes so much triangulation among us, Dionysos is, surprisingly, the only god who is faithful to his chosen bride – Ariadne. Ariadne was the daughter of King Minos and probably also the priestess – and originally the goddess – of the mystical rites of the labyrinth: dancing the labyrinth dance, winding into the center and out again. In the later Greek story, she gives Theseus the thread to find his way into the labyrinth to slay the Minotaur and to come out alive. Later, he abandons her, or is ordered to leave her, on the island of Naxos, and she becomes the bride of Dionysos – that is, if she was not his bride already.

There are many different tales about Ariadne, depending on who was telling them: whether it was the later Greeks (from c. eighth century BCE) or the earlier Mycenaeans (c. 1800–1500 BCE) or the original Minoans (c. 2500 BCE), insofar as it is possible to differentiate between them. After her death Ariadne becomes Aridela – a crown of stars placed in heaven by Dionysos. Many paintings on vessels from the sixth to the fourth century BCE show Dionysos and Ariadne dancing (Figure 2.18), or sitting together beneath the hanging vine (Figure 2.19), or ritually filling each other's cup (Figure 2.20).

FIGURE 2.18 Ariadne as maenad and Dionysos. Amphora, black figure, 510 BCE
(https://aras.org/ancient-greece-modern-psyche)

FIGURE 2.19 Dionysos and Ariadne beneath the vine. Lucanian red-figure volute
krater, fourth century BCE. Toledo Museum of Art
(https://aras.org/ancient-greece-modern-psyche)

FIGURE 2.20 Dionysos and Ariadne. Terracotta red figure, 520–510 BCE. The Louvre
(https://aras.org/ancient-greece-modern-psyche)

Dionysos's mother is called Semele, whose name means "seed." In one of the later Greek stories, Dionysos loves his mother so much that he goes down into Hades to bring her back to the upper world. But even he has to give a life for a life, so he gives Hades the myrtle tree and plants it at the entrance to Hades. So "the Seed" comes back as spring.

There is a rare Hellenistic marble sculpture from Herculaneum of a pensive young god lost in contemplation. Were it not for the panther by his side, the ivy in his hair, the thyrsus in his hand, and the *kantharos* of wine, he could be Apollo or any other youthful deity. Until their first contact with the Greeks, the Romans had almost no mythology. The Romans were not as interested in the narrative, the story, or the image in its own right, focusing more on the *numen*, the power of the gods in relation to themselves. Here, Dionysos is equipped with all the ritual paraphernalia that call upon the god's *numen* – the *kantharos* for wine and ecstasy, the thyrsus for phallic power, the panther for the dark and bestial force within his cult, and the ivy wreath of the rite. The cult of Dionysos was not as widespread in Rome as in Greece, not because it lacked followers, but because it was feared by the state. The Romans created their own rituals for initiation into the Mysteries.

Answering the stranger's call

For therapists, the ritual container is partially the psychotherapeutic container where all the dismembered parts can be re-collected. And then each individual has to find ways for his or her own containment. To conclude with my earlier examples of Dionysian visitations, what can I say? What does this have to do with us as individuals?

When the conscious attitude has become too rigid, legalistic, dried up, the stranger appears, often masked, in the form of something or someone foreign, the kind of person or event that we had never before seen, or paid attention to, or had even rejected outright.

In the case of the lawyer, mentioned earlier, the stranger appeared in the form of a young woman who seemed to contain all the libido that he had put aside in his race for success and in his being the perfect family man. Curious to him, he said, was that "she is not my type physically, not the kind of woman I'm ever attracted to, too chubby . . . So why then am I crazily, madly, in love with her?"

To the real-estate agent, the god appeared in the face of a drug: cocaine. This man had repudiated the shadow, the chthonic dark side, when he repudiated his father's alcohol addiction. And thereby he left himself vulnerable to the ecstatic in this undifferentiated way. He felt something that he had never felt before – rapture.

The stranger appeared to the librarian in the form of an adolescent, a boy living on the edge of Dionysian possession himself, dealing drugs, racing motorcycles. Not only was he a potential love interest by his age – no longer a child – but her possession threatened to draw her into degrading both herself and him in unthinkable and illegal ways. She was mystified, beside herself with her own fascination.

In these affairs of the heart, the problem of transformation – instead of addiction, destruction, or degradation – challenges the individual to hold the tension of opposites, rather than immediately answering the call of the god to simply abandon all and follow him into the woods and, as it were, dismember the previous life that he or she has created.

Again, there is no simple answer. The purpose of the psychological call, of the stranger's appearance, is to renew the too-limited ego, signaling that the individual has to encounter himself or herself by asking these questions: What are the outworn attitudes that need to be discarded? How is a woman who has suddenly fallen in love outside her marriage to know whether the outmoded, sterile form is the marriage itself or an inner attitude that keeps that marriage from flourishing? What is the man who is in love with cocaine lacking instead? The answer is unique to each situation that arises. What may be an internal problem for one individual is an external problem for the other.

If the impulse to movement, the maenadic dance in the woods, is to *bear fruit*, the individual must keep from doing irreparable damage to loved ones' or anyone's life. He or she must continually return to ordinary life or consciousness and face the one who has been betrayed – husband, wife, and family, or some dimension in the self – with courage and honesty. But then, what *is* honesty and how can those possessed know the truth? How do they respect themselves and their loved ones involved and not polarize and become destructive? How do they know what sacrifice is called for? Because a sacrifice will be called for. Once this Dionysian energy has erupted, there is no solution that does not hurt someone, including its victim. One of the lessons learned is often, "I am capable of hurting another." This may be an acknowledgment of harm done to self or other while in the throes of addiction or in the betrayal of a relationship.

Like worshippers of Dionysos, individuals in this situation are torn asunder by conflicting feelings and wishes and must sit still for many hours to pull all the different pieces of themselves together, and re-collect or re-member, so that they can gain sufficient integrity to make decisions and take measures. The deepest need is to concentrate on the work, to meditate upon it, and not to run away from themselves or the conflicting sides.

The obstetrician who is obsessed with the ecstasy of giving birth is arrested in her development. Her physician's skills are sophisticated and honed but split off from her own maternal instincts. In failing to see her own split, she has made herself and her son vulnerable to dark forces. He does not feel her love; he has no container for life. The obstetrician cannot move beyond birth – other people's births and her own role in them. She is sacrificing her child to her own euphoria, rather like a maenad who in a frenzy destroys her child. She has to stop being compulsively drawn to the high of the birth moment in order to grow into being a mother and rearing her own child for his own sake. Dionysos has appeared to her in the face of her son. She must listen to a deeper law.

On a more collective level, teenagers who succumb to ecstasy in its drug form and are possessed by raving and dancing also suffer arrested development. Finding an artificial escape from social discomfort, they no longer have to engage with people to learn how to relate to others. Instead, they stop growing. No transformation is possible for them as long as they repetitively engage in taking ecstasy, which gives them a sense of communion with others and a false, limited sense of identity, of being one of them.

The plethora of Alcoholics Anonymous (AA) groups in the United States, which has been life-saving for so many, is testimony to the dark toll of substance abuse on our historical national atmosphere of rationality and repression. Similarly, addictions to sex or money or, for instance, pornography, keep people stuck in an endless pursuit of ecstatic gratification. The Twelve-Step movement has become an invaluable adjunct to psychotherapy, a ritual container for women and men to acknowledge Dionysos and to stop their repetitive acting out in order to effect true transformation.

Yet abstinence without knowledge breeds more fascination, more possession. We cannot avoid a confrontation with Dionysos, once he has sought us out. We must look him in the eyes and know him. Dark, chthonic Dionysos must be allowed to move an individual's psyche, to find a balance with the other aspect of the Apollonian order that we so revere.

And when you have an initiatory dream that penetrates to your core and rocks the foundation of your psyche, you have no less an obligation to respond to the call of Dionysos than the person to whom he comes as an outside fate. To fail to respond to that visitation is to risk wasting away emotionally from the lack of the revitalizing energy that he offers or demands. Dionysos's way is the way of transformation, of dismembering and rebirth. In order to honor him, we must not only risk self-knowledge and challenge our outmoded assumptions, but also be willing to seek him out, find ritual containers for honoring him, in passionate dance or movement, in intimate emotional encounters with loved ones, in treasured initiation rites that we create for important passages, and continue to invite the depths of Dionysian emotion to invigorate us all through our lives.

> The mysteries remain,
> I keep the same
> cycle of seed-time
> and of sun and rain;
> Demeter in the grass,

I multiply,
renew and bless
Bacchus in the vine;
I hold the law,
I keep the mysteries true,
the first of these
to name the living, dead;
I am red wine and bread.
I keep the law,
I hold the mysteries true,
I am the vine,
the branches, you
and you.

(H.D.)[24]

Notes

1 From Hilda Doolittle, "The Mysteries," *H. D. Collected Poems 1912–1944*, New York: New Directions Publishing, 1983, p. 305.
2 Jane Harrison, *Themis: A Study of the Social Origins of Greek Religion*, Gloucester, MA: Peter Smith, 1974, pp. 442–3.
3 C. G. Jung, *Psychological Types: The Collected Works of C. G. Jung*, vol. 6, Princeton, NJ: Princeton University Press, 1921/1971, pp. 136–46. (Hereafter all references to *The Collected Works* appear as CW and volume number.)
4 Jung, "Individual dream symbolism in relation to alchemy," *Psychology and Alchemy*, CW 12, p. 90, ¶118.
5 *C. G. Jung Speaking: Interviews and Encounters*, ed. William McGuire and R. F. C. Hull, Princeton, NJ: Princeton University Press, 1957, p. 303.
6 Walter F. Otto, *Dionysus: Myth and Cult*, Bloomington, IN: Indiana University Press, 1965, p. 90.
7 Euripides, *The Bacchae*, Greek Tragedies, vol. 3, eds. David Grene and Richmond Lattimore, Chicago, IL and London: University of Chicago Press, 1964, p. 234, lines 922–4.
8 Jung, CW 12, p. 143, ¶182.
9 Otto, *Dionysus*, p. 106.
10 Jung, CW 6, p. 138, ¶227.
11 Otto, *Dionysus*, p. 138.
12 Jung, *Psychology and Religion: West and East*, CW 11, p. 263, ¶400.
13 Ibid.
14 Jane Harrison, *Prolegomena to the Study of Greek Religion*, London: Merlin Press, 1962, pp. 523–4.
15 Jung, *Symbols of Transformation*, CW 5, p. 423.
16 *Clement of Alexandria*, trans. G. W. Butterworth, Loeb Classical Library, volume 92, Cambridge, MA: Harvard University Press, 1919, Book 2.
17 Jung, CW 12, p. 131, ¶171.
18 Otto, *Dionysus*, chapter 7.
19 Otto, *Dionysus*, p. 146.
20 Marcel Detienne, *Dionysos at Large*, trans. Arthur Goldhammer, London and Cambridge, MA: Harvard University Press, 1989, pp. 37–8.
21 Plutarch quoted in Otto, *Dionysus*, pp. 161–8.

22 Otto, *Dionysus*, p. 96.
23 Otto, *Dionysus*, p. 110.
24 Doolittle, "The Mysteries," p. 305.

Selected bibliography

Bradway, Katherine. *Villa of Mysteries: Pompeii Initiation Rites of Women*. San Francisco, CA: C. G. Jung Institute, 1982.

Detienne, Marcel. *Dionysos at Large*. Trans. Arthur Goldhammer. London and Cambridge, MA: Harvard University Press, 1989.

Fierz-David, Linda. *Women's Dionysian Initiation: Villa of Mysteries Pompeii*. Dallas, TX: Spring Publications, 1988.

Graves, Robert. *The Greek Myths*. London: Penguin Books, 1992.

Hall, Nor. *Those Women*. Dallas, TX: Spring Publications, 1988.

Harrison, Jane Ellen. *Prolegomena to the Study of Greek Religion*. London: Merlin Press, 1962.

Harrison, Jane Ellen. *Themis: A Study of the Social Origins of Greek Religion*. Gloucester, MA: Peter Smith, 1974.

Jashemski, Wilhemina F. *The Gardens of Pompeii, Herculaneum, and the Villas Destroyed by Vesuvius*. New Rochelle, NY: Caratzas Brothers Publishers, 1979.

Kerényi, Carl. *Dionysos: Archetypal Image of Indestructible Life*. Princeton, NJ: Princeton University Press, 1976.

Lopez-Pedraza, Rafael. *Dionysus in Exile: On the Repression of the Body and Emotion*. Wilmette, IL: Chiron Publication, 2000.

Meyer, Marvin W. (ed.). *The Ancient Mysteries: A Sourcebook of Sacred Texts*. San Francisco, CA: Harper and Row, 1987.

Otto, Walter F. *Dionysus: Myth and Cult*. Bloomington, IN: Indiana University Press, 1965.

Reis, Patricia. "The villa of mysteries: Initiation into woman's midlife passage." *Continuum*, 1991, vol. 1, no. 3.

Villani, Silvano. *The Mystery of Room No. 5: What Strange Rites Were Performed in That Out of the Way Ancient Villa in Pompei*. Rome: ITER Roma, 1991.

3

THE MADNESS OF AJAX

Luigi Zoja

> Even a worthless man can triumph with the gods' help; I am confident of achieving glory even without them.
>
> *(Sophocles,* Ajax, *ll. 767–9)*

At the beginning of the play, the irreparable has already happened.

Ajax knows the end is near and believes it will be his triumph. With matchless strength and courage, his arm has wrought a warrior's duty. It has slaughtered the enemy. Why should the enemy's destruction not be his triumph? His arm had followed his mind, and his mind had followed suspicion. From that moment, he had cast aside facts and reason.

Ajax is only interested in one thing: being acknowledged as the strongest. And because he is only interested in one thing, because his life revolves around that one thing, his life is solitary. His thoughts are solitary.[1] But an absence of people and interests is contrary to the nature of the psyche, which reacts by filling the void. The presences that are rejected in reality gradually reemerge in the mind. Rejected as realities, they reappear as nightmares and obsessions. They become suspicion. In this guise, what the person had wanted to deny makes its triumphant return. Ajax's mental life is smoldering suspicion on the point of exploding.

But what are only mental images to us in the modern age were once apparitions of the gods. And the gods did not like this strong but obstinate, fair-minded but naive man. His feeling of being in the right was too simple. When the gods wish to destroy a man, they begin by making him lose his sense of proportion. Ajax does not seem to need the gods. He refuses their help.

A person like this – alone on earth and in heaven too – runs a grave risk. Human reason must bow to superior powers. Omnipotence is not a human quality.

If the mind is absolute, unrestrained by humans and gods, lacking any limitation or anchors, it can lose itself.

At the beginning of Sophocles' tragedy, the gods have made Ajax's mind fly away, free from any restraint, like that strong, proud, solitary bird (*aietós* or *aetós*, the eagle) after which, according to Pindar, Zeus had named him.[2]

Pindar loved Ajax – how he loved him! And we can understand this, for the feelings of the Classical world are so distant and at the same time so close to us. Homer, Pindar, and Sophocles are creators of that heroic world, but they are also heroes and characters in that world. Odysseus and Ajax are superimposed on one another, but so are Homer, Pindar, and Sophocles. We cannot have images of the characters without our images of the authors. Pindar fights against Homer just as Ajax crosses swords with Hector. Pindar's verses constantly attack Homer, reproaching him for bestowing fame on Odysseus and denigrating Ajax.[3]

Ajax is a solid, straightforward, simple character. He would not have fitted the infinite gradations of an epic poem. In the reciprocal flow of emotions between Homer and Odysseus, author and character, the latter embodies complexity, variability, adaptation. "Where cunning men are needed," Odysseus says even outside the *Odyssey*, "I am one such."[4] That was how tradition described him. He was the central character in a long poem marked by constant changes of style and content. He could not be merely masculine and warlike like Ajax: he had to have a feminine side too. He is favored by Athene, the Goddess of Intelligence, a faculty he himself possesses in the highest degree, and which consists first and foremost in having many different thoughts – not being obsessed by a single one. He is complex and rather perverse, like the gods themselves. He respects and fears them precisely because he understands them.

That is how the *Odyssey* came to be.

It would have been impossible to write an epic poem about Ajax. Just as it is impossible to write a symphony using only one tune. Ajax could only be the subject not of an epic but of a tragedy, where there is unity of time, place, and action:[5] a story that is solid, like the hero himself, short and intense. That is how the man who was probably the greatest of all tragedians came to devote what was probably the first of all his tragedies (c. 445 BCE) to Ajax.

In his first play, Sophocles depicts in a single work the greatness and the impossibility of tragic thought.

For tragic thought and paranoid thought are incompatible. They are opposites. The aim of tragedy was not only to entertain but also to educate, to teach people that life is contradictory: people desire good but foster evil; the human will counts for nothing because it does not know what it really wants.

Ajax goes wrong not because he makes any one particular mistake, but because, in succumbing to paranoia, he becomes obsessed with a single idea and deaf to human complexity. From the moment when that fixed idea is revealed to him, he believes that he has grasped what is most important in life.

By contrast, he becomes himself – a real character, possessing a personality – the first time he makes a choice instead of performing a duty. The moment is inevitably a fleeting one, for the choice he makes is to die.

In order to create this tragic character, Sophocles magnified Ajax's strength and arrogance to titanic proportions.[6] Pindar should have reproached Sophocles, rather than Homer: in Homer, Ajax is never arrogant toward the gods.

******

Sophocles' *Ajax* begins on the battlefield, with the Greeks besieging Troy. The first characters we see are not Ajax himself, but Athene and Odysseus. Odysseus tells the goddess that the army's animals have been slaughtered. Cattle and sheep all float in a sea of blood. The slaughter is said to have been perpetrated by Ajax.

Athene calmly takes the situation in hand.

After Achilles' death, the decision had to be made – which of the Greeks should be given his weapons? The choice was immediately narrowed down to Ajax and Odysseus. The jury, dominated by Agamemnon and Menelaus, Odysseus's constant allies, naturally preferred him. So Athene awarded victory to the most intelligent man, not the strongest.[7] Once again, Ajax's solitary position had told against him. But solitude foments suspicion, and suspicion magnifies the number and importance of one's enemies. And suspicion feeds itself. In order to survive in isolation, Ajax had to rely on fighting strength, of which Achilles' weapons were the supreme symbol. Ajax's mind gradually came to the conclusion that there was no alternative. Achilles' weapons were no longer a prize, a possibility; they were a necessity. Weapons are everything. And weapons are won by weapons.

Ajax came out of his tent in the night with his sword to kill all three of them – Odysseus, Agamemnon, and Menelaus. He must kill them at once. For paranoia is convinced that many people are enemies. Moreover, it has an impersonal enemy: time. Once it has conceived its central idea, paranoia wants to go straight into action. Just as it cannot tolerate a void in thought, so it cannot tolerate one in time. It will brook no delay.

How is it, then, that his three enemies are alive and the animals were killed? Athene had cast false images into Ajax's mind. She had entangled him, as she puts it, in a net of delusion and death.[8]

******

Ajax's mental landscape, deprived of its usual solitary habits, needed human images. The goddess Athene had supplied some. But the images she had supplied were fictitious. Ajax had killed the animals instead of his enemies. His trap was the self-deception of those who rely too much on solitude and suspicion.

Athene says to Odysseus, with a smile: "Is not laughing at one's enemies the sweetest kind of laughter?"[9] Paranoia makes a person laughable. But the perspective can also be reversed: the laughter of others reawakens sleeping paranoia. Anyone is likely to become anxious if others laugh at him and he does not know why they are laughing. Laughter infects the group, in the same way that aggression does. Often laughter is aggression under another guise. When suspicion sees enemies, the most terrible is the one armed not with a sword, but with laughter. Does suspicion *discover* enemies, though, or *create* them? Centuries later, Dante expressed a similar persecutory fear: "So that the Jew among you does not laugh."[10] The Christian's error attracts the Jew's scorn, before it attracts divine punishment.

An inability to laugh is the oldest symptom of paranoia. An ability to laugh is the most instinctive defense against this evil: significantly, it is a traditional defense of the Jews, a people who have often been the victims of paranoid attacks. As Shakespeare wrote, "The robbed that smiles steals something from the thief."[11]

******

The playwright of ancient Greece sought to achieve equilibrium by alternating sorrow, sublimated in the sad wisdom of tragedy, with conflict, sublimated in the liberating laughter of comedy. Tragedy and comedy were performed together. *Kômos* (the etymon of *comedy*) was the *group* (originally, a group of mildly drunk youths who roamed the streets at night) *infected by collective enthusiasm*. The equilibrium of comedy consists in transforming destructive derision into wise, benevolent laughter.

But in Sophocles' *Ajax* laughter cannot be redeemed by laughter. We, the audience of the play, know that Ajax's mind is laughable – lacking introspection, curiosity, and feminine sensibility. His mind is, to all intents and purposes, empty. Since natural law requires that a void be filled, there appears in his mind a sense that something is coming. An unknown novelty, which his mind is wary about but trusts in, because it needs it. As it waits for this novelty, the mind's anxiety grows. Eventually the simple-minded man will reach a point where merely being provided with an enemy would, paradoxically, make him feel more at peace; or rather more at war, for by this stage there is no difference between the two in his eyes. The important thing is no longer having to live in uncertainty. No longer having to make the terrible effort of trying to understand. The simplifying mechanism of paranoid logic will be able to work smoothly: the presence of an enemy explains everything. The suspicion that there has been a conspiracy has become certainty.

Athene calls Ajax out of his tent: "Ajax, my friend, this is the second time I have called you . . . But tell me, did you tinge your sword with the blood of Argive warriors?"

"It is a matter of pride to me, and I will not deny it . . . Now they can no longer cast aspersions on Ajax . . . Let them try to take away my weapons, now that they are dead."

"What about the son of Laertes? What have you done to him?"

"He is my welcome guest, in there, in chains."

"What are you planning for him?"

"First, the lash. Let him die with his back bloodied." Then Ajax goes back into his tent.[12] Athene had not really wanted to talk to him, but only to show him to Odysseus. The scene ends with a brief dialogue between the latter and the goddess. A dialogue that no longer concerns Ajax, but every human destiny.

Ajax seemed to have lived a just life. And yet, in an instant, his existence is shattered by the gods. We are shadows, obliterated by a brief gesture. Never be proud about what you are! In weeping for my enemy's fate, Odysseus acknowledges, I weep for my own.[13]

******

Night has ended. Light returns to the beach and to the shores of the mind. Tecmessa, Ajax's mistress, has heard about the slaughter of the animals, but does not know who they belonged to. The chorus of Ajax's sailors does know who they belonged to, but not who killed them. Tecmessa and the sailors exchange information and acquire the knowledge they lacked. With this, tragic truth is complete.

Seeing all the blood – blood and animal parts – Ajax asks what has happened and has been told by Tecmessa. His honor as a warrior now lies in pieces too. It is covered in ridicule. The strongest arm had raised its sword against goats and lambs. The situation is unbearable. "See how the wave of a murderous storm whirls around me, overwhelms me . . . Kill me here, among these animals."[14] Most unbearable of all is the idea of his enemies laughing at him.

His reawakening from paranoia occurs only after the slaughter: so waking up does not set him free, but locks him in an eternal prison of remorse.

Ajax asks Tecmessa to bring him his son. He speaks to him gently, expressing the hope that he will have his father's qualities but better fortune than he. Tecmessa speaks to Ajax, reminding him of the sweetness of having a family, of the things in life that are certain, of love. All these things are nourished by the relationship, within the relationship: should he die, she and the boy would be left with nothing but sorrow and shame. But these are human words, spoken by one who lives amid human complexity and among human beings. Such talk is doubly alien to Ajax.

In the first place, Ajax does not live among human beings; he lives alone, absorbed in suspicion and obsessed with a single idea. One who lives among human beings lives among the collective duties that link human beings: shared values such as respect for the family. But one who lives amid suspicion does not live among human beings; he lives among enemies. And his only duty toward those enemies is to defeat them.

Moreover, Ajax denies in himself all the psychological qualities that we call feminine; he can neither understand a woman, nor extract any emotions from his mind but warlike ones. Sophocles' narrative expresses this situation through clear symbols. As often happened in Mycenaean society, Tecmessa had been taken captive in war, later becoming Ajax's mistress and the mother of his son. But Ajax still treats her like a slave. He gives her orders. He finds some comfort in her but has no conception of holding a dialogue with her; perhaps he would find it dishonorable. Just as his relationship with this woman is the result of an act of force, so his relationship with the more feminine parts of his own personality is only a matter of force and domination. Those parts must be subjected to the masculine will, the only one that is allowed to manifest itself. Ajax is not interested in a feminine will that seeks ties, or in aesthetics or love, encounters or rituals: he is not interested in what, according to Pericles, the Greeks had created in order to banish sorrow from life.[15]

******

After so much suffering, the tragedy seems to be purified.[16] Ajax surprises us. He talks to himself wisely. We must respect the feelings of the family, he says, and do what is right for it. All things are relative. A storm is followed by calm, night by day, summer by autumn. Similarly, we must think that an enemy can become a friend, and a friend an enemy.

Ajax wanted more than anything else to receive Achilles' weapons as a gift from the Greeks, his own people. Instead, he received his last gift from an enemy, Hector. This is significant and symbolic: Ajax's mind opens to something and receives a gift only in a relationship with an enemy, not in a relationship of friendship or love. After an honorable duel, Hector had been given Ajax's belt and had given him his own sword.[17] Ajax says he will bury it on the beach, in a hidden place. It is shameful to receive gifts from enemies, he adds. But we who listen to his words are not so sure that it is shameful.

With these words the play stirs divided, ambivalent feelings in the audience. True to its vocation, tragic irony expresses itself in language that is susceptible to contrasting interpretations.

Ajax no longer speaks of death and blood. Is he making his peace with destiny? Does he allude to feeling at peace with himself? Has he given up the idea of suicide? Ajax's words are allusive and ambiguous. Tragedy often uses such language to keep us in suspense. But in this case, there is a deeper reason. Ajax's madness is the madness of solitude and suspicion. In order to understand his madness we must behave as it does, picking up hints and admitting our extraneousness; entering into the logic of its allusions, ambiguities, and indirect references, rather than trying to follow its explicit argument.

It is possible that humanity has insinuated itself into Ajax and induced him to look more kindly on his family, his noble enemy Hector, and his allies and friends Odysseus, Agamemnon, and Menelaus: for it is right that feelings should alternate like the seasons. A person who feels only a single emotion is unnaturally isolated: if that person returns to the society of human beings, he or she will resume the alternation of anger and love.

But his words might also be those of a man who has given himself up definitively to suspicion and death: for, since the truth was revealed, Ajax's most mortal enemy has been Ajax himself. In his simple, straightforward world, you must have an enemy to annihilate. And now that his colossal, ludicrous error has been revealed, shame and honor demand that the person annihilated be the one who perpetrated the error. A man must "either live gloriously," says Ajax, "or die gloriously; that is a brave man's duty."[18] It is up to us to decide whether this man is a man, since the laws that make him live or die concern him alone, not a community, nor an emotional tie.

Soon the tragedy makes it clear to us that the sword must be fixed in the beach, so that something – not a man, but the shore, the earth, the nature to whom we return when we die – will hold the hilt firmly while Ajax runs at it to impale himself. The sword's hilt must be buried so that the sword's owner can be buried. At this point we know that the foregoing eulogy of things that alternate was a eulogy not only of finiteness, but also of death. Ajax is already alone with his own death and sees around him only things that have a short life.

As the hero walks off down the beach, a messenger arrives. He reminds us that the transience of things can be something positive. The seer Calchas has announced that Athene's wrath, changeable like all the gods' emotions, will only pursue Ajax for one day. If he remains alive today, tomorrow he will be free.

Today the goddess is still angry at Ajax for offending the gods. When he had left home, his father had urged him: "Aspire to win with your lance, my son, but always to win with the gods' help." And what had his reply been? "Father, even a worthless man can triumph with the gods' help; I am confident of achieving glory even without them." And when Athene had come to encourage him during a battle, he had told her: "Lend your aid to the other Argives, goddess; the enemy will not pass where I am."[19] These are thoughts that exceed human measure, and a god cannot accept them.[20]

The end comes quickly. Before the edge of day touches night, Ajax fixes the sword in the seashore and with it his destiny. He bids farewell to the beaches and to the natural world around him: he has no farewells for his fellows. He asks the gods that his brother Teucer may find his body and that Agamemnon and Menelaus may be punished. Then he kills himself. Suspicion, solitude, and an obsession with a single aim, that of military glory, have made Ajax's mind monotonous: even as he leaves life, he is still wishing death on others.

Hector had tried to set life against death. Hector was the most human character in the harsh world of epic. He was strong with the sword, but he had feelings when he held it. Alone among the warriors of the *Iliad*, he fought not for glory but to protect the city of Troy – its women and children – from the slaughter the Greeks would bring. He does not survive, but his feelings do, for he has defeated solitude and the suspicion that is its fellow. Hector's sword is a great symbol. But Ajax plunges its hilt into the earth and its blade into his own breast: he makes reverse use of the sword. The *reversal of symbolic processes* is a tragic recurrence in paranoiacs of every age: in minds armed with suspicion, the creativity of symbols becomes destructiveness; a life-giving process becomes a deadly one. History provides more evidence of this than psychiatry.

Ajax recovers his honor but kills himself: he renounces the attention of others, which he had perhaps been unconsciously seeking when he had so desperately sought admiration. In the duel described in the *Iliad*, Ajax and Hector are linked by their destiny – to die: Hector because he is included among the Trojans who are destined to be defeated and slaughtered; Ajax because he has excluded himself from the Greeks who are destined to be victorious.

The gifts they had exchanged would become accessories to death. Hector's sword, which had kept Trojan children alive by defending them, brought death to Ajax. And Achilles, before his death, stripped invincible Ajax's belt from the defeated Hector's body. He used it to tie the Trojan hero to his chariot, turned him into a triumphal animal, and dragged him along at a gallop, torturing him to death.[21]

There are a few more scenes before the end of the play. Teucer, Ajax's half-brother, appears and organizes the sacred rites of burial. Tecmessa screams in despair over the body of the man she had loved. We too feel pity, and almost love, for this man who was so unable to love. What if instead of defying the gods, he had tried to embrace others? But perhaps no one had ever embraced him, even symbolically. Teucer dreads taking the news to Ajax's father, Telamon: "He is a man who is incapable of smiling even when he is happy."[22] We begin to get a sense of what a grim family this mighty giant had grown up in and what a frost of emotions had nurtured his suspiciousness, turning him into an emotional dwarf.

Agamemnon recalls that it is mental not physical strength that makes a man.[23] With his brother Menelaus he tries to prevent the sacred burial of the man who had wanted to kill them. Let dogs and birds tear him to pieces!

At this point Odysseus, Ajax's most uncompromising adversary, intervenes. Odysseus knows that death awaits them all. In the face of death, the rites of burial are a last, fragile redemption. With unexpected kindness he begs that these rites not be denied Ajax, and he persuades the other two Greeks not to offend the dead man and death itself.

Notes

1 Sophocles, *Ajax*, l. 614.
2 Pindar, *Isthmian Odes*, VI, ll. 49–64.
3 Pindar, *Nemean Odes*, VII, ll. 20–30; VIII ll. 24ff.; *Isthmian Odes*, IV, ll. 35ff.; VI, ll. 49ff.
4 Sophocles, *Philoctetes*, l. 1049.
5 Aristotle, *Poetics*, ll. 7, 18.
6 Max Pohlenz, *Der hellenische Mensch*, Göttingen: Vandenhoeck und Ruprecht, 1947, chapter 12.
7 Karl Kerényi, *The Gods of the Greeks*, Harmondsworth, Middlesex: Penguin Books, 1958, p. 335.
8 To the modern reader, Athene is an ancient symbol of the way the mind works. And the first rule of the mind is that its empty spaces must not remain empty. Like physical nature, mental nature eschews a void. Unoccupied spaces become sponges that absorb images from the unconscious. Even the mind at rest, when we are asleep, is filled with images. We call them dreams. Of course, these mental needs have always been known. But today we choose to ignore them. We do not try to understand mental activities; we try to organize them productively. We increasingly eliminate fantasy and meditation – activities in which the "empty" mind allows itself to be filled – for fear of encountering problematic images of our inner world. We prevent the formation of mental voids by using objects – television, videogames, magazines – which provide a never-ending supply of stereotyped, prefabricated figures from the outside world. In this way they fend off the inner figures and the intense emotions associated with them. We do not want to live. We want to watch, and listen to, things that imitate life. We avoid living in the first person.

 9 Sophocles, *Ajax*, l. 79.
10 Dante, *Paradiso*, ll. 5, 81.
11 Shakespeare, *Othello*, Act I, Scene 3, lines 207–8: "The robbed that smiles steals some-thing from the thief; / he robs himself that spends a bootless grief."
12 Sophocles, *Ajax*, ll. 89–117.
13 Ibid., ll. 118–33.
14 Ibid., ll. 350–60.
15 Thucydides, *The Peloponnesian War*, Book II, Chapter 38, Section 1.
16 Sophocles, *Ajax*, l. 646ff.
17 *Iliad*, Book VII, ll. 206–310.
18 Sophocles, *Ajax*, l. 479.
19 Ibid., ll. 767–9.
20 Ibid., ll. 748–77.
21 Ibid., l. 1131. The version of the story told by Sophocles is crueler than that recounted in book XXII of the *Iliad*.
22 Ibid., l. 1011.
23 Ibid., ll. 1250ff.

4

PERSEPHONE'S HEART

Craig San Roque

On the pragmatic uselessness of the mythic state of mind

Let us begin with Karl Kerényi on the Eleusinian Paradox in *Kore*, for his notion of a series of seeds and mothers and daughters in infinite cycle has been an inspiration in retelling this story in my own time and country. Kerényi writes, "every grain . . . and every maiden contains . . . all her descendants – an infinite series of mothers and daughters in one."[1]

There is no pragmatic value to this story, *Persephone's Heart*.[2] It is useless to anyone absorbed with the fast ratio, the political turnaround, and the daily demands of

FIGURE 4.1   Miriam Pickard as Persephone. Photo by Fiona J. Walsh

catastrophe or family. This project belongs in the category of the enigmatic, yet it may someday turn out that the neurological potency of the human brain cries out for the balm and surprise that nests in the mythic state of mind. Perhaps the music of it humanizes humans, alpha rhythms settle confusions, perhaps performance distills intense emotion, erotic dissolutions fluently activated, transformation and strange leaping provoked . . . perhaps this is good for us . . . who knows?

I acknowledge the danger of attempting to uncover the secret of Eleusis's greater mysteries. The rites, ceremony, and beliefs were kept confidential.[3] Death was a consequence for any initiate who broke that confidentiality. As far as I know, that restriction has not been lifted. Where we live in Central Australia, initiations into secret/sacred ceremony and cultural story (*tjukurrpa*) are still active, and thus we understand something of the reasons for the restriction of knowledge and the intensely personal dangers of trespassing, without preparation, upon the ground of original beings.

Exposure to Australian indigenous heritage has subtly influenced the way we formed the hypothetical travels of Persephone and the gathering of her humanized body through transformations of clay, rock, roots, salt, seeds, and geographic sites. Such a process mildly echoes the chthonic travels of mythic, serpentine, *tjukurrpa* beings with whom we have some acquaintance. Persephone's incarnation journey (as I tell it) is influenced by how creation stories among the old Europeans *and* among the first Australians are composed from landforms, water sites, the movement of plant beings, and the drama of creatures in metamorphosis. A glance through Ovid's *Metamorphosis* confirms the old European interest in the intrigue of trans-formations. Reassembling of the forms of human, fauna, flora, and landform takes place in human minds (and dreams) that are in intimate, reciprocal relationship with country. I suspect that my European ancestors lived in that same state of mind as do custodians of Australian mythic story and lore. It would be more accurate to say that exposure to *tjukurrpa* has helped me remember that state of being from which my own cultural, mythic stories arise. Having learned a little from our Australian countrymen and women, we take part in a synthesis and share it here with you. By referencing indigenous creation stories and *tjukurrpa* states of mind, I am also hop-ing that this might encourage fellow Australians to value more deeply the states of "embodied imagination" out of which our local cultural stories are born.

Persephone and Demeter, as personified forces of nature, are part of a richly layered heritage that includes the elegant Minoan flowerings of perhaps 2000 BCE, and linking back 10,000 years BCE into dimly known Neolithic transitions between hunting, gathering, and the settled cultivation of cereals. Many icons of those early periods feature female forms, phases of the moon, young men, bulls, animals, birds, and sea creatures in graceful evocative shapes with gestures that suggest participa-tion in nourishing cultural activities and vibrant flows of life, even though times may have been hard.

European Mysteries are embedded in specific geographic sites, some in the Mediterranean regions – Enna, Eleusis, Knossos, Palaikastro, and Delphi among them. Such sites I have visited, along with Miriam Pickard, Fiona Walsh, and others connected in the Persephone project. We have researched images, artifacts, and archaeologies, and found or invented theories. Yet, I believe, now, that it is discourteous to go hunting after Demeter/Persephone's Eleusinian secret. Her intimacies are her own. Better to prepare the ground and wait for her. Thus, our method of looking into these intimate matters has been guided by a sidelong glance, an ethic of discovery through creating a performance.

With introverted intuition in body and feeling, we rehearse, discern, perform. We take notice, throughout the empathic action of developing a performance, of the strange things that appear in our sensibilities, in our intensities and confusions. The logic of this approach is that if there is an old mystery to be found, a touch of it may be revealed through such a participative approach in the retelling. This method, insofar as it can be called a "method," is a form of transference relationship between the past human and the present human imagination. It is a form of "participation mystique." It does seem, from our joint experiences, that, while dwelling upon Persephone, a dynamic force of nature comes alive in oneself and within group interactions, as the performance develops.

We have found this procedure to be nourishing and beautiful and alarming. I am supported in trusting such an approach by my experience of ceremony in Central Australia. Here, humility, good humor, preparation, and knowledge of the storylines are crucial, and so too is the moment of letting go, incarnating qualities of mythic beings upon whose territory one is moving. Such an experience of participation may be akin to the experience of a Mystery revealing itself during participation in the dark and light of the original Eleusis gatherings.

The trick for us, now, is of letting once secret things reveal, innocently, by a naive ontopoetic approach – that is, marking out a place (*temenos*) and stepping off a cliff; creating an event of contemporary, yet ceremonial nature and waiting for what comes to meet us out of that creation itself. I think of this as psychological work done among companions open to cultures hybrid, past, present, and future. "Hybrid" because few of us comply with what passes for the fixed idea of the fixed tradition, and some of us, where I live, are anarchic most of the time.

So – to sum up. Recomposing a myth for performance could be seen as a version of archeology, putting together broken mosaic and fragments of graffiti, imagining an original shape. The ontopoetic method implies research, yes; and composing something, yes; and feeling and enacting it; and also waiting for the mythic state of being to come and work on one's present contemporary mind (often at night or at dawn). Additionally, I have found it fertile to compose in wild country. Doing this "ontopoetic thing" sometimes feels as though one has taken some subtle homeopathic intoxicant. A little of the past permeates one's present neurological synapses and new combinations fire.

In Alice Springs, Central Australia, a loosely held group of about twenty-five people have delivered versions of Persephone twice. *Persephone's Dog*, in the Ilparpa Quarry site, August/September 2015, and then *Persephone Goes Under*, in an industrial shed, April 2016.[4] *Persephone's Heart* is a development from these two, but reformed and distilled into the recitation for two persons that we presented in Santorini.[5] Much has been found and created among our friends in Australia, through the process of participating in the story of Persephone and her imagined travels through the country where we now live. My gratitude is endless for our multicultural heritage, Eurasian and Australian; and the fact that it is still available to us and that friends can meet and share without constraint. Please enjoy our hybrid version of this maybe 10,000-year-old story of women traveling, and please forgive our naivety and our hazard.[6]

Note on performance text

This text is a sequel to Persephone's Dog *as published in* Ancient Greece, Modern Psyche: Archetypes Evolving *(2015).[7] Whereas I take responsibility for the overall concept and written composition, the Santorini text is a result of collaboration with Miriam Pickard and Fiona Walsh, and the influence of Jules Cashford. In this text music, images, cues, actions, and the original range of performance characters, such as the Seven Sisters, have been removed or simplified so that the reader can follow the story as a single narrative rather than as theatre work. The story here is told by Persephone and the linking narrator – the spirit of her dog.*

Persephone's Heart

Part one: the world as it is

1. Persephone's son
2. Persephone to the people
3. She begins her story
4. The cave
5. The form of snakes/going down the hole
6. Sites of destruction
7. Tea in Babylon
8. The decision
9. The Pleiades gather her

Part two: gathering the body

1. Sites of creation
2. Spleen bones skin guts
3. Black stone/lymph node
4. Liver and kidney
5. Water
6. Heart brain and rigmarole
7. Gratitude
8. Return
9. To Eleusis

We begin with a lament for a lost girl. It is based upon a true event that took place on the airfield of a western desert Aboriginal community. A medical emergency plane arrived at night. When the airfield lights were lit and the plane landed, her body was seen in the glare. Some say this was a deliberate display by the lonely girl. Some say she intended to be found just as the lights on the airfield were turned on, but the plane came late. It was too late to revive her. Sometimes a young person will intentionally, sullenly walk past family with a rope or electric cord – this signals an intention to suicide. Sometimes people might ignore the display. The reasons for this are complex. Sometimes unexpected or unexplained deaths, such as this, are attributed to sorcery or the presence of malevolent vengeful male spirits. Woven here is an acknowledgment of her loss, her tragedy, with the return of the young girl – Kore. Mythic event and airfield event echo, and begin our story.

Persephone's Heart/Airfield Lament

Sometimes the plane arrives too late. The lights on the airfield turn on too late.

Sometimes she hangs herself on the airstrip. The girl on the airstrip. Thirteen years old. We didn't know where she'd gone. She walked with a rope. She went too far. We didn't see her. Sometimes the lights on the airfield turn on too late. The plane comes too late. Sometimes Kore falls down in the dark. No dogs howl for her. No dogs find her. The plane comes too late.

But another time, I tell you – this time, tonight, we can say, thank God.

Our Kore came back. She came up out of the hole in the ground. Her face was covered in concrete. Her skin was covered in lime. She did come back. The young girl walked into camp in the morning. She took the rope away from her neck. Stay strong, she said. Live long, she cried.

> When Kore came back from the dead, her mother washed off the white lime, she rubbed her skin with oil. Her skin is shining. Her eyes are shining.
> All the mothers and sisters smile. Their skin is shining, their eyes are shining.
> The birds begin to sing such sweet song in the trees. The seeds unwrap.
> The roots begin to move their little toes.

> When Kore came back up the street, the old men smiled sweetly to each other. They remembered her. They remembered her story. They began to tell it again, telling each other, "Remember when Kore came back? That was a good day. I remember that day."

Part one: the world as it is

1 Persephone's son

Persephone. My son said to me, "How did you become a human?" I said, "So that you could be born." My son said, "No. I dreamed that once upon a time you were something else; a snake crawling through rock." "My son, I should not tell you.

It will change the way you think of me." He said, "I will not turn away. You must tell me the truth . . ." "Well then – I will tell you the story of how I became a woman, and who is your father and how you were born – so that you can be happy in the dark night and the hard light of day."

2 Persephone to the people

I told you before. I tell you once more. The form you see here is not my original form. The form you see here is the form you see with human eye. The voice you hear is not my original voice. You hear the voice of a young woman. It is she who speaks and I, Persephone, speak through her.

3 She begins her story

I have already told you the story of how, when I was young and named as Kore, my mother and I walked the country, and how I learned from her the use of fruits and seeds, and how it was that she made things grow. I have told you how my dog and I traveled the country alone and learned more of what could be eaten and what should not be eaten by the people yet to come. I told you how I learned from the dog. If the dog stopped to sniff something his tail wagged; I noted that as good to eat. If he sniffed and turned away I knew that humans would have to be careful. But I did not tell you of that terrible day when my dog made a mistake.

Walking toward Eleusis in the morning, my dog stopped to sniff something. What's that, said Kore. Don't know, said the dog, smells good. It tastes ok, like old meat . . . and ate it, just like that. The dog staggered on its feet, the dog's eyes went white. The dog staggered and rolled over. The dog tried to vomit but it was too late. The dog lay still. Everything stopped.

Kore looked in the mouth of the dog. She found that deadly thing. She tore it from the tongue of the dog. This is poison, she said, you stupid dog, it makes you sick. She cursed the fungus – she gave it a name, *amanita phalloides (deathcap)*. She cried out for her dog. Her dog did not move. The wind moved, the sea moved, but her dog did not move. What is this, said Kore, I have never seen this before.

She held her dog in her arms, she walked into the rocks. She laid her dog down in the shade. In a cleft in the rock, she laid her dog. She saw the spirit of her dog move. Where are you going? I'm going to Aidos, he's whistling me. I'll come too, said Kore. She went down, following the spirit of the dog, she carried the body of her dog in her arms. She went down through the crack in the rock. She walked into the dark. This is how Kore went down. Remember this.

4 The cave

It was there that Aidos came to meet my dog and I. I walked into a cave. I made a fire. I looked around. I cried out. All the walls are black with smoke. There are drawings on the wall. What are those marks?

And then I heard his voice. I could hear his voice all around me. I could not see him. He would not show himself; but Aidos spoke. They are for you, these marks are there to teach you. Look, these are the plants, the ones you see up on country. These are the plants from outside, the plants from up above, the ones you see when you follow your mother. Here are the plants from inside. Here are the marks. Here are the plants inside the skin of the world. These are the roots of things, the seedbed. He showed me drawings, charcoal on the red walls of the cave. Charcoal and red and ochre white. Here, he said, here, are all the animals with blood. Here is the serpent brain, and the lizard. The people have come from this beginning; he said, touching all the marks of plant, insect, serpent, fish, bird, animal. The people still are coming from this. All these things die. And begin again.

He drew circles on the wall of the cave, he drew circles and lines turning and turning. And it was then that Kore and the spirit of the dog traveled to the underworld with Aidos. For it is he who takes care of the roots of things and the richness that comes from the earth beneath your feet. My son, you need not be afraid of your father. It is true that, by this journey, I, Kore, changed from my original form so that I, Persephone, may understand the life of all creatures and take care of you as you die and change into other forms. People call me many dark things, they are afraid of your mother, but you should know – I carry love for living things. Remember this.

5 The form of snakes/going down the hole

Dog. Among the rocks, within the site of Eleusis, there is a hole now known as the Maiden's Well. It is near here that Kore went down. It is near here that Aidos called her. It is from here that Kore and Aidos began their long travel underground in the form of snakes. Aidos showed her the life and the death of the world. He opened the eyes of Kore, he opened the ears of Kore. He made her into the one who could manage destruction. Do not be afraid of her, it is she who gathered me, she who carried me, who brought me to you now. It is this story that I tell you now.

Some say these things happened before people began – that two serpents traveling the world marked out the sites of cities to come – foreseeing also their end. Some say these two were two unseen winds passing through the skin of the world, heaving, weaving, revealing the shape of things to come. Some say this . . . some say that . . . who knows, all I know is where they went. Like a dog, I followed their scent.

6 Sites of destruction

Dog. From Eleusis, Aidos took her down under the crust of rocks, under the sea and down below islands. Two serpents swimming beneath Delos, Melos, Naxos, Ios, Thera, Ikaria, Chios . . .

Persephone. Kore, looking up beneath islands, said, "They are like stars above, floating on the sea."

Dog. We passed under Lesbos, approaching Anatolia. Look again, he said. Those are not stars. Those are people in boats fleeing the war. There will be deaths and more deaths. Many souls will fall into your care, Persephone. Remember this place. We burrowed underground coming out on the shore of the Black Sea. We looked over that great lake, seeing mountains in the distance.

Caucasia, he said – from here many people will come.

We drank the water, fresh and sweet. He said, Around these sweet waters are the beginnings of your people. They will settle here. You will feed them. From here plants will flow all over the world. They will love this place. Remember this.

And then; Aidos looking over this great lake bowed low saying, From this fresh water, your people will draw comfort. But I tell you – coming upon your people there will be a great flood. The mountains will rise up and crack. Salt sea will break through the Dardanelle. Plants will quake. Fish die. People calling out, Help us Persephone . . . Help us. Your head will shake. You will not see what to do. Remember this.

Persephone. We turned south, underground into the belly of Anatolia. We burrowed beneath mountains, and down into Syria. We passed under cities yet to come, Aleppo, Damascus . . . then south through Phoenicia and Byblos. Beneath Beirut I looked up and saw a young man being killed by pigs. "Why are pigs killing him?" I said, "He is too beautiful for slaughter . . ."

Aidos turned his head away in sorrow. His name is Adonis. His mother is Myrrha. It is a sad tale, Persephone; along this shore you will see the young men all torn apart for thousands of years to come.

I cried then, I said to him – How can such things happen? These men are too beautiful for slaughter. Too beautiful for slaughter . . .

We came to Jerusalem. Aidos held me calmly to him, the coils of his body wrapped around me. I said to him then, "I feel the weight of the dying upon me."

Look, he said, here is a place where many souls will fall to your hands. This is the place. The city of Jerusalem to come. This is a hole in the life of the world through which will fall the generations of men. From this place, for ages to come, women and children will fall to your hands. You will make a net to catch them. You will make a net to console them.

"I have no hands," I said. "How can I catch these people who fall? To my left I feel the net to catch the people falling. To my right I feel a basket, fertile with seeds. Yet, I have no hands to hold these things. I have no hands."

Dog. Crossing into Assyria . . . (some men name this the cradle of civilization.

And you will see how such hands rock the cradle). A king of Assyria. His name Ashur-nasirpal, attacked the city of Suru. Listen to this exactly as written, 2,865 years before our present time. The time in which I tell this story.

I built a pillar over against the rebel city gate,
I flayed all the chiefs who had revolted,
And covered the pillar with their skin.
Some I walled up within the pillar,
Some I impaled upon the pillar on stakes
And others I bound to stakes round about the pillar.
And I cut the limbs of the officers.
Many captives from among them I burned with fire
And many I took as living captives.
Of many I put out the eyes.
Their young men and maidens I burned in the fire.
Their warriors I consumed with thirst in the desert of the Euphrates . . .

Persephone. Hearing this, turning to Aidos I said, These are not human. These are not animal. These are not birds . . . What is it in the minds of men that would do such a thing? He said to me then, This is the world as it is. Remember this.

I turned away. We went south into Iraq. We passed broken cities, the rivers, Tigris, Euphrates, smelling of sulfur burning in the night. And there I saw my mother raped again and again by some beast whose face I cannot see. His smell arouses terror. Bromide and blood. Fire after lightning; sacrificial flesh. Have I come into earth for this?

Turning to my son, I saw the fear in his eyes . . . My son, I should not tell you these things. It will change the way you think of me. And he said, "I will not turn away. You must tell me the truth. Is there more?" Yes, there is more. "Is my father the king of Assyria?" No, I said, you need not be afraid of your father.

7 Tea in Babylon

Persephone. It was early in the morning, we walked into Babylon. I remember then, it would have appeared that we were two people, sitting at a table, drinking tea, staring into each other's eyes. At that time my human form had not been fixed into place but I could appear in any shape I wished. Two people sitting at a table drinking tea.

You will hear people say that he took me away as though I were a child, that he brought black horses and ripped me from my mother's side; but your father spoke to me then at that table, the words that turned my life around. He said – People speak of you as Kore, but I know you as a force of nature, a force wrapped now in the skin of a serpent. Could you become that force wrapped in the body of a woman?

A strange fire ran through me – I turned to him and said, "Yes, I could become human." "And why is that?" So I said to him, "The seeds who fall to your domain, are they not lonely, are they not cold? How could I truly care for such souls if I do not know their pain, if I do not feel their grief, their fear, their hope?"

I saw Aidos pause. He looked away, as though he were looking far, far away.

He took a breath. "There is more for you to know. I am taking you to see your sister, Ereshkigal; your sister Inanna. I am taking you to Eridu, to the gate of Sumer's Underworld."

He took me to the gates, he made himself invisible. I could hear his voice humming in my ear as though it were a fly, but I could not see him. It was so dark, I could see nothing. "Where have you brought me?"

He said, "What do you hear?" "I hear a voice reciting . . ." "Well then – Recite . . ."

And I repeat these words –

> *"From the Great Above she opened her ear to the Great Below.*
> *From the Great Above the goddess opened her ear to the Great Below.*
> *From the Great Above Inanna opened her ear to the Great Below.*
> *When Inanna arrived at the outer gates of the underworld. She knocked loudly and*
>   *cried out in a fierce voice. "Open the door, gatekeeper! I am Inanna, Queen of*
>   *Heaven, On my way to the East." The gate opened for her.*
> *She passed through seven gates. At each gate her sister Ereshkigal, Queen of the Un-*
>   *derworld, bitterly ordered the removal of Inanna's powers, her garments, her jewels,*
>   *her crown. At the last gate, naked and bowed low, Inanna entered. Ereshkigal, her*
>   *sister, rose from her throne. She fastened on Inanna the eye of death. She spoke*
>   *against her the word of wrath. She uttered against her the cry of guilt. She struck*
>   *her. Inanna was turned into a corpse,*
> *a piece of rotting meat, and was hung from a hook on the wall."*

Aidos spoke – "What do you see?"

> "I see my sister in a cave in Sumer. She hangs on a hook on the wall.
> Flies part as I come to her. Whose face is this? Is it hers; is it mine?"

Aidos said, "What do you hear?"

I hear Inanna's voice. "Sister, take care," she says, "This pain of being human is hard to bear. Learn my story. I, who am Queen of Heaven, the morning star, I fell in love, I married, I bore a son. I went to the underworld to console my sister. And now I hang on this hook. Tell me, where is my hope?"

And I, Persephone, said to her. "Inanna, I know your story. Life comes back to you. Flies will bring you the water of life. Flies will bring you the bread of life. You will arise, star of heaven."

Inanna moaned . . . she said, "You know nothing! The Queen of Heaven is dead."

8 The decision

After I had seen my sister Inanna, even after I had learned the whole story, I found myself troubled, I found myself uncertain. I felt that strange fire whispering at my skin.

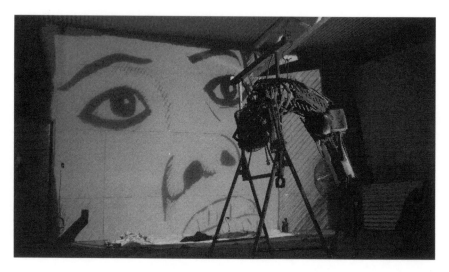

FIGURE 4.2 Stage setting to *Persephone Goes Under* performance with Innana graphic by Joshua Santospirito and *Innana on the Hook* sculpture by Dan Murphy. Photo by Fiona J. Walsh

I went to Aidos. I gathered my serpent form in coils around his and I said, "Is there some way that I could fall in love, in the way that humans do?" And he said, "You would have to take on human form, not the appearance of it, when it suits us, as you do now. You would have to become human."

I looked then to the shadow in his eye. The valley of his mouth, the caverns of his hand. I could feel my rivers filling him. I saw him look to me with that face of his that could swing like a flock of birds and break up into nothing but sky or dark. "Are you ready for that?" he said. And I said, "I am."

Aidos uncoiled himself. He lay still for a long time. He lay still for so long that I thought he had forgotten. And then he turned his eyes toward me and I could see deep inside him. If I told you what I saw then it would make you afraid. You would call out to me, "Mother do not go there. Do not do this." And I would say to you. "If I do not go there, how will you be born?"

Aidos, turning to me then, said, in his gentlest voice, You will go south to the oldest land on earth.[8] The seven Pleiades sisters will be with you. They know the places of the most pure ingredients. They will help form you out of earth, water, salt, and the secret parts of plants. You will have within your human body every element of creation. You will be full of life. You will be beautiful.

9 The Pleiades gather her

There were stars gathered around me. Stars like flies, gathered around my serpent head, humming. "Who are you moaning, groaning, sighing with me?" And they said, "We are sent to bring you hands. To bring you feet and human form." "Who sends you?" "Quiet Persephone, the ways of the underworld are perfect, they may not be questioned!" "Where is my husband, where is Aidos?" "There is no one here by that name. Your husband has left you." "I tell you, where is he?" "Quiet Persephone!"

Dog. The Pleiades seized her. They carried her into the air above Uruk, high above Iraq. As they carried her high into the air, her hands came into being. They took her hands in their hands. As they carried her high into the air, her feet came into being. They held her feet. She rose up, above Euphrates, a snake form with hands and feet, high into the northern sky. A great black snake twisting, with hands and feet, carried by the Pleiades. High into the night sky.

Persephone. I can see the whole turning globe, I cried, I can see the whole earth turning. Who are you who hold me so strongly to my fate?

Dog. The Pleiades said – "We go with you; you and the dog star. We will help you gather your human body, piece by piece. You who have seen the dismemberment of men. You who have seen the shattering of children. You who have witnessed the breaking of women. You who have foreseen the ravage of earth. Now you will know how to gather, you will know how to bind, to console. You will have hands to carry the basket. You will have hands to hold the seeds. This was your wish. We help you, Persephone. You are honored among women."

Persephone. I fell from the sky. I came down like a meteor. I hit the sea in the Persian Gulf. I went down. The Pleiades covered me like fish, like fish we swam southeast through sea to an old, old country. And so it began – the trek to gather a human body. To clothe me.

Part two: gathering the body

1 Sites of creation

Dog. We came ashore on the northwest coast of a far country. It is a place now marked with iron mines, all dug out by the Caucasus people who live there now. In those days it was not disturbed. In those days there are stories of how the Seven Sisters came up out of the sea. These are things that some of you cannot see and cannot say. But I say, as a dog, if you do not know these things you will never know how the world came into being. You will never know how it was dogs who helped you become human.

The Pleiades sisters came up out of the sea. They left her lying there on the beach. They looked around. They started calling out to someone, I don't know who. They dragged her up the beach. She'd been under water for five-thousand nautical miles. They made a fire, wrapped her up, laid her down and waited.

Persephone raised her head. "I can hear singing," she said, "a long way away." From among the rocks, seven dark women came slowly into the firelight.

They smelled of stars and smoke and lizard. They all sat down together. They looked at you. They looked sorry for you. They started rubbing you. Singing to you . . . I went to sleep. Not my business. Women's negotiation taking place in the dark; all the women whispering in a strange language. Not the business of a dog.

When I woke up everyone was happy. The local sisters said, "We cleared the way for you. We can help you. We can help your people, poor things, there will be trouble for you all for a long time." They drew a map on the sand. Here, they said, here is where you find all the parts for a woman's body. It's laid out in the country for you, in every hill, in every rock. Follow this line here, this riverbed, this salt lake, this ochre mark, these plants, these deep holes, here – be careful here – this cave . . . this and this . . .

2 Spleen bones skin guts

Persephone. The Pleiades dragged me across the hot sand. They dragged me to that heap of ironstone. They gathered up the red iron. Rolling the iron in their hands with clay and water. Forming the dark shape of the spleen to filter my blood. They hurt me, trying to push it into my snake body.

The dog pulled them away. Don't you girls know anything? You got to give her bones in the shape of a woman. The Pleiades shouted. What would you know dog? I know about bones, he said.

The dog grabbed me, he dragged me, he laid my snake body down beside a salt lake, crystal white on top, black mud beneath. It was full of old bones left over from God knows when. He gathered delicate bones from the wings of old creatures. He chose my lovely bones with care. He laid out the bones upon the salt. He formed them in the shape of a woman.

Dog. The sisters got the idea. They made ligaments and muscles from their long black hair. Singing love songs, weaving their hair into string, joining up all her bones. They wrapped her in skin, they stretched the skin of the snake and wound it around her inside and outside her. From her snake skin and snake guts they made her into the first shape of a human. There she was laid on the salt. The most beautiful shape you ever saw.

Persephone. What!? Are you kidding me, Dog? Me in all that pain while those women poke and pull and sew my skin together! Beauty; don't talk to me about beauty. What would you know, Dog? The ways of the underworld are not perfect. They should be questioned!

Dog. The sisters looked at the map. "Where's that place the local girls told us; limestone caves, tunnels running underground? She needs human stomach, bowels, urinary tract. Caves of belly, greater and lesser intestine . . .?"

They got me to grab all that stuff from under the ground and pull it out. There I was backing across the plain with all her guts in my teeth. I left it to them to work out how to get the guts inside her. They did get that bit right, but messed it up again.

They tried to make her walk too soon, she fell all over the place, bits falling out of her. They never tied her up properly.

3 Black stone/lymph node

Persephone. They dragged me northeast – it was raining. Pelted down, then stopped. I was rolling about like a snake and woman all at once; mud, every-where, tracks filled up with water, looked like a string of mud lakes right across the country. The sisters got fed up with getting bogged, they wheeled into the air, they carried me through the sky, they came down on a shining plain of little black rocks, polished, looking like they fell from the night. They gathered and spat the little stones inside me all the way through my body, the pain like lightning hitting me all over. Dog barked at them. "Don't worry, dog," they said, "these pretty little stones are the lymph nodes, her immune system is going in."

Further on we came across a creek bed covered in little plants, "*yalka*," the local girls told us, root system all connected underground, good to eat. Use them for the gland network. Bush onions. Good for thyroid. That'll settle her down. Keep her steady. And we should pick up some honey ants to sweeten her up. She's a bit rough on everyone. They started digging like the local sisters told them. Bringing the sweet honey ants out from the ground.[9]

4 Liver and kidney

Persephone. We stayed by the creek for the night. Dog kept me warm. In the morning we went east into long red-sand hills. Seven women walking and me, walking, falling, carried in their arms.

I can hear an old lady singing behind a hill. I don't know her language. She is singing out to me, in her language. Then I understand. I hear this. She is singing in my serpent tongue.

> "*Kidney and liver are crying out, they cry out for you*
> *Over here behind the sand hills we're waiting for you, too long.*
> *Where is that woman, we've been waiting here too long.*"[10]

The old lady carried the liver and kidney to me. She passed them so smoothly though my skin I felt no pain. She breathed into my lungs. "What is your name?" She said, "One day I will tell you, it is enough to know you have family in this country who take care of water, your liver and your kidneys."

Walking back to camp I said to the girls, I need water. My body's crying out for water. They said, "Sorry sis, I can't see any water." "Why is there no water in this godforsaken country?"

"Maybe ask the old lady." The old lady was smiling, she nodded. "That way," she said, pointing with her lip, a lift of her chin; "My brother over there, that old man, he's waiting for you. See the smoke coming up."

5 Water

Dog. She took off. She ran straight to where that fire is burning. She ran so fast flies couldn't catch her. She ran straight for the fire. A man sitting there? She ran up to him, sitting by that little fire. He looked at her a long time. She looked at him a long time. He leaned a long black hand down into the rock. She heard the sound of water.

> **Persephone.** He is shaking water on my lip. He is shaking water on my eye.
> He pours water on my hands. He pours water on my tongue.
> My tongue loosens. I find human words. I cry in front of him.
> I have no family in this country. This country is empty for me.
> He pours more water upon me. He pours the water of life upon me.
> Who are you, I say, caring for me so? Who are you, he says, that I care for you
>   so? In my country I am the daughter of growing things. In my country
>   my father is the moving rain. In my neighbor country, my uncle Enki
>   cares for the rivers.
> In my neighbor country, my sister Inanna cares for the plants
>
> I have no family here. There is nothing in this country. There is pain, only pain.
> My promised husband fastened upon me the eye of death. He has left me.
> I am alone. Tell me, where is my hope?
>
> He smiles. Into the rock he dips again his long black hand. No, he says, I know
>   you. I set my ear to his words. You are the snake running with water.
> In your right hand you gather seeds. In your left hand you gather spirits – falling.
> Here you also have a name. It is marked upon your skin. You are not alone.
>
> He poured water upon me, He poured life upon me.
> He said – Tell your family I live in a dry country. In this country the water lies
>   beneath the ground. Beneath the skin. He smiled. With a cheeky smile,
>   he reached out to touch me. I felt a strange thing, like water, like fire run-
>   ning together, filling me. Do not be afraid. Water from this country now
>   lives beneath your skin. With this water you will bring your country life.
>
> With this smile I was satisfied. He filled me with waters. My human form filled.
> He took my serpent head in his hands. He gave me a human face. I arose. I
>   thanked him. He said, You will need a woman's heart. Where will I find that?
> A little way, he said pointing north.

Dog. She came back in the morning. She walked into camp. The sisters smiled sweetly at her. Where you been, they said. None of your business. Today you don't drag me, I can walk on my own two feet. Her skin was shining. Her eyes were shining. Maybe, said one of the sisters, spitting on the ground. You don't have a heart yet. Well, you have a snake heart – not a human heart.

6 Heart brain and rigmarole

Dog. I can't tell you where we found the heart. We had to go north. It was a dangerous job. That mixed-up woman went really wild. She tried to push the heart in herself. She rose up hissing, slashing this way and that. You couldn't tell what she was – snake or woman or what – fighting herself all the way – mad as a cut snake. She kept bashing her head against a rock. The snake brain wanted to get away, go back to where she came from, back to the roots in Babylon. The woman heart kept trying to come in, the snake heart fighting it. The wound in her chest wide open. Then it just slipped inside her. She was shaking, shaking. All the voices started talking at once, her voice, the sisters and god knows what else.

  Persephone – *deranged, dissociated, in different voices, her own and the Pleiades.*

I hate this, I hate this, there is no order in this – just get me my fucking brain and I'll get on by myself.

Fucking brain . . . hmmm, that reminds me. She needs "a wondrous vulva" and all the rigmarole that goes with it.

Wondrous . . . fucking vulva; who needs it . . .?

Listen Sis, You can't take off till we fix you up with the vulva. And that, my girl, is that.

Thing is, do we get her a brain before she gets all the rigmarole?

Or do we get her the rigmarole first and the brain after?

If she gets the wondrous vulva first we'll never get a brain into her . . .

Ok, ok, so get the brain. Where do we find a brain in this godforsaken country?

(Persephone, calming down, seeing a vision.) There is an old lady in a cave, over near Chilla Well, the walls all black with smoke. She is drawing fine white lines on the roof of the cave. On the walls of the cave, fine white lines.

  Dog. The sisters gathered her up. They took her to the old lady at Chilla Well.

Persephone, breathing deeply, her blood beating slowly, her body pulsing and open.

  Persephone. I sat there very calm while that old lady drew the lines of my nerves, all the glimmering points and links and lines and the flow of thought,

  running through the fine texture. The brain coming in, the brain coming in.

All the constellations flowing in, long fingers finding patterns, weaving me together. And it was then, in the dark, in the cave, among the beautiful lines, that the woven vulva descended with all the rigmarole of fertility, longing, conception, compassion and taking care . . .

Human life finally found its place in my body. Life came into me like a river in flood. It was a wondrous night, a night of wonder, the light flowing in. The eyes of Persephone coming alive in a manner never ever seen before.

7 Gratitude

And when it was finished, I went to all the sisters. In the dark of a cave, I thanked each of the seven sisters from the north and each of the seven sisters from the south.

I kissed them. I spoke to them the words of gratitude. I spoke to them words of love.

"You I will set as a constellation in my heart. You are with me always. You, I will remember."

The ladies were smiling. The birds began to sing. And like birds, the Pleiades and I flew north. Home – to my own country.

8 Return

When I had gathered my human body, when it was all over; I came to Aidos.
I called to him saying – The love in my body is so immense, I am afraid.
He took up a pomegranate, opening it. Smiling, he chose a seed, giving it to me.
I chose a seed, giving it to him; Five times we did this.

Then taking the pomegranate, I said, consider this open fruit, this is a gathering place of life. I love this place. See that our children do not destroy it.

In the morning, I rolled over in bed and I said to him.
How could I have loved like that if I had no human body?
Now I have hands to hold the net, hands to carry the basket
To catch the souls falling. To gather and scatter the seeds.

I must return to Eleusis. I have work to do.

9 To Eleusis

Dog. You remember the Maiden's Well, near the crack in the rocks where Kore went down? You remember that well where her mother sat and waited, crying; and the young women of Eleusis came and took her home, feeling sorry for her? You remember all that? Nowadays, there's a hotel there, the Maiden's Well Hotel.

Persephone. I said to Aidos my husband, I said; "In the Maiden's Well Hotel there is a room with a single bed. There I must leave you." He said; "We could meet again in the winter, I will wait for you . . ." and I said, to my surprise, "That remains to be seen . . ."

As I left him there, the room darkened; his shape became shadow; I saw his heart beating, dissolving, and his eyes . . . never have I seen such sorrow and I knew that both of us had become human, no matter what else we might be.

I walked out through the door of the Maiden's Well Hotel.

Coming up by the rock hole in the morning. Persephone, water shining along the roots, water shining on the roots of the tree, birds flickering . . . I can feel on my tongue the taste of my country. I am coming out, she cried. I am coming out.

In the street, I saw my mother. My mother looked at me. She looked closely at me. "You are pregnant," she said. Mum, I said, can we not talk about this here?

She smiled at me. "Show yourself to the people," she said. "They are waiting for you. They love you."

And to you the people I say, I say this. I know now what it is to be human,
And the pain it brings. And the compassion.
A force of nature became a woman. I fell in love. I slept with death. I conceived.
I am pregnant always with death, yet I live. I gave birth to seeds whose shape can always change; now a child, now the pomegranate, now the vine, now the heartfelt falling in love.
Each year I go to your father and each year I return to you. I come and I go, I return and return. I love this place. See that your children do not destroy it.
Dog. When Kore came back up the street, the old men smiled sweetly to each other. They remembered her. They remembered her story. They began to tell it again, telling each other, "Remember when Kore came back?"
That was a good day. I remember that day.
I remember that day.

End

Acknowledgments

To Jungarai Wanu, in memory of Andrew Japaljarri Spencer, 1954–2015

And to Napaljarri Jurra of Chilla Well for her stories and Dorothy Napangardi, artist. Her images courtesy of Palya Gallery, Alice Springs.

Photography and icon works courtesy of Fiona Walsh, Rusty Stewart, Josh Santospirito, Sia Cox, Dan Murphy, and Dave Nixon, and special thanks to Ruth Apelt and the musicians.

With infinite appreciation to all the performers and production crew on the Persephone, Ilparpa, and Hele Crescent events, 2015–2016.
This version completed March 1, 2018.

Notes

1 Karl Kerényi, "Kore," in C. G. Jung and Karl Kerényi (eds.), *Essays on a Science of Mythology: The Myth of the Divine Child and the Mysteries of Eleusis*, Princeton, NJ: Princeton University Press, 1973, p. 153.
2 *Persephone's Heart* is a work of fiction. Exact locations in her travels in the southern hemisphere are undisclosed and remain a mystery. They are based upon true stories. *"These things never happened yet always are."* – Sallust (86–35 BCE).
3 The Persephone/Demeter ceremony took place at Eleusis near Athens for perhaps 2,000 years until, in 389 CE, the Christian Roman Emperor Theodosius shut down all temples and ceremonies. The Final Oracle from Delphi goes thus: *Go tell the king the temple has fallen to pieces, the Gods dwell here no more. There is no oracular laurel, no talking spring, and the voice of the water has been silenced. All is finished.*
4 See Kieran Finnane's review of *Persephone Goes Under* in "Show Me Another Way to Live," *Alice Spring News*, May 5, 2016, www.alicespringsnews.com.au. She writes, "It seems to me that Persephone goes through her arduous deconstruction/reconstruction,

pushing to the brink of renunciation her relationship with Aidos, before she can in freedom choose to love him. It's an incredible metaphor for the constant task of women in 'the patriarchy.' For me its shape was transmitted through religion. The pinnacle of womanhood, the Virgin Mary and Mother, was the shockingly destructive way that the Christian patriarchal order subverted the earlier Mother–Daughter pair, stole from them their generative power, and rendered Woman as unknowing, passive, a receptacle, who has only to submit and suffer. I see Persephone's getting of a body as a fierce act of repudiation of all that, of being ready to travel to the end of the earth, to the edge of the mind's limits, to be *her self*."

5　The Form of the Performance: Nomikos Centre, Santorini, 2017. Part one was introduced with aerial film of the Australian desert and salt lakes and then a recapitulation of key scenes from the Alice Springs event in the mountain-set fire-lit quarry. For the travel of *Sites of Destruction*, maps were projected of the Mediterranean/Middle East along with incidents of war by photojournalist Rusty Stewart. Arriving in Sumer, Persephone finds Inanna in a cave, featuring Dan Murphy's metal figure of Inanna, Josh Santospirito's graphics, and Sia Cox's *Goddess*, with selected scenes from the May 2016 performance. In Part two, "Gathering the body," the imagery is Australian desert forms. As Persephone gains her neurological and generative system the overlaid imagery is the exquisitely lined network paintings of Dorothy Napangardi. Soundtrack music pieces included Hainides (traditional Greek), Astor Piazzolla's *Milonga del Angel*, Tinariwen's *Tassilli* (Track 8), Ibrahim ag Alhabib's *My Secretive Girlfriend*, Johnny Cash's *Help Me*, and Paul Kelly's *Summer Rain*.

6　Key references used as background include the following: Craig San Roque, *ARAS Connections*, special edition on Indigenous Australia, 2014, no. 4, aras.org/.webloc. On the Persephone events in Alice Springs, 2016, see Craig San Roque, "Introduction to the Kore Story/Persephone's Dog," *ARAS Connections*, 2016, no. 2, aras.org/ 2.webloc. Jules Cashford (trans.), *Homeric Hymns*, London, Penguin Classics, 2003. Issue 13, 2017, of *PAN: Philosophy Activism Nature*, edited by Geoff Berry, features Persephone and related events, www.panjournal.net.webloc. George Mylonas, *Eleusis and the Eleusinian Mysteries*, Princeton, NJ: Princeton University Press, 1961. George Roux, *Ancient Iraq*, London: Penguin, UK, 1980; see, in particular, p. 269 for the declarations of Ashurnasirpal. Diane Wolkstein, and Noah Kramer, *Inanna, Queen of Heaven and Earth: Her Stories and Hymns from Sumer*, New York: Harper and Row, 1983.

7　The introduction and text of *Kore Story/Persephone's Dog* by Craig San Roque may be found in *Ancient Greece, Modern Psyche: Archetypes Evolving*, eds. Virginia Beane Rutter and Tom Singer, London and New York: Routledge, 2015.

8　The constellation known as the Pleiades has equivalent stories in Australia. The pursuit of the women by a hunter, Orion, is similar to versions of the Australian Seven Sisters, known as *Kungarangkalpa*. A major exhibition in the National Museum of Australia, Canberra, September 2017–February 2018, featured the adventures of the sisters and drew comparisons with the European sisters. See Kungarangkalpa: Seven Sisters Songline at sevensisterssongline.com.webloc and Margo Neil, "Songlines: Tracking the Seven Sisters at the National Museum of Australia," *The Canberra Times*, September 14, 2017, www.canberratimes.com.au#4B8E19.

9　Where Persephone hypothetically entered the country is a mining area in the Pilbara region of Western Australia. The little black stones are polished fragments of meteor found in certain parts of the central desert. *Yalka* (bush onion) is an edible native lily (*cyperus bulbosus*), with a widespread network rhizome root system, often found in sandy watercourse and salt-lake areas. Honey ants, uniquely, form a capsule of delicate nectar attached to their bodies. They are good to suck.

10　The "Liver and kidney" excerpt is adapted from Nancy Nangala's traditional Pintubi song, recorded May 1996, as part of the Sugarman/Dionysos project.

5

ORPHEUS REMEMBERED

Jules Cashford

Shakespeare in *Two Gentlemen of Verona* gives us the magic of Orpheus:

> For Orpheus' lute was strung with poets' sinews,
> Whose golden touch could soften steel and stones,
> Make tigers tame, and huge leviathans
> Forsake unsounded deeps to dance on sands . . .[1]

Orpheus was a man who sang like a god (Figure 5.1). He first appears in the mid-sixth century with the poet Ibycus, who calls him "Orpheus-famous-of-name" (Homer and Hesiod do not mention him), and then a fragment from Simonides of Chios in the early fifth century says simply:

> And countless birds flew above his head
> and fish leapt straight up from the dark-blue water
> in time with his lovely song.[2]

After this, it is as though the excitement of this possibility – that a singer could draw the creatures of air and sea toward him, that the natural and human worlds might sing together to the same song – sends everyone off imagining in their own way, so that the story of Orpheus grows and grows until it reaches the boundaries of life and death.

Then the lyric poet Pindar calls Orpheus the "Father of Songs" and names him the son of the Muse Kalliope and the Thracian king Oeagrus, who was sent by the god Apollo to play the lyre among the Argonauts in their quest for the Golden Fleece. Aeschylus has trees follow after him, charmed by his lyre.

FIGURE 5.1 Orpheus playing to entranced Thracians, with their fox-skin caps and long heavy embroidered cloaks. Orpheus, by contrast, is dressed as a Greek. His left hand has the look of a bird with outstretched feathers, singing as he plays. 440 BCE. Antikensammlung, Staatliche Museen zu Berlin

Euripides' Chorus, in *The Bacchae*, search for Dionysos in the forests of Olympus where "once Orpheus, playing on his lyre, gathered the trees with his song, gathered the wild animals."[3] By the time of Ovid, in his *Metamorphoses* (8 CE), even "insensate rocks" follow him.

We might say that with Orpheus we are given an image of the ecstatic power of Imagination – the magic of his lyre, which sang the Song of the Universe – so that the hearts of all who heard him came alive and were brought into harmony with each other and with the whole. It made no difference whether they were humans, animals, birds, fish, trees, or rocks – all were purified and restored to their original participation in the eternal, which gave them the freedom to change their natures. This is a story with the consciousness of the *Unus Mundus*, the essential unity of the world. Philosophers described themselves as returned to their divine nature, to *Arche*, the first principle, from which all else follows. The Pythagoreans, followers of Orpheus, expressed this as Number; whereas for Plato, often known as the Orphic's philosopher, the *Arche* was Harmony and the Music of the Spheres. *Harmonia* was his term for the right tuning of the Soul.

The Egyptian scholar Schwaller de Lubicz writes of this:

> The principle of harmony is a cosmic law, the Voice of God. Whatever be the disorder that man or fortuitous natural accident may provoke, Nature, left to herself, will put everything in order again through affinities (the consciousness in all things). Harmony is the a priori Law written in all of Nature; it imposes itself on our intelligence, yet it is in itself incomprehensible.[4]

In Shakespeare's *The Merchant of Venice*, this vision of harmony is expressed by Lorenzo to his love Jessica:

> How sweet the moonlight sleeps upon this bank!
> Here will we sit and let the sounds of music
> Creep in our ears: soft stillness and the night
> Become the touches of sweet harmony.
> Sit, Jessica. Look how the floor of heaven
> Is thick inlaid with patines of bright gold.
> There's not the smallest orb which thou behold'st
> But in his motion like an angel sings
> Still choiring to the young-eyed cherubins.
> Such harmony is in immortal souls.
> But whilst this muddy vesture of decay
> Doth grossly close it in, we cannot hear it.[5]

In these terms, perhaps, Orpheus, playing his lyre, allows us to hear the harmony of the universe in our own immortal souls, leading us from *Bios*, the personal and finite reality, to *Zoe*, infinite life – the soul remembering itself. Orpheus would then be the initiator into unfathomable depths, whose power transforms the whole of the natural world, including ourselves. In his myths there is a search for what that secret is, asking: what is the essence that can bring about transformation?

Mnemosyne, Goddess of Memory

In the origins given to Orpheus we can see the magnificent Greek idea of the lineage and power of poetry, music, and song: Orpheus was the son of a Muse, Kalliope, and the grandson of the Goddess of Memory – Mnemosune, or Mnemosyne, as she becomes in English. Karl Kerényi suggests that Mnemosyne originates in Mycenaean times under the name *Manasa*, who, like many of the other Greek goddesses and gods, may have come from Crete (c. 1500 BCE)[6] – the older story, as so often lurking beneath the later myths, one closer to the soil and the rhythms of the Moon, often only visible through its underlying images, rites, and etymology. There is a Late Minoan picture of a lyre player enchanting birds in the Museum of Chania in Crete, who has been suggested as Orpheus or Apollo, though only the name of Apollo appears in Mycenaean Linear B script from Knossos under the name Paean. Bulls' horns with the double axe between them – a Minoan image of wholeness – point to the sacred character of the scene (Figure 5.2).

FIGURE 5.2 Lyre player from Kalami enchanting birds. c. 1300 BCE. Late Minoan IIIB. Museum of Chania. The singer is often called Orpheus or Apollo, though only Apollo appears in Mycenaean Linear B script from Knossos under the name Paean. Bulls' horns with the double axe between them are a Minoan image of wholeness

(https://aras.org/ancient-greece-modern-psyche)

The etymology of Mnemosyne leads us far back into the mists of a lunar culture that existed a long time before the Aryans, whose chief god was Zeus, arrived in Greece around 800 BCE. Mnemosyne's name derives from *Mene*, Moon, and *mosune*, "wooden house" or "tower," so her name literally means "the House of the Moon." As Plato said, the Moon can teach even the very slowest creature to count, watching the waxing and waning, and counting from Moon to Moon, giving us a past, present, and predictable future.[7] Practically all the words in Greek concerned with measurement and mind, wisdom and mania, have the Moon/mind root of *me*, *men*, or *ma* in them from the Sanskrit (*Mene*, Moon; *mneme*, remembrance; *mnesthenai*, remember; *anamnesis*, recollection; *metis*, wisdom; and so on). In the *Aitareya Upanishad*, for instance, when the heavenly bodies are asked to find an abode within the human being, "the Sun became sight and entered the eyes, and the Moon became mind and entered the heart."[8] Mnemosyne carried all these resonances in ancient times.

The symbolism of the Moon contains without contradiction the ideas of visible change and invisible perpetuity: the *Bios* of the ever-moving phases and the *Zoe* of the changeless cycle of the whole – for the numbering of days was always resolved into the "eternal return" of the New Moon, which, for Plato, was the closest thing there is to eternity.[9] In many myths across the world the Moon is the abode of souls, the place where the ancestors live, holding the memory of the laws of the tribe and the world. And in its image of the eternal, the Moon – especially the Full Moon, when *Zoe* and *Bios* seem to come together as one – has always been a Muse, an inspiration leading us beyond the boundaries of time.[10]

Mnemosyne belongs to the Olympian story of creation, first given in Hesiod's *Theogony*, written around 700 BCE, where she is named as one of the original children of Earth and Heaven. Gaia, Earth, the first to arise from Chaos, gives birth to Ouranos (Latin, *Uranus*), Heaven, and Pontus (Sea). In the tradition of son-lovers of the goddess, Ouranos becomes her consort, and together they give birth to the twelve Titans, among whom are Kronos (Time), Themis (Law), Rhea (the Flowing One), and Mnemosyne (Memory). This tells us that the idea of Memory, along with Time, Lawfulness, and the "Flow of Life," among others, belongs to the structure of consciousness – the archetypal realm of the psyche – such that consciousness cannot be conceived without them.

In the next stage of creation, Rhea and Kronos give birth to three daughters – Hestia, Demeter, and Hera – and three sons – Poseidon, Hades, and lastly Zeus, whose name, from its Indo-European roots, means "Light" and "Day," or, in its original verbal form, a "Lighting Up." Zeus unites with two of the Titan daughters of Earth and Heaven – first with *Themis* (Law), who brings forth the *Horai* (the Seasons) and the *Moira* (the Fates), and then with *Mnemosyne of the Beautiful Hair*, who gives birth to the Muses.[11]

The story, in Hesiod, went that Zeus and Mnemosyne lay together for nine nights and later, on snowy Olympos, she delivered nine daughters, one for each night, all of one mind, their one thought singing and dancing, and their hearts free from care. In a fifth-century BCE red-figure painting on a *lekythos* – a vessel for storing oil – Kalliope, the first-born Muse, "She of the Beautiful Voice," is drawn playing the lyre, seated before her mother who stands looking down on her, holding the scroll of Memory. Kalliope looks only at her lyre, not at her mother, as though she is playing "by heart" the song inscribed on her mother's scroll. Kalliope herself became the mother of Orpheus, uniting either with the Thracian king Oeagrus, as Pindar says, or the god Apollo, as others say, or, as it were, both – giving Orpheus human *and* divine parentage, as though he were indeed half man, half god (Figure 5.3).

FIGURE 5.3 Mnemosyne, standing, holds the scroll of Memory, looking down upon her first-born daughter, Kalliope, She of the Beautiful Voice, who plays the lyre without looking at her mother, as though she is playing the song inscribed in her mother's scroll, knowing it by heart. Fifth century BCE. Lekythos, Museo Archeologico Nazionale di Siracusa

(https://aras.org/ancient-greece-modern-psyche)

There is an *Orphic Hymn to Mnemosyne*, written sometime between 300 BCE and 300 CE:

> Mnemosyne I call, the Queen, consort of Zeus,
> Mother of the sacred, holy and sweet-voiced Muses.
> Ever alien to her is evil oblivion that harms the mind,
> she holds all things together in the mind and soul of mortals,
> in the same dwelling place, she strengthens
> the powerful ability of humans to think.
> Most sweet, vigilant, she reminds us of all the thoughts
> that each one of us is for ever storing in our hearts,
> overlooking nothing, rousing everyone to consciousness.
> Blessed goddess, awaken for the initiates the memory
> of the sacred rite, and banish forgetfulness from them.[12]

We can see that Mnemosyne is a more comprehensive idea than our memory, closer to what Yeats calls the *Great Memory*, which he refers to as "the Memory of Nature."[13] She is conceived not only as an inexhaustible store of all the facts in the world, but also as the timeless figure of origin pregnant with the forms that are to come. So she contains in herself both what we might in general terms think of as analogous to the *human* faculty of memory, which stores and restores the past and so structures categories of perception and thought, and also she gives birth to the Muses, her children, whom we might more usually associate with Imagination. The Muses were often called not just *Mousai* but *Mneiai*, a plural of Mnemosyne herself, suggesting an even closer relation to the origin of the world and the structure of the psyche.[14] The mythic image of Mnemosyne asks us to consider this relationship between Memory and Imagination as it unfolds through the Muses and Orpheus – from the archetypal realm to the human particular.

In one way it makes sense that, in an oral tradition that recited long epic poems, goddesses of the arts were the daughters of Memory. Though, on the other hand, Plato has Socrates tell Phaedrus a tale of an Egyptian king, Thamus, who forbade the lunar god Thoth, who had invented writing, to teach it to anyone, saying that "writing would implant forgetfulness in their souls, for they will no longer call things to remembrance from within themselves."[15] Yet for the Egyptians, a thousand years earlier, calling things to remembrance from within themselves was the same as remembering the gods and aligning the soul to the cosmic order.

A fourteenth-century BCE black basalt statue, in the Louvre in Paris, shows Thoth, the Lunar God of Eternity, Time, Imagination, Hieroglyphs, and Scribes, in his baboon form, inspiring the scribe, Nebmeroutef, as he writes down the hieroglyphs sent to him by the god. Thoth, more usually drawn with the head of an ibis, is married to Maat – Goddess of Truth and the Right Ordering of the Universe, whose symbol is the ostrich feather – and the scribe has himself to be "in Maat" – personally in harmony with the universe before Thoth will come to him. The inscription around the base of the statue says that Thoth "brings back Maat every day" – Imagination brings back Truth: it could be Keats speaking: "What the imagination seizes as beauty must be truth."[16] The sculpture shows the god looking at the scribe; the scribe is simply engrossed in his work (Figure 5.4).

FIGURE 5.4   The scribe Nebmeroutef and the god Thoth in his baboon form. Schicht statue. 1391–1353 BCE. The Louvre

(https://aras.org/ancient-greece-modern-psyche)

However, for the Greeks it was Mnemosyne who was ritually invoked before telling a story, as she was in the Healing Temples of Asklepios, God of Healing, where she would be offered a cake by the supplicants about to enter their incubation and would receive their last prayer so they would remember the visions they had while sleeping. Many of the supplicants carved their names and their gratitude on the stone wall beside the sleeping couch. One in particular, Archinos, who lived in in the fourth century BCE, dedicated a votive plaque in which Asklepios and his familiar snake are shown healing the dreamer of a wound on his shoulder. While the young man, Archinos, lies asleep and dreaming on the stone bed, a snake rises out of his body and licks the wound. Reading the picture dramatically, as though re-enacting the dream that he remembered, we then see Archinos standing on the floor before the god Asklepios who is touching his shoulder in precisely the same place. The coincidence suggests that healing arises from a union of body and soul. Archinos wrote his name on the rectangular plaque on the wall above him, which was ritually left empty so the dream could come (Figure 5.5).

FIGURE 5.5 Asklepios and his snake healing the dreamer of the wound on his shoulder. Both snake and god touch the same place, suggesting that healing arises from a union of body and soul. Archinos, the name of the dreamer, wrote his gratitude at his cure on the rectangular plaque on the wall above him, ritually left empty so the dream could come. Votive plaque dedicated by Archinos, the dreamer. c. 380 BCE. National Archaeological Museum, Athens

(https://aras.org/ancient-greece-modern-psyche)

Mnemosyne's nine daughters, the Muses, came still closer to human beings, and their presence was felt whenever life lit up and became iridescent, when you could hear Nature speaking and thinking – the word "muse" comes from the Proto-Indo-European root of *men*, meaning to "think." Muses could assume the shape of birds, messengers of the unknown, and were seen in mountains and fountains, just as Mnemosyne, like the Moon, was always linked with water, the mysterious source of springs and rivers in the outer and inner worlds, above and below. The Muses live beside Desire, *Himeros*, and their companions are the Three Graces. From their shrine in their dancing grounds – the *Museion*, from which our term "museum" comes – they can be glimpsed going back and forth in procession to Olympos, wrapped in veils of white mist.

When the Muses sang about the immortal gods – Hesiod continues, "telling of things that are, that will be and that were" – everything stood still: sky, stars, sea, and rivers. And, conversely, the mountain that does not move, Mount Helicon, began to grow in rapture up to heaven, until the winged horse Pegasus, soaring from the severed neck of the Gorgon of fear, struck the mountain with his hooves, and the cascade of water arising from his blow was called *hippou krene*, the "fountain of the horse."[17] Around this spring the Muses danced, and its waters brought inspiration to all who drank from it. Thus Keats, in his *Ode to a Nightingale*:

> O for a beaker full of the warm South,
> Full of the true, the blushful Hippocrene,
> With beaded bubbles winking at the brim,
> And purple-stained mouth;
> That I might drink, and leave the world unseen,
> And with thee fade away into the forest dim.[18]

The magical nature of the Muses is celebrated here, mirroring the magical nature of their gifts to human beings. The *Homeric Hymn to the Muses and Apollo* points to the difference between poets and kings: "It is because of the Muses and the archer Apollo that there exist on earth people who sing songs and play the lyre; kings come from Zeus."[19] They bring honor to statesmen, availing them of "soft words" to ease conflict and reach sound judgment. When they watch a heaven-favored Lord being born they pour sweet dew upon his tongue and honeyed words flow from his mouth. The *Orphic Hymn to the Muses* says to them:

> Daughters of Mnemosune and loud-thundering Zeus,
> Pierian Muses of great name and glorious fame,
> the mortals you visit long for you, appearing
> in your many shapes, giving birth
> to unblemished virtue in every discipline,
> nourishing the soul, setting thought right,
> becoming leaders and rulers of the power of the mind,
> teaching mortals the sacred and mystic rites.
> Kleio and Euterpe and Thaleia and Melpomene
> and Terpsichore and Erato and Polymnia and Ourania
> and mother Kalliope and the mighty goddess Agne, come.
> Sacred goddesses, come to the initiates in all
> your manifold forms, bring honour and loving rivalry,
> and may you be sung in many songs.[20]

We have to imagine seeing these Muses outside, embodied in Nature, as well as those who come into our minds in solitude. They come from a time when divinity was immanent in natural life, so they were seen dancing in the waters when they sparkled and in the mountains when they shimmered in the evening light. Numinosity was the sign of their presence (literally, "the nod or wink of a god" – *nouein* – the awakening of the divine). Our term "musing" may have gained overly inward overtones, but there is also music, which was always played when Apollo gave the oracle at Delphi.

In Boeotia, Hesiod's own country, the Muses were said to be originally only three in number and had names that came from the craft of poetry: *Melete*, "Practice"; *Mneme*, "Memory"; and *Aoide*, "Song." But, for Hesiod himself, there were nine Muses and he gives them names eloquent of their natures. Their particular domains came later in Hellenistic times:

> Kleio, "the Giver of Fame" – who became Muse of History
> Euterpe, "the Giver of Joy" – Muse of the Flute
> Thaleia, "the Festive" – Muse of Comedy
> Melpomene, "the Singer" – Muse of Tragedy
> Terpischore, "She Who Enjoys Dancing" – Muse of the Lyre
> Erato, "the Awakener of Desire" – Muse of the Dance
> Polymnia, "She of Many Hymns" – Muse of Sacred Storytelling

Ourania, "the Heavenly" – Muse of Astronomy
Kalliope, "She of the Beautiful Voice" – Muse of Epic Poetry and Heroic Song.[21]

The leader of the Muses in the dance was Apollo, son of Zeus and Leto – and the divine father of Orpheus. He was called *Apollo Mousagetes*, Apollo of the Muses, the only god to know the mind of Zeus and so to have the gift of prophecy. In the winter Dionysos becomes ruler of Delphi and Apollo goes north to the land of the Hyperboreans, beyond the North Wind. A very old eighth-century vase shows Apollo playing the lyre while three Muses are dancing together, holding hands between serpentine rivulets of water, with the sun below the horizon, suggestive of rain in winter (Figure 5.6).

FIGURE 5.6   Apollo with his lyre dancing with the Muses – "Apollo Mousagetes."
The sun below the horizon shows that it is winter, when Apollo leaves
Delphi and goes north, to the land of the Hyperboreans, beyond
the North Wind, and Dionysos takes over the rulership of Delphi.
The serpentine rivulets of water suggest rain. c. 750 BCE. Staatliche
Kunstsammlung, Dresden

(https://aras.org/ancient-greece-modern-psyche)

Back in Delphi, in the summer, however, when Apollo passes by the gods, everything changes:

> Suddenly the gods think only of the lyre, think only of song,
> and at the same time and all together the Muses sing,
> voice to sweet voice answering,
> they sing of the divine gifts of the gods
> and of the suffering of human beings
> which the gods bring upon them,
> how they live, mindless, helpless,
> how they can't find a cure for death, can't stop old age . . .[22]

Yet, "If the Muses love you then you are blessed and sweet sound flows from your mouth."[23]

The Muses' relation to memory

In Book 2 of the *Iliad*, the Poet asks the Muses to tell him who went to fight in the Trojan War: "For you are goddesses, watching all things, knowing all things, but we have only hearsay and not knowledge." He ends with the plea that it is the Muses who have to remember and give *him their* memories of it because he could not do this by himself.[24] He is asking for an actual vision of the past re-created in the present, so he can see things in truth. Again, in the *Odyssey*, when Odysseus says that Demodocus can sing about the war of Troy "as if he had been there or heard about it from an eye witness," he concludes that a Muse or Apollo must have "taught" it to him.[25]

When the Muses, as daughters of Mnemosyne, are asked to *remember* the past, they are asked to bring back not just the facts but the original structure of feeling in which these facts made sense and had value, that which makes them *worth* the remembering. The original value, implicitly evoked by the Muses who graced the Poet with their presence, infuses the theme and manner of his song so it becomes poetry. Klio, who later became the Muse of History, is often shown reading from her large scroll (Figure 5.7).

FIGURE 5.7   The Muse Klio, later known as the Muse of History, reading from her scroll. Attic red-figure Lekythos, c. 430 BCE, Boeotia

(https://aras.org/ancient-greece-modern-psyche)

The gift of the Muses was then the power of true speech, and the poet was known as the servant of the Muses, dependent ultimately on "the Muse" for inspiration, as poets have said ever since. They point to the dimension in any creative work, which is not chosen but "given" – it comes upon us and takes us away – and for the Greeks "given" meant "divinely given." So poet and seer, the oracular voice, are allied here, as they are, etymologically, in many Indo-European languages. Both reveal hidden truth and, even for Virgil in the *Georgics*, the secrets of nature.[26]

But there is a warning: the Muses tell Hesiod they can also lie. In fact, they seem to tempt him with lies first: the truth, the reservations of the prose imply, is more difficult. As they say: "We know enough to make up lies which are convincing, but we also have the skill, when we've a mind, to speak the truth."[27] So is this mind of theirs arbitrary and unpredictable, or can it be intuited and anticipated? The stories suggest that it is *our* relation to the Muses that calls forth from them truth or trickery – and even punishment for abusing their gifts.

When the nine daughters of the Macedonian King Pierus challenged the Muses to a contest, and lost, the Muses turned them into chattering magpies. When the Sirens (the half-bird maidens against whose irresistible song Odysseus strapped himself to the mast of his ship) competed with the Muses and lost, the Muses plucked out the Sirens' feathers to make themselves crowns. When Marsyas, the flute player, boasted that he was better than Apollo and was judged the loser by the Muses, he was flayed alive. However, these punishments could not have been avoided by winning – for how could anyone win? – it was because the participants invoked the Muses and Apollo with the spirit of competition in their hearts. In one vase, even Apollo himself seems to be approaching the Muse Kalliope with due ritual, holding his laurel staff respectfully between them, while she sits on her chair offering him the lyre (Figure 5.8).

FIGURE 5.8   Kalliope holding out the lyre to Apollo who is approaching her ritually, holding his laurel staff between them. c. 430 BCE. Staatliche Antikensammlungen, Munich

(https://aras.org/ancient-greece-modern-psyche)

Approaching the Muses, as any other god or goddess, with *hubris* – the arrogance of the ego – turns their powers against us. So it is that Homer, Virgil, Dante, Milton, Shakespeare, and D. H. Lawrence begin their poetry by invoking the Muses, the Muse, or Memory, Mnemosyne herself. Dante begins the *Divine Comedy*:

> O Muses, o high genius, aid me now,
> O Memory that engraved the things I saw.

As Shakespeare begins *Henry V*:

> O! for a Muse of fire, that would ascend
> The brightest heaven of invention.[28]

And D. H. Lawrence begins his poem, "Song of a Man Who Has Come Through":

> Not I, not I, but the wind that comes through me.

Yet this radical uncertainty – is the mind pure enough? how can we know? – pervades many such tales. The bee-maidens, whom Apollo gave to Hermes, teach divination and speak the truth graciously after they have fed on golden honey. "But if they are deprived of the sweet food of the gods they tell you lies, swarming to and fro."[29] How can we tell if they have had their honey? Perhaps by their swarming, their not being in the mood? Likewise, Apollo expects humans to know their place. Some human beings, he says, "shall profit from my oracular voice":

> Those who come guided by the cry and the flights of prophetic birds,
> but those who trust in twittering birds and want to question my oracles
> against my will, in order to know more than the ever-living gods,
> these people will come on a wasted journey.[30]

And even Hermes: "A few he helps, but he endlessly beguiles the race of human beings in the darkness of the night."[31] Similarly with dreams: do they come from the Gate of Horn or the Gate of Ivory, the one true and the other deceitful? It was the same with the blood of the Medusa – the Gorgon, whose look turned heroes to stone, whom Perseus slew with the help of Athena's mirror and Hermes's sword and sandals. Blood from her veins went to Asklepios, the God of Healing, and with blood from one side he heals and with blood from the other he slays. But then, which side is which?

Perhaps the tales themselves suggest to us the way of right approach? For while the poet asks the Muses to remember for him so he can repeat it, the first gift of the Muses to the poet, in direct inversion, is forgetfulness – *Lethe* or *Lesmoysne*. *Lesmoysne* is the sister of Mnemosyne, suggesting how inextricably the two ideas are linked and valued. When the Muses, or their bard, sing:

> At once that man forgets his heavy heart,
> And has no memory of any grief,
> So quick the Muses' gift diverts his mind.[32]

The same word for "forgetfulness" is used here as in the Orphic Hymn – *Lethe* – and while there, for the initiates, it was to be shunned; here, for the poets, it is to be welcomed. So as well as more than one meaning for memory, we have, predictably enough, more than one meaning for forgetfulness. We might read the Muses' gift of forgetfulness as diverting and so redirecting the troubled conscious mind, afflicted by its own personal memories that keep it focused on itself alone. This self-forgetting seems to be a more relaxed classical version of the Virginity of Mary, symbolically closed to all that is not God – the virgin soul open to Annunciation. Yet forgetfulness can also be blessed in its own right. *Lethe* was a healing gift for Orestes when pursued by the Furies:

> O magic of sweet sleep, healer of pain,
> I need thee and how sweetly art thou come.
> O holy Lethe, wise physician, thou,
> Goddess invoked of miserable men.[33]

Virgil also talks of "the waters that quench man's trouble, the deep draught of oblivion." And Dante, in his *Purgatorio*, emphasizes the unity and dual activity of Lethe and Mnemosyne by drawing one river that divides into two streams: Lethe, taking away the memory of all sins, and Mnemosyne (which he calls *Eunoe*, Good Memory), restoring the memory of all good deeds.[34]

Lethe and Mnemosyne are given further meanings in practical ritual, in the oracle of Trophonios – a half-brother of Asklepios. The oracle was given in the subterranean Cave of Trophonios in the land of the Muses near the slopes of Mount Helicon in Boeotia, where there were two springs, one of Lethe and the other of Mnemosyne. There, the initiates must first ritually drink of the waters of Lethe, in order to forget everything they have previously had in their minds – like a catharsis, a purification – and only then may they drink of the waters of Mnemosyne, which will allow them to remember the visions they are about to have in their journey into the underworld. Even so, they cannot remember them when they come back, and they are made to sit in the Chair of Memory to be questioned by the priests, who interpret what Trophonios, in the shape of a serpent, had revealed to them.[35]

> I can only say, *there* we have been: but I cannot say where.
> And I cannot say, how long, for that is to place it in time.[36]

So all the stories explore this relation, almost a dance, between remembering and forgetting, with the two terms expanding in meaning until they invoke the whole person, our unconscious as well as our conscious selves. We might even wonder if, between them, it is remembering and forgetting, in their daily dance, which creates the underlying and dynamically ever-changing reality of the present for each person. "Those images which yet / Fresh images beget," as Yeats has it in his poem *Byzantium*.[37] But when the story is one of the ego that has been persuaded or beguiled to forget itself, what – or who – takes its place?

Hermes, God of Imagination, flying above the clouds in a flurry of wings and feet, holding his lyre, the caduceus leading the way, was often known simply as the "Slayer of Argus" (Figure 5.9). *Argus Panoptes* (All Seeing) was the giant with a hundred eyes who never slept – always had one eye awake, never, like the over-alert mind, stopping watching. Hermes lulls him to sleep with his music, and when the last eye shuts he slays him (his only violent act) and frees the Moon Cow Io whom Argus was imprisoning. What Hermes kills is the literal mind as a condition for his being there at all. At one day old the playful child Hermes even beguiles a furious Apollo, his elder half-brother, whose cattle he has just stolen and who has been found out. Laying aside his trickster mode and assuming his role as artist to quell Apollo's rage, he takes up the lyre he has made from the hollowed shell of the tortoise of the mountains and sings. He sings of "the immortal gods and the black earth, how they came into being in the beginning, but first among the gods he praised in song Mnemosyne, Mother of the Muses, for the son of Maia belonged to her by lot."[38] Apollo is instantly enchanted and *gives* him his cattle, the caduceus, and the uncertain prophecy of the bee-maidens, and in return Hermes gives the lyre to Apollo.

FIGURE 5.9 Hermes, the Messenger, with lyre and caduceus. c. 450 BCE. The British Museum

(https://aras.org/ancient-greece-modern-psyche)

Like the Muses, Hermes charms people into forgetting themselves with his lyre, while drawing others gently across the boundary of life and death. Now, although Apollo is the god who strikes from afar – an image of the highly focused but uninvolved mind – he is also the god who sings the Paean, the song that heals, when he dances rhythmically with the Muses at the feasts. Apollo gives this same lyre to his son Orpheus, who was taught to play the lyre by the Muses, and later the son or disciple of Orpheus was called *Musaios* – meaning "of the Muses." Plato refers to people who believe that Orpheus and Musaios are both sons of the Moon as *Mene*.[39] This same lyre will eventually find itself set into the heavens by Zeus at the request of Apollo and the Muses, where it becomes the seven stars of the Pleiades, one of whom is Maia, the mother of Hermes who invented the lyre in the first place – the story coming round again, rather bewilderingly, to its beginning.

Can we not feel an archetypal forcefield at work here? Stories and images echo each other, cross over and tangle and disentangle, all the while following an invisible thread that winds its way through them all. It is like a mind exploring ever new ways of trying to get at an essence that, in the end, always escapes us, must escape us, because it can only be glimpsed indirectly through its symbols, which never completely reveal their meaning. What we do know is that, although Hermes was the god who invented the lyre, Orpheus was the man who perfected it, and in his hands, the lyre made the universe translucent to his song.

Orpheus

In Greek legend, Orpheus came from Thrace, though Kerényi and the classical scholar Jane Harrison believe he came originally from Crete, and traveled north, along with Dionysos, to Thrace and only later came down into Greece. The last syllable of his name – *eus* – points to him being quite old, like Atreus of Mycenaean times.[40] He is typically pictured playing his lyre to Thracians while dressed as a Greek, as though he has a double allegiance (Figure 5.10).

FIGURE 5.10 Orpheus playing the lyre between two Thracians holding spears. c. 430 BCE. British Museum

(https://aras.org/ancient-greece-modern-psyche)

Orpheus' story, like that of Plato and Pythagoras, says he went to study in Egypt. When he came back he joined the Argonauts, and, in Apollonius of Rhodes' Hellenistic version (c. 300 BCE), he stopped a fight between the sailors by singing of the origin of creation, after which their oars pulled to the rhythm of his song. Later, in a fierce storm, he sang more sweetly than the Sirens, those who had lured Odysseus's men and ships to their death – and the waves calmed down.[41] On his return he married Eurydice, who was an oak nymph and/or a daughter of Apollo. After a short time she died.

Virgil, in his *Georgics* (29 BCE), was the first to look for a reason. Eurydice encountered yet another son of Apollo, Aristaeus, a man versed in the practical arts of the Earth, especially the keeping of bees. Aristaeus molested her and, as she fled from him, a serpent, sheltering in the grass, bit her in the ankle and she died of the bite.[42] If this were a dream, we might wonder if the serpent biting the heel were an image of something neglected trying to come back into consciousness, perhaps to compensate for a too extreme conscious attitude. And perhaps again, it invites us to think about whether art and initiation require some sacrifice of instinctual energies that may themselves require honoring in some other way. The alchemists called their work *Opus Contra Naturam*, the work against nature.

Ovid (forty years later) saw Eurydice as a newly wedded bride walking through the grass with her friends the Naiads, water nymphs, when she disturbed a snake sheltering there, as the omens of Hymen conducting the ceremony in his saffron robes – the torch sputtering and not lighting, the tear-provoking fumes – had foretold at her wedding.[43]

The story of Orpheus's descent into the underworld first appears in Euripides' play *Alcestis* (438 BCE) and is elaborated in Virgil and especially Ovid, among others.[44] Orpheus went down to the underworld to ask Hades to let Eurydice come back to him, and when he sang he entranced the entire world of the dead. Charon, the Ferryman, and Cerberus, the three-headed dog, allowed him to enter the underworld without protest. The cheeks of the Furies were wet with tears for the first time. Sisyphus ceased rolling his stone uphill. Tantalus stopped being thirsty. Ixion stepped off his wheel. The vultures did not pluck at the giant Tityos's liver. His song changed the reality of all who heard him. Hades and Persephone were delighted to see him. No one could resist him. But Hades made one condition: walk ahead of her and don't look back until you are both in the Upper World.

A fifth-century marble relief, now in the Louvre, shows Orpheus and Hermes on either side of Eurydice, in her journey out of Hades (Figure 5.11). Orpheus, on the right, unusually wearing a peaked Thracian cap, holds his lyre in his left hand and is now facing Eurydice, their heads bowed together in grief. Hermes stands waiting on the left. Both Hermes and Orpheus are tenderly touching Eurydice, who is veiled, the central figure and the visual focus of the composition. This is the moment when Orpheus has just turned to look back for Eurydice, and Hermes is laying his hand gently on her arm to take her back down to the underworld. The figures of Orpheus and Hermes are almost a mirror image of each other – Orpheus with his arm raised to clasp the hand of Eurydice, who is brushing his shoulder as if to comfort him, while the downward gesture of Hermes on her other arm draws her back.

FIGURE 5.11 Orpheus, on the right, dressed unusually in a peaked Thracian cap, holding his lyre in his left hand, bringing Eurydice out of Hades, with Hermes on the left. They are both tenderly touching Eurydice, who is veiled, the central figure and the visual focus of the composition. Marble relief. 420 BCE. The Louvre

(https://aras.org/ancient-greece-modern-psyche)

Rilke's poem, *Orpheus, Eurydice, Hermes*, ends on this moment:

She was already root.
And when abruptly,
the god had halted her and, with an anguished
outcry, outspoke the words: He has turned round! –
she took in nothing, and said softly: Who?
But in the distance, dark in the bright exit,
someone or other stood, whose countenance
was indistinguishable. Stood and saw
how, on a strip of pathway between meadows,
with sorrow in his look, the god of message
turned silently to go behind the figure
already going back by that same pathway,
in paces circumscribed by lengthy shroudings,
uncertain, gentle, and without impatience.[45]

But why did Orpheus look back? The story is often taken as a myth of failure: that he didn't love her enough or didn't have the courage to die for her himself, as Alcestis had offered to do for her husband, Admetus. This is the view of Phaedrus in Plato's *Symposium*.[46] Admetus himself, who had happily accepted his wife's offer, manages to convince himself that if *he'd* been Orpheus, he would have brought her back![47] Virgil puts it down to "a sudden frenzy" (*dementia*) that seized him, "unwary in his love . . . and he halted at the very verge of light . . . unmindful, alas, and vanquished in purpose." Then, "Suddenly she vanished from his eyes, like smoke dissolving in a sigh of air."[48]

As though in answer to Phaedrus, Ovid has Orpheus telling Persephone – playing the lyre as he speaks – that he came to the underworld because Love *won* over Death, and he would not return without her: "You can delight in both our deaths," he says. Yet, "drawing near to the threshold of the upper world, afraid she was not there and eager to see her, the lover turns his eyes."[49]

Or, we could simply say with Craig San Roque, in his "Invocation to Orpheus," he "slipped and fell."

Taking the myth personally allows the thought that if some slight adjustment could be made – a different character perhaps? ours maybe? – all would be well. But if we stand back, we might wonder if the myth of Orpheus and Eurydice could be seen as a *tableau of consciousness*, one that warns and reminds us of the laws and conditions of the underworld or the unconscious: that those who enter it must go with utmost attention and respect, so as to discover and remember its laws. It is only when returning – like waking from a dream, reaching for a fleeting image, words of a poem, the fading glimpse of a wholly new thought – that we realize we had received a *gift* – one far beyond us – and frequently receding in proportion to the consciousness we bring to bear upon it, as it vanishes back into . . . wherever it was it came from.

It must be significant that Orpheus looks back at Eurydice just *after* he crosses the threshold into the Upper World – entering at the same time the daylight consciousness that goes with it. Yet it was, inevitably, *before* Eurydice had joined him, as Hades knew it would be. The offer was not, could not be, to go side by side, hand in hand. It is tempting to think that at this point Orpheus must be at his most vulnerable, just as he is caught back into the senses and their polarizations: suddenly she has to *be there* or *not there*. And he *has* to know. So, forgetting the law, the condition, he turns and looks with his eyes – no longer holding her, seeing her in his Imagination – and loses her – his wife, his muse, his soul, and eventually his life. Yet the condition was that both of them must cross the threshold, so he has to wait until she is there too. The question then becomes: why could he not wait? Is it that falling back into the senses too precipitately, *and without awareness* – without, as it were, "postponing" their claims for as long as possible, refusing their immediate demand for clarity, for orientation, for gratification, peace of mind, illusion, anything – is it *that* which prevents him from remembering the law of the Self, the condition he once accepted, but now, in the light of day, feeling it, somehow, not so real as before, almost unreal even, and soon . . . impossible? It no longer matters more than anything else.

In Blake's terms, he looks with "Single Vision and Newton's sleep" (the Newton crouched over his protractors, dividing the visible from the invisible world), not with "Double Vision," which holds the inner and outer eye together without having to distinguish between them.[50] Could he, once he was out into the sun, no longer *feel* Eurydice walking behind him, no longer share *as his own* her last slow steps out of the gloom, so close – did he now have to *see* her to know? Was this *his condition*, which he had no right to make? Distrusting, in that terrible moment of anguish, his own unsurpassable gift of Imagination, and losing, in that same moment, Imagination's own gift of compassion that would have saved them both?

Hence Coleridge's continual practice of "suspension of disbelief for the moment" and the habit of "leaving room" for the unimaginable to be imagined, in the way that the pupa leaves room for the wings of the butterfly to come.[51] As Plotinus says, "It either appears to us or it does not appear. So that we ought . . . to watch in quiet till it suddenly shines upon us."[52] Or Keats's "Negative Capability": "the ability to rest in doubts, uncertainties, mysteries, without any irritable reaching after fact and reason."[53] Or Eliot: "And what you do not know is the only thing you know . . ."[54]

Had Orpheus forgotten that he was permitted to enter the underworld as a poet – his lyre and his singing opening the way for him, allowing him to move ever deeper down into its dark unconscious depths – but, returning, once he had crossed the threshold back into the light of the conscious mind, he was but a man?

Death of Orpheus

Orpheus was slain and dismembered by the Maenads, followers of Dionysos, and then re-collected by the Muses (Figures 5.12 and 5.13). There are many attempts to make sense of the violence of the Thracian women. Was it Orpheus's inconsolable grief which made the Maenads jealous, since he sang no more songs for them? Did he, as Ovid suggests, transfer his affections to young boys, enjoying their "brief springtime"?[55] Were the Maenads set on him by Dionysos because Orpheus had disdained his own "raw and bleeding feasts," as Euripides calls them in *The Cretans*? Was Orpheus once a Priest of Dionysos, who had reformed and purified the more savage rites of Dionysos, moving away into what they saw as an otherworldliness, which now preferred Helios and Apollo?

FIGURE 5.12 Orpheus dismembered by Maenads. Painted dish by the Louvre Painter. 480–470 BCE. Cincinnati Art Museum

(https://aras.org/ancient-greece-modern-psyche)

FIGURE 5.13 Maenad slaying Orpheus. Lekythos. c. 450–440 BCE. Boston Museum of Fine Arts

(https://aras.org/ancient-greece-modern-psyche)

Mythologically speaking, was he also caught in the lunar pattern of the dying and resurrected god, in the tradition of Osiris, Dionysos, and others, dismembered into the fourteen pieces of the waning Moon, and so an inevitable part of death and rebirth in Nature? In Orpheus's case perhaps – reading it symbolically – following a marriage in the underworld with Eurydice, she whose name means "the wide-ruling one," an epithet of the Moon, just as his name may have come from *orphne*, "darkness."[56] But then the man disappears back into the myth and we lose the claim of the story upon us.

Unless, again, we might wonder whether this dimension of the myth is also offering an insight into the state of one who has forgotten or transgressed the laws of the unconscious, or temporarily lost sight of them in themselves: that dismembered, disembodied reality when the ego is severed from the Self like a song cut off from its source, soon to fall silent because no longer inspired. Or even the creative process itself – deeply at home in the unconscious, and bereft, disoriented, when abandoned by it. As in the ending of Yeats's "Leda and the Swan": "Did she put on his knowledge with his power / Before the indifferent beak would let her drop?"[57] The myth makes a distinction between Orpheus who dies when he can no longer sing, and the lyre that lives on in new form – awaiting, it may be, a new song (Figure 5.14).

FIGURE 5.14   Maenad severing the head of Orpheus. Red-figure vase painting. 480 BCE. Cabinet des Médailles, Bibliothèque Nationale

(https://aras.org/ancient-greece-modern-psyche)

The Muses collected Orpheus's limbs and buried them at the foot of Olympos where the nightingales now sing sweeter than anywhere else in the world. His head floated down the River Hebrus across the sea to the island of Lesbos where it prophesied and sang so sweetly that Apollo stood over it and commanded it to be silent, as no one came to Delphi anymore to listen to his own prophecies. He cried: "Cease from interference in my business" – upon which the head fell silent forever[58] (Figure 5.15).

FIGURE 5.15   Orpheus singing with oracular voice to a young man who is taking it down with a stylus and tablet. Apollo, with his commanding gesture, is telling the singing to stop, demanding his godly powers back from him. Red-figure vessel. 410 BCE. The Fitzwilliam Museum, Cambridge

(https://aras.org/ancient-greece-modern-psyche)

But Orpheus's lyre was not to be silenced and sang its way into the music of the universe. Drifting to Lesbos, following the head, it laid itself to rest in the Temple of Apollo. Apollo and the Muses then interceded with Zeus, who placed the lyre in Heaven as the constellation of the Pleiades, or the Seven Sisters, known in Bronze Age Celtic times as the stars of mourning, since they then rose at Samhain, our day of Hallowe'en, at the meeting of the souls of the dead. The Pleiades were sometimes called by the name of Maia, the mother of Hermes, in the plural form of *Maiores*, which then means "Ancestors." So it is that the tale comes round to its beginning, and the Arts, given by the Muses, bring us back to the Great Memory.

Orphism

Orpheus was said to be the author of some of the Orphic Hymns and also the founder of the mystic cult of Orphism. Those who called themselves Orphics also called themselves ascetics, though Orpheus and his songs do not feel ascetic, suggesting that more rigor was expected of initiates than of poets. The term *soma-sema* – the body a tomb – was attributed to them by Plato, an idea close to his own thinking in the *Phaedo*, among other books, where the true philosopher longs for death.[59] The relation between myth, hymn, and cult is problematic, however, and there was no lack of persons and cults claiming his name for poems and rituals alike.[60] The Orphics were early, belonging in feeling to the participative age of the Mother Goddess, before the Olympians came in to Greece, as we can see from their own creation myth, composed of the Cosmic Egg and the Wind:

> In the beginning, Black-winged Night laid an egg, born of the Wind, in the dark depths of Erebos, and from there, with the rolling of the seasons, sprang Eros, Love, his golden wings gleaming like the whirling of the Wind:

> Then in Tartaros, Love lay down to sleep with Chaos,
> and we, his children, nestled there, fluttering
> till he led us upwards into the light of air.[61]

The transformative nature of the lyre of Orpheus, and many of the Orphic Hymns, is close to the elation of some Dionysian rituals. "Wholly Orphic is the mystical joy with which the hymns brim over," Harrison says.[62] Yet there was an inner stillness in Orphic thought that tempered a wilder enthusiasm. Orphic Hymns were to be sung at rituals with specifically prescribed herbs to accompany them, suggesting a precise relation between poetry and the daily rituals of living a good life, including the refusal to harm animals and eat meat. The devotion of the Orphics was to "wineless Mnemosyne" – a mystical union, brought about through rites of purification – as opposed to the wine-filled rites of Dionysos, which, for the Orphics, had too much of *Lethe* in them, too much of the "wrong kind" of forgetfulness, allowing the Maenads – standing outside themselves in their ecstasy – to rend animals and humans apart (Figure 5.16).

FIGURE 5.16 Dionysos dancing with his Maenads. 490 BCE. Antikensammlung, Staatliche Museen zu Berlin

(https://aras.org/ancient-greece-modern-psyche)

Orpheus weaves in and out of Dionysos in many, sometimes baffling, ways, so it may be better to talk of an Orpheus/Dionysos complex of ideas, and then the question of a balance between them comes in – a holding of the tension between their extremes. The violence of the Maenads toward Orpheus is arresting in the light of Heracleitus's aphorism that "Hades and Dionysos are the same."[63] Does this alliance suggest that Orpheus had broken the laws of "both" of them at once? The *Homeric Hymn to Dionysos* ends with the warning: "Anyone who forgets you cannot remember sacred song."[64] The Maenads who express the will of Dionysos are undeniably enraged, as though something sacred had been betrayed, and Orpheus becomes for them the animal rent apart in the extremity of their rites. It is as though, in forgetting the laws of the underworld, Orpheus loses not only Eurydice, his love and muse, but also, at the same time, his "sweet song," his poetic voice, and, altogether, this tears his life apart.

Yet if we could say that Orpheus is ultimately a symbol of Imagination in all of us, we might expect that "he" – as it were – would be the one uniquely able to, in Blake's phrase, "cleanse the doors of perception" so that everything appears "as it is, infinite."[65] If we consider Orpheus and Eurydice together in love – the singer at one with his song – is it not Orpheus's state of mystical rapture that is so enthralling, so often drawn with his head thrown back in the trance of music that the Muses are playing through him? "Where you are is where you are not"[66] (Figure 5.17).

FIGURE 5.17   Orpheus playing his lyre (closeup of Figure 5.1). The wreath of ivy leaves round his head is evocative of Dionysos rather than Apollo, whose leaves were of laurel

(https://aras.org/ancient-greece-modern-psyche)

In Jean Cocteau's 1950 film *Orphée*, Orpheus has to sign in to the functionaries of the Realm of Death, seated formally upright behind a long table in black suits and ties. "Profession?" they ask, their pens raised. "Poet," he says, slightly taken aback. "Ah, a Writer," they say. "No," he says, "A poet is not a writer, yet he writes." This Orpheus insists on the dynamic present, the verb, the act – not the noun that names and fixes, the concept that stands apart – rather, the moment itself, beyond classification – "the music while the music lasts," "the dancer as the dance." This is the original god, *theos*, shouted out at the theatre in moments of revelation. It moves; it flows. If a tragedy wasn't cutting it, the people would cry: "*ouden Dionisos*." "It is not Dionysos." There's no god here.

"Save me from the 'about' consciousness," Goethe writes, may I never be in it, though, like all of us, he is in it as soon as he talks about it. So perhaps the rapt presence that is Imagination may be known only in the *act of experiencing* a poem, a play, a song, a dance, which is to say this poem, this song, this dance, this image in the mind – this act of loving anyone or anything – whenever we become one in art and life with the vision disclosed by the Muses, who themselves come to us from Mnemosyne – or rather, as Yeats says, from "some mysterious tide in the depth of our being."[67]

The Orphic tablets

Mnemosyne also lies at the heart of the journey into the afterlife, as the Orphics conceived it, and their rituals reveal a deeper meaning to the idea of Memory. Eight inscribed tablets of very thin gold were found in South Italy, Rome, and Crete, rolled up and worn as amulets round the necks of the deceased.[68] The Pet-e-lia Tablet from Italy, inscribed sometime between 300 and 200 BCE, is now in the British Museum. What is fascinating is that the case in which the tablet is enclosed is Roman, 500 years later than the tablet itself, possibly suggesting it had been treasured, and maybe even worn, for 500 years, handed down from one generation to another (Figure 5.18).

FIGURE 5.18   The Pet-e-lia Tablet from Italy. c. 300–200 BCE. British Museum. The case in which the tablet is enclosed is Roman, 500 years later than the tablet itself

(https://aras.org/ancient-greece-modern-psyche)

Initiates are told that they will find two well-springs, one on the left of the House of Hades, and another beside the Lake of Mnemosyne – as though a choice between them is being offered, one for which they should be prepared. They are to drink only from the cold water flowing forth from the well-spring of Mnemosyne:

> Thou shalt find on the left of the House of Hades a Well-spring,
> And by the side thereof standing a white cypress.
> To this Well-spring approach not near.
> But thou shalt find another by the Lake of Mnemosyne,
> Cold Water flowing forth, and there are guardians before it.
> Say: "I am a child of Earth and of Starry Heaven;
> But my race is of Heaven. This ye know yourselves.
> And lo, I am parched with thirst and I perish.
> Give me quickly the cold water flowing forth
> from the Lake of Mnemosyne."
> And of themselves they will give thee to drink
> from the holy Well-spring.
> And thereafter among the other Heroes
> thou shalt have lordship.

The first well on the left – other tablets make clear – is the Well of Lethe, beside the white cypress, bleached of its living green life. The sacrament of this ritual is the drinking of the water from the well-spring of Mnemosyne, which grants them consciousness of the whole, awakening to the mystery, as the *Orphic Hymn to Mnemosyne* says. Another Orphic tablet ends with an image of bliss: "A kid thou art fallen into milk." They remember what they once knew.

The Eleuthernae Tablet from Crete contains the essence of the Pet-e-lia Tablet:

> I am parched with thirst and I perish. – Nay, drink of Me,
> The Well-spring flowing for ever on the Right,
> where the Cypress is.
> Who art thou?
> Whence art thou?
> I am son of Earth and Starry Heaven.

The soul speaks to the Well of Living Water that, in relation to the other tablets, must be the Well of Mnemosyne, and the Well answers. It is as though the initiates are being asked to affirm their divine nature, the part of their nature they share with the gods, and also to express their longing for this union: "I am parched with thirst and I perish." It has to matter more than anything else. The initiates are to understand that the essence of who they are comes from Heaven – *Zoe*, their archetypal core – as it is expressed through Earth – *Bios*, their individuality – and, it is implied, the *harmony* between them both, which is evocative of Jung's idea that we are all, in our individual natures, the Self's unique experiment.[69]

Although the Orphics' initiation is portrayed as taking place in the next life, we can understand it as an image of the choices available to us in this life, next lives characteristically forming the tableaux in which to explore the dramas of this one. Especially, perhaps, at moments when a choice can initiate us into one or another reality – a "life or death" choice, as it might seem. So, in this context, *without* the mediation of the Muses, Lethe here becomes unconsciousness of the Self, a diminishing of humanity, and Mnemosyne becomes consciousness of the Self, a symbol of transformation. The overtones of the image are such as to define this Memory as Remembrance of Origin – "I am a child of Earth and starry Heaven," they must reply – opening the soul to its earthly and heavenly inheritance or, as we might say, opening the psyche to the archetypal images of the collective unconscious and the way they are embodied in life, the Great Memory. As Harrison comments:

> That Memory, the mere remembering of facts, should be the Mother of the Muses is a frigid genealogy . . . the Mnemosyne of initiation rites, the remembering again, the anamnesis of things seen in ecstasy when the soul is rapt to heavenly places, she is surely now, as ever, the fitting Mother of all things musical.[70]

This parentage belongs also to the Immortal Gods. At the beginning of his *Theogony*, Hesiod bids the Muse:

> Sing the holy race of Immortals ever existing,
> Who were born from earth and starry Heaven.[71]

Remembrance of origin also closes the nine-day journey through death and rebirth in the Eleusinian Mysteries. The priest raises one cup of water to Heaven and points another cup of water toward Earth, then pours them both upon the

Earth in a ritual celebrating the Sacred Marriage of Heaven and Earth, which brings forth the "child" of new life. The people cry "*Hye, Kye*" ("Rain, Conceive.")[72]

The idea of the Orphic Well of Memory lives on indirectly in Plato's Myth of Er at the end of the *Republic* where Er, a brave man killed in battle, comes to life again and tells the story of what he saw in the other world. Souls choose the life they wish to lead, and when about to be born, they must drink of the Waters of Lethe to forget their heavenly origins, as a condition for entering life on Earth.[73] But some do not drink so deeply as others and do not entirely forget, and so this makes it clear why, for Plato, knowledge is remembering what we once knew – *Anamnesis*. The word for truth is *Aletheia* – not forgetting – a double negative. So here we are to forget the eternal realm to be born into time, and, once incarnated, we are to forget time to remember the eternal out of which we came, allowing the unconscious to speak to us.

The symbolism of the Water of Life is familiar from *St. John's Gospel*, where Jesus says: "If any man thirsts, let him come unto me and drink" (John 7:37); "the water that I shall give him shall become in him a well of water springing up unto eternal life" (John 4:14).[74] In the Gnostic *Gospel of Thomas*, Jesus says: "Whoever drinks from my mouth shall become as I am and I myself will become he, and the hidden things will be revealed to him."[75]

In the Hellenistic age (c. 300 BCE to 300 CE), when the Greek and Egyptian minds came to know and value each other, a way of thinking, called *syncretism*, became possible. Syncretism was the ability to search for the underlying unity beneath divinities from different cultures or, from within one culture, embracing alternative modes of expression. The religious impulse was one of joyful recognition of a common exploration of the sacred dimension in life. There is a remarkable cylinder seal from around 300 CE that embodies this. Jesus hangs on the Cross, which is crowned with the Crescent Moon, for millennia the symbol of rebirth, and arching over him are the seven stars of the Pleiades, known as the Lyre of Orpheus, thrown into the heavens by Zeus at the request of Apollo and the Muses, originally made by Hermes and given to Apollo. The inscription in capital letters across the lower half of the seal reads: "*Orpheos Bakkikos*," where Bacchus was the Roman name for the Greek Dionysos, who was identified with Osiris by the Greeks (Figure 5.19). The image invites us to see through the outward names and forms to the shared essence within every one of them, so that all these manifestations of the sacred are enriched through their mutual affinity. It has the feeling of all the "Sayings *(Logion)* of Jesus" in the *Gospel of Thomas* (c. 150 CE) – which could be described as a theology of immanence:

> Jesus said: "I am the All . . . Cleave a piece of wood, I am there.
> Lift up the stone and you will find me there."[76]

FIGURE 5.19   Jesus as one with Orpheos Bakkikos, with the Crescent Moon of
             Rebirth as the crown of the cross, and the seven stars of the Pleiades,
             the Lyre of Orpheus, arching over him above. The syncretic feeling is
             one of joy. Cylinder seal, c. 300 CE

(https://aras.org/ancient-greece-modern-psyche)

Syncretism did not, however, survive the Roman adoption of Christianity, or not for long. In the description of the following three pictures we can trace the lyre of Orpheus growing increasingly silent by the time of the fifth century. Orpheus was one of the inspirations of early Christian thinking in its original lyrical mode. A mosaic from Palermo from between 200 and 250 CE celebrates Orpheus with all his animals clustered around him, wild and tame alike – snake and leopard, lion, boar and tiger, bull, monkey, deer and birds – all brought into harmony through the spell of his lyre, all, in the language of the new vision, loving one another (Figure 5.20).

FIGURE 5.20   Arte romana. 200–250 CE. Mosaico pavimentale, marmo, 150 × 150 cm. Palermo, Museo Archeologico

(https://aras.org/ancient-greece-modern-psyche)

But after the Roman Emperor Constantine legalized Christianity as the official religion in the early fourth century, and the new Roman Church began to polarize itself to those it called Pagans – *paganos*, meaning, merely, "of the countryside" – it was soon pointed out that Christ could bring back *all* the souls from Hell whereas Orpheus could not even manage one.

In the late fourth century, a marble table support from Asia Minor depicts Orpheus seated, playing his lyre, with carved animals twisting round him, as though he is sitting in the space of an alcove between them: a lion seated on his left, two deer on either side of him, curious gargoyle figures with an owl perched on the lyre, and upon his head an eagle sits, with imperial-looking wings – perhaps the eagle of the Roman Empire – while animals, including a tortoise and a lizard, swim beneath his feet. Either Orpheus is still enchanting wild animals with the magic of his song, or the figure of Orpheus is serving as an allegory of Christ taming the wild hearts of the pagans, exemplified as wild beasts. Or again, was there an intentional ambiguity allowing for either interpretation, anticipating spectators of different persuasions? But even if this gentle figure of Orpheus is seen by some early Christians as allegorical, the lyre is still there, still being played to the animals gathered around him. It is now, fittingly perhaps, in the Byzantine and Christian Museum in Athens (Figure 5.21).

FIGURE 5.21   Either Orpheus is still enchanting wild animals or "Orpheus" is serving as an allegory of Christ taming the wild hearts of the pagans. Different people saw different things. Marble table support from Asia Minor. Late fourth century. Byzantine and Christian Museum, Athens

(https://aras.org/ancient-greece-modern-psyche)

But by the fifth century, the lyre has gone, and with it all the joy of harmony with the natural world. In a Roman mosaic in a mausoleum in Ravenna, built by the Emperor Theodosius for his daughter, Galla Placidia, Christ is still conceived in the tradition of Orpheus, though now given the role of the Good Shepherd who cares for his sheep. He is no longer surrounded by wild animals on their own terms, but by the devotional faces of the tamed sheep of his flock. There is no lyre to summon the song of the universe or play the music of the spheres for animal and human, rock and plant, alike. The symmetry of the composition is one of impe-rial majesty rather than a symbol of the divine poet who moves all hearts. Christ, robed in purple and gold, turns – almost twists – his body away from the lamb his hand is touching, while looking in the other direction, far into the beyond. Christ's other hand, stretching upward, holding onto a large golden cross blending into his golden halo, draws the focus away from Earth – reaching for Heaven (Figure 5.22).

FIGURE 5.22   Mausoleum of Galla Placidia, daughter of the Roman Emperor Theodosius. Fifth century, Ravenna

(https://aras.org/ancient-greece-modern-psyche)

It is no coincidence that Theodosius was responsible for the closure of many non-Christian sacred sites. He prohibited non-Christian customs in public (in 393 CE), probably including the Olympic Games, and he made the Nicene form of Christianity compulsory. This was the time when the Gnostics hid their scrolls in jars and urns and buried them in caves and desert cliffs.

Orpheus was to sing no more. Even the expectant sheep have become allegories of themselves.

Conclusion

Jung says:

> We have actually known everything all along; for all these things are always there, only we are not there for them . . . Originally we were all born out of a world of wholeness and in the first years of life are completely contained in it. There we have all knowledge without knowing it. Later we lose it, and call it progress when we remember it.[77]

In Yeats's terms this is a joining of the personal memory to the Great Memory: Our little memories, he says,

> are but a part of some Great Memory that renews the world and men's thoughts age after age, and . . . our thoughts are not, as we suppose, the deep, but a little foam upon the deep . . . Memory is also a dwelling-house of symbols, of images that are living souls.[78]

This is memory not only in the sense of remembrance of things past but also as the original pattern holding all the forms that have been and are yet to come. In his "Essay on Magic," he writes that "Whatever the passions of man have gathered about, becomes a symbol in the Great Memory," and this Great Memory or Mind or *Anima Mundi* may itself be evoked by symbols.[79] This helps to explain why the story of a poet, singer, and musician, such as Orpheus was, never dies out and is remembered through the generations as a symbol that returns those passions back to us thousands of years later, as we in our turn, through our own rekindled passions, light up the symbol again in the Great Memory, in an unending communion of souls nourishing each other in the Soul of the World (Figure 5.23). Like Jung's collective unconscious, Yeats's Great Memory is not set apart from us, for our own memories and dreams are a part of it as well. It is of us, all indissolubly entwined and so continually, if imperceptibly, changing. We reach it through our passions and dreams, and then, again, we invoke it by engaging with symbols through Imagination. For this Memory is, as he says, "still the Mother of the Muses, though men no longer believe in it."[80] And, he adds, is not "Imagination . . . always seeking to remake the world according to the impulses and the patterns in that Great Mind, and that Great Memory?"[81]

FIGURE 5.23   The Poet waiting for the Muse, with the empty scroll before him. The eleventh-century Dutch/German Poet Hendrik van der Veldeke. Codex Manesse. 1305–35. Heidelberg University Library

(https://aras.org/ancient-greece-modern-psyche)

Notes

1 Shakespeare, *Two Gentlemen of Verona,* Act III, Scene ii, lines 78–81. References to Shakespeare's plays hereafter indicated by act, scene, lines.
2 Simonides, Fragment 62 (c. 556–458 BCE). From *Greek Lyric III: Stesichorus, Ibycus, Simonides, and Others,* Loeb Classical Library, trans. David A. Campbell, Cambridge, MA: Harvard University Press, 1991.
3 Euripides, *The Bacchae,* trans. William Arrowsmith, in David Grene and Richmond Lattimore (eds.), *Greek Tragedies,* Vol. 3, Chicago, IL and London: Phoenix Books, 1960, p. 217, lines 560–4.
4 R. A. Schwaller de Lubicz, *Le Roi de la theocratie pharaonique,* quoted in Lucie Lamy, *Egyptian Mysteries,* London: Thames & Hudson, 1981, p. 17.
5 Shakespeare, *The Merchant of Venice,* V, i, 52–63.
6 Karl Kerényi, *Zeus and Hera: Archetypal Image of Father, Husband and Wife,* London: Routledge & Kegan Paul, 1975, p. 79.
7 Plato, *Epinomis,* 978b–9a.
8 Quoted in Jules Cashford, *The Moon: Symbol of Transformation,* revised color edition, Carterton, Oxfordshire: The Greystones Press, 2016, ch. 5, pp. 133–7.
9 See Henri-Charles Puech, "Gnosis and Time," in Joseph Campbell (ed.), *Papers from the Eranos Yearbooks,* pp. 38–84, Princeton, NJ: Princeton University Press, pp. 40–1.
10 Cashford, *The Moon,* pp. 296–330.
11 Anne Baring and Jules Cashford, *The Myth of the Goddess: Evolution of an Image,* London: Penguin, 1993, ch. 8, pp. 299–310.
12 Translation by Jules Cashford, from Apostolos N. Athanassakis (ed. and trans.), *Orphic Hymns,* Atlanta, GA: Scholars Press for the Society of Biblical Literature, 1977, no. 77, pp. 99–101.
13 W. B. Yeats, *Essays and Introductions,* London: Macmillan & Co. Ltd., 1961, p. 50.
14 Plutarch, *Moralia,* 743D: "Actually all the Muses are said to be called *Mneiai* (Memories) in some places."
15 Plato, *Phaedrus,* 275b–e.

16 John Keats, "Letter to Benjamin Bailey," 22 November 1817, *Letters of John Keats,* ed. Robert Gittings, Oxford: Oxford University Press, 1970, p. 36.

17 Hesiod, *Theogony,* trans. Dorothea Wender, London: Penguin Classics, 1976, lines 53–65.

18 John Keats, "Ode to a Nightingale," in M. Robertson (ed.), *Keats: Poems Published in 1820,* Oxford: Clarendon Press, 1909, p. 107. Available Project Gutenberg, www.gutenberg.org/files/23684/23684-h/23684-h.htm.

19 Jules Cashford (trans.), *The Homeric Hymns,* London: Penguin Classics, 2003, p. 130, lines 2–4.

20 Trans. Cashford, from Athanassakis, *Orphic Hymns,* no. 76, p. 99.

21 Hesiod, *Theogony,* lines 77–99. Pausanias, *Description of Greece,* 9.29, 2–3.

22 Cashford, "Homeric Hymn to Pythian Apollo," *The Homeric Hymns,* p. 38, lines 185–93.

23 Ibid., "Homeric Hymn to the Muses and Apollo," p. 130, lines 4–6.

24 *Iliad,* Book 2, 484–92.

25 *Odyssey,* Book 8, 487f.

26 Virgil, *The Georgics,* Book 2, 475ff.

27 Hesiod, *Theogony,* lines 25–35.

28 Shakespeare, Chorus, *Henry V,* line 1.

29 Cashford, "Homeric Hymn to Hermes," *The Homeric Hymns,* p. 84, lines 560–63.

30 Ibid., pp. 83–4, lines 541–80.

31 Ibid., p. 84, lines 577–8.

32 Hesiod, *Theogony,* 105–8.

33 Euripides, *Orestes,* line 211.

34 Dante, *Purgatorio, The Divine Comedy,* Canto *XXVIII.* In the last lines of *Purgatorio,* Dante talks of the "sweet draught" of *Eunoe,* writing of the water that "never would satiate me." Canto XXXIII, line 138.

35 Walter Burkert, *Greek Religion: Archaic and Classical,* Oxford: Basil Blackwell, Ltd., 1985, p. 115.

36 T. S. Eliot, "Burnt Norton," *Four Quartets,* London: Faber and Faber Ltd., 1944, lines 67–8.

37 W. B. Yeats, "Byzantium," in R. J. Finneran (ed.), *The Poems of W. B. Yeats: A New Edition,* London: Macmillan Publishing Company, 1933.

38 Cashford, "Homeric Hymn to Hermes," p. 77, lines 426–34.

39 Plato, *Republic,* Bk 2, 364e.

40 Jane Harrison, *Prolegomena to the Study of Greek Religion,* London: Merlin Press, 1980, p. 459.

41 Apollonius Rhodius, *Argonautica.* First half of third century BCE.

42 Virgil, *Georgics,* IV, lines 458–10.

43 Ovid, *Metamorphoses,* X, 1–85.

44 Virgil, *Georgics,* IV, lines 453–527 (70–19 BCE). Ovid, *Metamorphosis,* X, 1–85; XI, 1–66 (43 BCE–17 CE).

45 R. M. Rilke, "Orpheus, Eurydice, Hermes" (1904). Available Project Gutenberg, www.gutenberg.org.

46 Plato, *The Symposium,* 179c–180e.

47 Euripides, *Alcestis,* in David Grene and Richmond Lattimore (eds.), *Greek Tragedies, Vol. 3,* Chicago, IL and London: Phoenix Books, 1960, pp. 265–311.

48 Virgil, *Georgics,* IV, lines 486–90.

49 Ovid, *Metamorphoses* X, 1–85.

50 William Blake, *Blake: Complete Poetry and Prose,* ed. G. Keynes, London: Nonesuch Press, 1961, p. 860.

51 Samuel Taylor Coleridge, *Biographia Literaria,* London, J. M. Dent & Sons, Ltd., 1975, ch. XIV, pp. 169 and 173.

52 Plotinus, quoted in Coleridge, *Biographia Literaria,* p. 139.

53 John Keats, *The Letters of John Keats,* ed. M. B. Forman, Oxford: Oxford University Press, 1952, p. 71.

54 T. S. Eliot, "East Coker," *Four Quartets,* III, line 324.

55 Ovid, *Metamorphoses* X, lines 84–5.
56 See Cashford, *The Moon*, ch. 9, pp. 257–67.
57 Yeats, "Leda and the Swan," *Collected Poems*, p. 241.
58 For all the many variants on the Orpheus myth, see Robert Graves, "Orpheus," *The Greek Myths*, London: Penguin, 1960, chapter 28.
59 Plato, *Phaedo*, 65e–69e; *Cratylus*, 400c, *Republic*, 442a–b, *Gorgias*, 492e–3a.
60 E. R. Dodds, *The Greeks and the Irrational*, Berkeley and Los Angeles, CA: University of California Press, 1951, p. 147: "Orpheus . . . is one thing, Orphism quite another . . . and the more I read about (early Orphism) the more my knowledge diminishes."
61 Translation from Aristophanes, *The Birds*, by Jules Cashford.
62 Harrison, *Prolegomena*, p. 265.
63 Logion 74, *The Fragments of Heracleitus*, Bray, Ireland: The Guild Press, 1976, p. 24.
64 Cashford, "*Homeric Hymn to Dionysos*," *The Homeric Hymns*, p. 4, line 23.
65 Blake, "The Marriage of Heaven and Hell," p. 154.
66 Eliot, "East Coker," *Four Quartets*, III, line 326.
67 Yeats, *Essays and Introductions*, p. 92.
68 Details of the tablets can be found in Harrison, *Prolegomena to the Study of Greek Religion*, pp. 573–99.
69 Jung, referred to throughout his published works.
70 Jane Harrison, *Themis: A Study of the Social Origins of Greek Religion*, London: Merlin Press, 1977, p. 513.
71 Hesiod, *Theogony*, lines 43–5.
72 See Baring and Cashford, *The Myth of the Goddess*, pp. 364–90.
73 Plato, *The Republic*, trans. H. D. P. Lee, London: Penguin Classics, 2003, lines 393–401.
74 See also Hugo Rahner, *Greek Myths and Christian Mystery*, New York: Biblo and Tannen, 1971.
75 *The Gospel According to Thomas*, Coptic Text established and translated by A. Guillaumont et al., Leiden: E. J. Brill, 1976, Logion 98.
76 *Gospel of Thomas*, Logion 77–8.
77 Jung, "Letter to M. R. Braband–Isaac, 22.7.39," in C. G. Jung, *Letters*, eds. Gerhard Adler and Aniela Jaffe, Vol. 1, London: Routledge & Kegan Paul, 1973–6, pp. 274–5.
78 Yeats, *Essays and Introductions*, pp. 28, 50.
79 Ibid., p. 50.
80 Ibid., p. 91.
81 Ibid., p. 52.

6

PAUL AND PERPETUA

About cultural complexes in early Christianity

Joerg Rasche

In memory of Virginia Beane Rutter

When St. Paul was traveling in the Mediterranean world, from Syria to Greece and Italy, and across the sea in the first century CE, preaching and speaking about his own personal experience, the ancient Greek and Roman culture in its Hellenistic stage was in deep crisis. The Roman world had been united since the Battle of Actium in 31 BCE; the Roman Empire of Augustus stood for stability and balanced powers under the hegemony and leadership of Rome. Augustus started a program of restoration and revitalization of old Roman values, of its religion and rituals. Nevertheless, the traditional basis of the antique culture was weak, and the early Christian ideas found receptive ears among many educated people and philosophers but also among poor people, soldiers, slaves, and women.

Religion is a process, and its concepts change and develop through the centuries depending on cultural circumstances. The epochal shift and turn to Christianity had many roots from earlier times: there was the messianic prophecy in Jewish traditions, and there was the Hellenistic vision of a rebirth of the mythical Golden Age and the Divine Child – as expressed by Virgil and personified in Augustus. With the divination of the emperor Augustus the thrilling idea of a divine human became a central issue in the religious practice of the many. The stories of Paul and of the Christian martyr St. Perpetua show how deeply the Christian transformation of the antique culture that emerged resulted from streams and groundswells in the collective unconscious of their times. On his missionary travels Paul spoke about his own experience with Christ whom he had never seen personally in the flesh; with Paul, a new concept of religion and ethics began. Even if Paul seemed to be ambivalent in this regard, the Christian idea of equal rights of men and women before God became influential for what we may call an Early Christian Women's Liberation Movement: The traditional role of women had been to produce children, and most of them had nearly no rights. But now hundreds of Christian women died as martyrs because, rather than marrying a pagan Roman (in many cases, an officer or soldier) to produce children, they preferred a life in the new religion. This material is already in the background of Paul's statements in his letters. We are well informed about the inner motivation of these heroic women by the dreams of Perpetua, a young Roman mother who became a martyr in Carthage in 203 CE. She told her dreams to her father confessor (it is said that he was Tertullian), and so they came down to us. Marie-Louise von Franz wrote a study about the "passio perpetuae" showing the emerging Christian symbolism out of the religious cultural complexes of the late antiquity. When listening to these dreams and moving narratives we are close to the birth process of our modern times.[1]

Introduction

Why this essay about St. Paul and the cultural complexes around early Christianity?

I was brought up in the Christian atmosphere of an old city in Bavaria/Germany, a Lutheran protestant among many Roman-Catholic pupils. Traditionally my family also had a close relationship to Jewish culture. I learned the Christian prayers and the stories of the Bible in the translation of Martin Luther, and in my humanistic school also in the Latin and the original Greek version of the New Testament: The Gospel and the letters of Paul.[2] There are sentences that became fundamental for my spiritual life:

> *Nun bleibet Glaube, Liebe, Hoffnung, diese drei; aber die Liebe ist die größte unter ihnen.*

> But now abide faith, love, hope; but the greatest of these is love.
> *(1 Cor. 13:13)*[3]

> *Ist aber Christus nicht auferstanden, so ist unsere Predigt vergeblich, und auch unser Glaube vergeblich . . . Nun aber ist Christus auferstanden von den Toten und der Erstling geworden derer, die schlafen. Denn wie durch einen Menschen der Tod gekommen ist, so kommt auch durch einen Menschen die Auferstehung der Toten. Und so in Adam alle sterben, so werden sie in Christus alle lebendig gemacht werden.*

> If Christ has not been raised, then our preaching is in vain, your faith also is vain . . . But now Christ has been raised from the dead, the first fruits of those who are asleep. For since by a man came death, by a man also came the resurrection of the dead. For as in Adam all die, so also in Christ all shall be made alive.
> *(1 Cor. 15:17, 20)*

These sentences I found again and again in the compositions of J. S. Bach and Handel's *Messiah*, expressed in the most beautiful music I ever knew. Resurrection from death and individuation seem to belong together. Other words that spoke to me:

Ich lebe; doch nun nicht ich, sondern Christus lebt in mir.

It is no longer I who live, but Christ lives in me; and the life which I now live in the flesh I live by faith in the Son of God, who loved me, and delivered Himself for me.

(Gal. 2:20)

Ihr seid teuer erkauft – werdet nicht der Menschen Knechte.

You were bought with a (high) price; do not become slaves of men.

(1 Cor. 7:23)

All these quotations are from St. Paul's letters. It was a book by the French philosopher Alain Badiou that recently re-stimulated my interest and research: *Paulus: The Foundation of Universalism.*[4] Here, he emphasizes that the central idea for Paul was resurrection and the longing for Jesus's return during his lifetime. I am neither an academic scholar of theology nor of history, and I beg your pardon for errors and misunderstandings about the theology of Paul and his followers. Somehow I follow C. G. Jung, who in "Answer to Job" gave a quite individual view of his search for the meaning of the Christian myth.[5]

Another stimulus for my research is the growing impact of religion-motivated politics, violence, and forced or voluntary martyrdom. It is about the painful transformations of the God-Image and the role of humans in this epochal transformative process in the collective unconscious – people who happen to get in between the millstones of G-d's own transformation.[6] The fate of the early Christian martyrs – often they were women – shall put the spotlight on the changing constellations. At the end it will be about the *Anima Mundi*, the soul of the earth. I'll also speak about Jewish religion – Jesus from Nazareth and Paul were Jews and rabbis (even if not officially) – and I beg your pardon for projections and misunderstandings. One can understand deeply only the religion in which one was brought up – we can say the same about cultural complexes.

Religion as a process

In this essay I talk about religion as a process.[7] Under Jungian perspectives symbols of the Self and of G-d can't be differentiated, at least not empirically – or, as we can ask, only empirically, namely by revelation? On the other side, believers usually will not agree that the image of G-d is a mere psychological function. "You shalt not make an image of G-d" is one of the basic commandments – we could translate this: "With all your imagination and images of the Self you will never get an entire and complete picture of the Self." So, in fact, it is not a commandment but a statement – as often in Jewish thinking. The answer out from the burning bush to Moses – "I am who I am; or: I am who I will be" – emphasizes the continuity behind the images we may create for our orientation. Nevertheless, in monotheistic traditions we find many different pictures of the divine. I will reflect on how these images have changed over the centuries, how the archetype of the Self was expressed in these different concepts and contexts, and to what extent we can regard and study them as what we call cultural complexes.[8] Archetypal images are often shaped by culture; therefore, they show many aspects of cultural complexes.

The central object of my study will be the time and culture of the first two centuries of early Christianity. It will be about Paul and about the social and psychological situation of women. St. Paul was born under the name of Saul (*Schaul*) in Tarsus in Cilicia (today Turkey), in 6 or 7 BCE, and died around the year 60 CE. He was a Jew and a Roman citizen; maybe the Roman citizenship was bought by his father. He was well educated and spoke Greek. Paul became the "Apostle to the Gentiles," famous for his travels and his letters to the early Christian communities in Rome, Corinth, Thessaloniki, and others. Many of these Christian communities were inaugurated by Paul who mostly spoke in the local synagogues, but also in public places like in Ephesus or Athens. Some of Paul's epistles are not authentic and were written later under his name: Timothy, Titus, Colossians, and others. These "false" pastoral letters, attributed to Paul, also included in the Christian Bible, show the changes and the creation of the early dogma of the Roman Church – and there you find some controversial statements about women. The original letters of Paul were written between 40 and 60 CE, somewhat earlier than the four Gospels of Mark, Matthew, Luke, and John and also before the Acts of the Apostles. The earliest gospel (Mark) was written, after decades of oral tradition, around the year 70 CE. So the letters of Paul are the first Christian texts we have; they were read throughout the Mediterranean world and are *the* founding documents of the Christian Church.

Religion as a process means change – inner transformation in the individual life and individuation process, as well as in the collective unconscious of a culture. Paul writes about his own development:

> When I was a child I used to speak as a child, think as a child, reason as a child; when I became a man, I did away with childish things. For now we see in a mirror dimly, but then face to face; now I know in part, but then I shall know fully just as I also have been fully known.
>
> *(1 Cor. 13:11 ff.)*

And then he writes the famous conclusion: "But now abide faith, hope, love, these three; but the greatest of these is love." The images or concepts we create about the Self are changing during our lifetime, in relation with the changing constellation of archetypal concepts in our culture.

The concepts of all religions were created and changed over the centuries. After critical events they had to be reconstructed or reinvented. There the impact of the other contemporary cultural complexes can be seen. We find examples of this process in the Greco-Roman world and on the Jewish side around the beginning of the Aion of the Fish, 2,000 years ago. Today we are confronted with changes and redefinitions of Islam and the dangers of eruptive and destructive apocalyptic contents of this third Abrahamic religion.

Cultural complexes around Jesus and Paul

The dawn of Christianity took place in the decline of the antique world. And, in a remarkable parallel to our times of today, humankind had to invent, or reconstruct, itself anew. There were mainly two great cultures suffering from inner destruction and unsolved problems and, at the same time, pregnant with new perspectives. These two worlds were the Roman–Greek–Antiquity, then coagulated in the form and the multifaceted culture of the Roman Empire under Augustus; and on the other side the Jewish world at the border to the Eastern cultures, reined by Jewish-Hellenistic families and longing for a new self-definition.

To start with the Roman world: It was polytheistic to the extreme; in the first century more than 200 gods and deities were worshipped in Rome. There were temples for Egyptian, African, Asian, even Celtic gods; for Isis and Hathor, Horus or half gods like Heracles; for the great mother goddess Cybele, Artemis from Ephesus, Serapis, and so on; not to forget Mithras, the Sol Invictus, Zoroaster, and in a special position, the Emperor and divine human Augustus. St. Paul on his travels one day (it was in Athens) came across an altar of the "Unknown Gods": "As I was passing through and considering (looking) I even found an altar with this inscription 'To the unknown God'" (Acts 17:23). It is very likely that he saw some of those altars mentioned by Pausanias – it should be noted that in the late antique period many people would dedicate altars and offerings to "unknown gods," either from superstition, or because they wanted to pre-empt the consequences of neglecting gods that they were not aware of.[9]

The inflation of religious idols and rituals was an expression of deep uncertainty, also in regard to the entire concepts of life. Everything and nothing seemed possible. Human life was of no value after hundreds of years of civil war and moral devastation. The public entertainment was of an incredible brutality, with its killing performances in the big arenas. The great philosophy, inherited from the Greeks, in its actual form was reduced to helpless humanistic attitudes. Depression and suicide were common among intellectuals. Plutarch wrote about the cry of the deserted nature, when his ship sailed along the coast of southern Italy: The Great Pan is dead! The magic voice made it known to the world: The age-old antique god of the nature is no more alive, and nature is suffering from unquenchable pain and thirst.

The unquenchable thirst for meaning was addressed especially by thinkers and poets around the young Octavian, the later Augustus. Virgil was the poet who created a new myth for the Roman culture. In his *Aeneid* he linked the Asian origin and the Western development of his culture. Aeneas, the Trojan warrior who escaped from the burning city of Troy, became the mythical founder of Rome. In the words of Anchises, Aeneas's father, Virgil told Octavian, after he was victorious at Actium, how to behave as a responsible leader of the now unified and appeased empire. Virgil also wrote poems about a sustainable agriculture (*the Georgics*) and about the dawn of a New Age: the birth of the Eternal Child as a kind of Messiah – thirty years before Jesus was born far away in Bethlehem in Judaea and without knowing anything about the Jewish myth. Obviously the idea of the divine human was constellated.

The reforms of Augustus finally led to an unforeseen stable political system (the *Pax Augustea* of the Roman Empire), but the longing for meaning was not sufficiently satisfied. One aspect was the social and economic situation of the many: the slaves, the soldiers, the poor, and those who came under Roman government and exploitation all over the world. There were many slave revolts and uprisings, to name only the one led by Spartacus or that led by Eunous (the "good willing") in Sicilia. The punishments for the rebels were drastic, and many thousands of them were crucified. It was a system of terror. Mostly forgotten is the situation of the women who had quasi no rights in the patriarchal society outside the family sphere. They were married very young and had to produce children. Many died during their first pregnancy. To draw a conclusion: Roman culture had to reinvent itself.

On the other side of the empire was the Jewish country, the small district between Syria, Gaza, and Egypt. Jewish culture was experienced in reinventing itself several times. This remarkable and pioneering process started in (quasi) prehistoric times with the monotheism of Abraham. With Abraham a new and revolutionary concept of the divine was created, different than the animistic and polytheist neighborhood. Ages later, after the exile from Egypt in the desert, the codex of Moses established a new formulation of the meaning and rituals of the Jewish religion. Later, the temple in Jerusalem became the center of Jewish life, its rituals and hopes. After the destruction of Solomon's temple in 586 BCE and the forced exile of the people to Babylon and their return three generations later, the temple had to be rebuilt and the rituals newly formulated. The original texts were lost and had to be reconstructed. The prophets emphasized the importance of the fulfillment of all of G-d's orders and laws – to prevent another catastrophe with a second destruction of the temple. A period of decay followed, but then the Maccabean rebels restored the religion and the temple. Later, under the Idumean king Herod, the temple was again rebuilt and became the center of public and religious life in Israel. Jerusalem was the center of the world, where, at the end of the days, the Messiah would come.

Life changed remarkably under the Romans and Herod. King Herod the Great renovated the temple again and introduced a kind of Hellenistic atmosphere. The renewed Jewish self-definition became critical, with the emergence of sects besides the priests of the temple: the Pharisees, the Zealots, and the Essenes in Qumran. The Jews now had two masters: the Romans and G-d (hence Jesus's famous answer: "Give the emperor what is his, and G-d what is G-d's"). The Roman Empire had serious military problems with the Parther (a strong empire in Iran, northeast from Syria); Rome needed Egypt for its wheat, and the small land bridge of Palestine and Gaza was the weakest point in Rome's geopolitical and military sphere and concept. The Romans installed and guaranteed a kind of self-administration of the Jews; King Herod the Great was the representative of both, the Roman Empire and the Jewish self-administration. The shadow side of his successful era was that the religious dimension of life in Jerusalem was replaced more and more by secular attitudes and corruption. Many Jews withdrew in resignation and protest from the service and identification with the temple, as it was now. Many Jews hated Herod. After Herod's death in 6 BCE, the Jews asked for a direct government by Rome, but Rome continued his politics with Herod's family. Finally, in addition to the Jewish Tetrarch, a

Roman ambassador was installed who lived most of the time in Caesarea. This is the time we know, more or less and with some one-sided projections, from the Gospels. Pontius Pilatus was one of these ambassadors. The Pharisees were deeply concerned about the meaning and definition of Jewishness and of the perspective of Jerusalem, if once again the people would not fulfill the orders of G-d properly. Their focus was purity: What one is allowed to do and not to do on Shabbat, and so on. Jesus, as we know him by the Gospel, argued in this discussion. Historians like Pinchas Lapide say that the historical Jesus was probably a rabbi and a Pharisee himself (and that he, like all rabbis, was married or widowed!). Many years after his crucifixion the Gospels (Mathew, Mark, Luke, John) were written, and the emerging dogma claimed Jesus as the Pharisees' opponent. Others, like Pinchas Lapide, say that Jesus was a member or associate of the radical sect in Qumran, like John the Baptist, and that they never wanted to become the founders of a new religion.[10]

This fragile stability ended in 66 CE when one of Rome's ambassadors, Cestius, a successor of Pontius Pilatus, was killed on his way from Jerusalem to Caesarea. The revolution broke out, and finally in 70 CE under Emperor Titus the temple was definitely destroyed. The shock went deep; it was like a repetition of 586 BCE when Nebuchadnezzar had destroyed Jerusalem and led the Jews into the Babylonian exile. What was the meaning of this catastrophe? After the repeated destruction of the temple, the Pharisees began step by step to reconstruct a new Jewish identity. The temple was lost; now the weekly service (like the Shabbat rituals) had to be performed at home. To become an acceptable replacement, it had to fulfill especially the tasks of purity: regarding food, rituals about the Shabbat, and the holy days. What the priest or high priest of the temple had been before was now left to the rabbi. The most prominent figure (even if not historical) was Rabbi Hillel. Some of his sayings are close to Jesus' words: *Don't harm your neighbor in a way you don't want to be treated yourself.*[11] Or in another saying: *In a time when the temple is lost, we have got another chance to pray and to do something for G-d: namely selfless compassion.*

Therefore, Jewish culture had to reinvent itself several times. After 70 CE the new Rabbinic Jewish culture was created and then prevailed for centuries. In those times the Mischnah and Talmud were formulated. Gerhard (Gerschom) Scholem has studied such processes in the rabbinic circles of the first century after the destruction of the temple.[12] The situation repeated itself later in Spain in the Jewish Diaspora, with the anti-Jewish persecution in the Islamic massacre of Granada in 1266 and under the Almohads in Andalusia in the twelfth century. In 1492 Jewish life was forbidden in Spain and Portugal by the Christian King. Under the long repression much of the tradition was lost. The Sephardic Jews, in exile in other European countries, had to re-create their religion. It was the time when in his *Tractatus Theologico-Politicus* (1670) Baruch de Spinoza wrote critical comments on the reinvented narratives. Gershom Scholem has written about the "mythologization" of religion and spoke about it several times in Eranos (1949, 1950, 1953, and 1957). The traditions that Jews nowadays perform and keep in honor are the result of several reconstructions. Religion is a process. It reacts and changes its *Gestalt* and meaning following the changing needs of the people. The God-Image changes in response to the development of human identity and self concepts.

In the critical periods of transformation, the people often find them painfully, as C. G. Jung said, between the millstones of the changing G–d. In some understandings, G–d himself is a process, or better: the G–d concept represents the evolution or involution of our mind.

Paul and the creation of Christianity

In Christian development, the central figure is the Messiah. The messianic idea was developed during repeated times of existential crisis in the Jewish culture. For St. Paul the crucial point, nevertheless, was the resurrection. I already mentioned:

> If Christ has not been raised, then our preaching is in vain, your faith also is vain . . . But now Christ has been raised from the dead, the first fruits of those who are asleep . . . For as in Adam all die, so also in Christ all shall be made alive.
>
> *(1 Cor. 15:15, 17, 20)*

This statement makes the essential difference to the Jewish view, in Jesus's time and today. Pinchas Lapide, the Jewish scholar, would concede that Jesus from Nazareth was crucified in the year 30 CE, like 2,000 other insurgents against the Roman occupation in the years around that time, but the resurrection is – of course – not part of his religious concept.[13] The legend of Paul shall be shortly retold: When the first martyr, the deacon Stephan, was stoned by Jewish believers (a group of Pharisees) some years after Golgatha, a young man stood there and agreed to this ritual murder (Acts 7 ff.). This man was Saul, who then became a declared enemy of Jews who confessed Jesus as the Messiah. "And Saul was in hearty agreement with putting him to death . . . But Saul began ravaging the church, entering house after house, and dragging off men and women, he would put them in prison" (Acts 8:3).

> And it came about that as he was approaching Damascus, and suddenly a light from heaven flashed around him; and he fell to the ground, and heard a voice saying to him: Saul, Saul, why are you persecuting Me? And he said: Who art Thou, Lord? And he said: I am Jesus whom you are persecuting. But rise, and enter the city, and it shall be told you what you must do. And the men who traveled with him stood speechless, hearing the voice, but seeing no one.
>
> *(Acts 9:3–7)*

Lapide does not deny the event of Damascus: the famous conversion, when Saul fell off his horse and all the people around him heard the voice. But the event, he argues, happened not there but in Qumran in "Araba," the desert at the edge of the Dead Sea. Damascus was a code name of Qumran. The idea is that in Qumran among the sect of the Essenes, there was a tendency to venerate Jesus as the Messiah and to believe in his resurrection. Jesus himself, following Lapide, was attached to the Qumran movement. Saul, the Pharisee, wanted to stop this heresy. Paul's eternal merit, after Lapide, nevertheless, was that he brought the idea of monotheism to all the Roman Empire, to the gentiles and the end of the world, but, unfortunately, in the Christian version – with Jesus's resurrection in the center of his message.

Lapide is a linguist and discovered many "false" quotations of Jewish texts by Paul and false translations in the Christian texts in the New Testament. These corrections are important also for the interpretation of Jung's "Answer to Job." For example, Jung describes Jahweh of the Old Testament as a wild and barbaric storm-god who has to learn about human consciousness (this would be the "answer" to Job). It is about the *tremendum*: to love and to fear G-d. An example is in the Paternoster: following the Latin version (*vulgata*) and the usual translation, the two final requests are "Do not lead us into temptation, but deliver us from evil" (Matt. 6:13). A god who leads us into temptation would be, in fact, a terrible one. The correct translation from the Greek original is "Lead us, if we fall in temptation, and protect us from the bad" (this then means from misfortune and accidents). This version is quite different and, following Lapide, close to the rabbinic tradition. The fear of God, Lapide says, is a later Christian idea, created by the Roman Church a long time after Jesus and Paul. But we may ask Lapide: what shall a "wrong" translation be? If religion is a process, then, of course, each stage of this process will shape its own version of the delivered concepts. It is about changed concepts and narratives. Faith doesn't care about correct translations, and language is a flexible carrier of changing meanings.

The cultural complex that shines through Paul's letters can be seen in sentences like this:

> There is neither Jew nor Greek, there is neither slave nor free man, there is neither male nor female; for you are all one in Christ Jesus. And if you belong to Christ, then you are Abraham's offspring, heirs according to promise.
>
> *(Gal. 3:28)*

This shows an egalitarian philosophy, not far from the Stoic, but different from Paul's Jewish heritage. For the Jewish complex this was and still is a heresy. Martin Buber is said to have criticized Paul especially for this sentence.[14] For the Roman slave system it was a provocation; for underdogs of every kind a glimmer of hope for a better world.

> Now concerning the things about which you wrote, it is good for a man not to touch a woman. But because of immoralities, let each man have his own wife, and let each woman have her own husband. Let the husband fulfill his duty to his wife, and likewise also the wife to her husband. The wife does not have authority over her own body, but the husband does; and likewise also the husband does not have authority over his own body, but the wife does . . . But I say this by way of concession (proposal), not of command.
>
> *(1 Cor. 7:1–6)*

Again, an egalitarian concept; it was revolutionary in those times, when women had no rights, were married early, and had no voice in the synagogue. Paul said that there are some complementary aspects between women and men, and he even addressed sex. Important also that Paul doesn't command but emphasizes solutions. The not authentic letter to Timothy, written decades after Paul's death, reads differently:

> For it was Adam who was first created and then Eve. And it was not Adam who was deceived, but the woman being quite deceived, fell into transgression. But women shall be preserved through the bearing of children if they continue in faith and love and sanctity with self-restraint.
>
> *(1 Tim. 2:13–15)*

This falsification and inversion of the original meaning then became a dogma in the Roman Church and remains in place today.

Paul's original message was different. In his authentic letters like that to the Romans and the Corinthians he says that it is better not to be engaged in earthly things like marriage, instead of preparing oneself for the day when the Messiah will return. Nevertheless, in all his authentic letters he shows a warm and confidential relation to women – like his master Jesus himself.

The background of Paul's real statement is in his and his followers' expectation and belief that Jesus will return soon, during their lifetime. "Behold, I tell you a mystery; we shall not all sleep [= *koimethesomatha* means to die, to pass away], but we shall all be changed, in a moment, in the twinkling of an eye, at the last trumpet" (1 Cor. 15:51). It was an apocalyptic anticipation based on Jesus's words:

> For the Son of Man is going to come in the glory of His Father with His angels, and will then recompense every man according to his deeds. Truly I say to you, there are some of those who are standing here who shall not taste death until they see the Son of Man coming in His kingdom.
>
> *(Matt. 16:27)*

In St. John's gospel, Jesus says to Marta, shortly before he reanimated his friend Lazarus three days after his passing away: "I am the resurrection and the life; he who believes in Me shall live even if he dies. And everyone who lives and believes in me shall never die. Do you believe this?" (John 11:25). The anticipation of the Messiah's return was an essential element in early Christianity, even though Jesus said, questioned by (other) Pharisees as to when the kingdom of God was coming: "The kingdom of God is not coming with signs to be observed, nor will they say, 'Look, here it is,' or 'Look, there it is.' For behold, the kingdom of God is in your midst" [*enthos hymon estin* = "inside yourself"] (Luke 17:20).

It is a moving study to see how step by step this early security and hope was to be replaced by the experience that the Last Judgment didn't come in the expected time. We can follow this disillusionment in the Gospels, which were written decades after Paul's preaching and letters. The dogmatic fixation of Christianism and new interpretations of Jesus's orally delivered sermons and deeds by the emerging and stabilizing Roman Church was an answer to the crisis of the physical nonappearance of the resurrected Christ. The psychological situation became worse and more complex after the destruction of the temple in Jerusalem in 70 CE by Titus. The Christians began to accuse the Jews of not having accepted Jesus as the Messiah, and the Christian anti-Jewish complex began to emerge. The destruction of the temple was seen, from both sides, as a punishment by God. The last gospel (John), written between 90 and 120 CE, is full of anti-Jewish sentences. Much later it became an inspiration for anti-Semitism. For the Jews the loss of the temple became the impulse for an introverted development.

Paul and the martyrs

Saul, after the Damascus event also called "Paul," went on four missionary journeys. He preached over many years in Syria, Asia Minor, Macedonia, Greece, and finally in Rome. Maybe he also passed Santorini on his travels? Often, he was in prison because he refused to adore the Roman Emperor (the other "divine human") or was attacked by the servants of the local pagan deities. He was also in prison because the Jews in Jerusalem wanted to have him killed. He pleaded that he was a Roman citizen and, therefore, had to be tried in Rome, and that's why he was taken to Rome by the Roman soldiers. Special events were his failed first performance in Ephesus (the place of Artemis) and in Athens. In Rome he is said to have met St. Peter; in Rome he was sentenced and killed (like many others) in the name of the Emperor (it is said that this happened under Nero). According to the tradition he had even traveled to Spain.

One of his early followers was a woman named Thecla. We know the legend from a novel of the second century called *Acts of Paul and Thecla*. Thecla, a lady in Ikonium, heard Paul preaching, and when Paul was put in prison by the government she visited him there, was baptized, and followed him when he managed to escape. She refused to marry her fiancé and promised solemnly to live as a virgin following the message of Christ, in expectation of his return at hand. She was caught and sentenced to death in the theater, but the lions did not touch her (did not even look at her naked body!), and also snakes couldn't harm her. She also survived a second martyrdom (to be thrown into a basin of seals), and she became a respected teacher and made long missionary travels. *Martyr* in Greek originally means somebody who testifies and bears witness, somebody who openly declares his or her views, not necessarily somebody who has sacrificed him- or herself and is killed for confession. Thecla's reputation as the first female martyr didn't last long (in Milan, Italy, there is a miraculous memorial still today). Already Tertullian, an important priest in the second century, criticized the somehow funny novel about her.[15] The crucial point was that Thecla was said to have taught and preached in public. This was certainly not well appreciated, if not forbidden. In one of Paul's falsified letters, we find the sentence that women shall not preach and not speak in the synagogue. This was and is originally the Jewish attitude but was then adopted by the more and more patriarchal Christian Church. Today Thecla is nearly forgotten.

The martyr I turn to now is Perpetua, a noble young woman from Carthage, who became a devotee, was baptized in prison, refused to live with her husband, and was killed as a martyr in 203 CE, together with her friend Felicitas and other Christians.

The *Passio Perpetuae et Felicitatis* is a unique document, different from the many written legends about the early Christian martyrs, because it contains personal feelings and dreams. It is a moving work and was recently again studied by feminist scholars. Marie-Louise von Franz wrote an impressive study about the inner life of the saint, the *Passio perpetuae: Das Schicksal einer Frau zwischen zwei Gottesbildern (Fate of a Woman between Two Images of God)*.[16] It was possibly Tertullian who, as her father confessor (*Beichtvater*), wrote down the dreams and made a theological interpretation.

There were many female martyrs in the first centuries; all reports about their life and religious conversion are connected with their denial and refusal of the expected role as a woman: to marry, to produce children (boys better than girls), and to stay at home. St. Augustine in the fifth century wrote about these early martyrs, saying their time was of the past – the time of persecutions was over, and the church was so well established that the heroic fights belonged to another time – we would say another cultural complex. Nevertheless, in the second and third century CE the original certainty of the coming end of time was still present. One of the representatives of this stream was Montanus. It is said that Lucius Montanus was a priest of Cybele (the mother goddess of Asia Minor) before his conversion to Christ. Montanus had ecstatic visions, and together with his followers Maximilla and Prisca (both women) he preached the soon coming end of the world. Montanus referred especially to a saying of Jesus, as written in the Gospel of John: "And I will ask the Father, and He will give you another helper, that He may be with you forever. That is the spirit of truth . . . I will not leave you as orphans" (John 14:16–18). Montanus claimed to have visions of this spirit of truth. In his group women played an important role. Eve was respected because she had eaten from the Tree of Consciousness (The Tree of Knowledge of Good and Evil), and St. Mary was adored as the mother of Christ.[17]

We see how the expectations changed and how in this process the new religion was shaped. It must have been an atmosphere of extreme confusion and devotion. Tertullian, for example, finally left the Roman Church and became an adept of Montanus himself. He sacrificed his intellect, as C. G. Jung said about him,[18] and even committed a self-castration like the priests of Cybele! He encouraged martyrdom. He is famous for his statement *"anima naturaliter christiana"* – the soul is Christian by nature. The complexity of his personality can be understood only in the context of the chaotic fermentation and clearing process of the new religion.

There was an earlier stream of female emancipation in Alexandria. A group of wealthy and educated women used to live around Alexandria in monastery-like dwellings, without men, not married or widowed; they were called the *Therapeutes*. The philosopher Philo from Alexandria wrote about these emancipated women. The Hellenistic atmosphere was open for experiments – but only to a special limit. The first generations of early Christianity were a kind of laboratory for the new religion. Especially, as I said before, women felt inspired by new perspectives.

> The positive view of their religion towards virginity of men and women and to sexual abstinence in marriage allowed the Christians for the first time to

speak in public about the sacrifice which the antique society claimed from married women: from death in childbirth and -bed, the pain during delivery and breastfeeding, the infection with child diseases, the shame of the unfertile and the misery of older women whose husbands turned towards prostitutes or younger slaves.[19]

Women were the property of their fathers or husbands. Many women died during their first pregnancy or childbirth. Nearly 50 percent of twelve- to fourteen-year-old girls were already married and had to become pregnant. The omnipresence of mother goddesses for fertility and childbed was an expression of the suffering of women and their children. Virginia Beane Rutter, who knew quite a bit about the situation of girls and women in antique times, mentions "Aristotle's view in classical Greece that a girl's menarche brought her into the category of a sacrificial beast until she married."[20] In Roman times it was even worse. The comparatively liberal and democratic concept of an eternal life, without looking at the person's gender and status, and the utopia of love made the young Christian religion very attractive for women.

The diary of Perpetua

In 203 CE and in the wake of a local flaring up of anti-Christian sentiment, a group of young catechumens (confessors and teachers) were incarcerated in Carthage in Africa because of their Christian faith.[21] They were condemned to participate in one of the hugely popular spectacles of those times: fighting with wild beasts in the amphitheater. Thus they merited their undying fame as valiant and intrepid martyrs in the eyes both of believers and the Church as a whole. The account of their famous martyrdom, probably written shortly after the event, survived under the title of *Passio SS Perpetuae et Felicitatis* (*The Passion of Saints Perpetua and Felicitas*).[22]

It is a deeply moving story and report, unique also in its direct and authentic style. Vibia (Lady) Perpetua, a twenty-two-year-old educated woman of "noble birth" and mother of a baby, and her friend Felicitas, as well as her teacher and co-martyr Saturus, obviously belonged to a circle of Montanus's followers in Carthage. Perpetua's report moves us not only because of her fate, but also by the simplicity of her style. The young catechumens were taken to the public prison where Perpetua was shocked by the circumstances:

> A few days later we were lodged in the prison, and I was terrified, as I had never before been in such a dark hole. What a difficult time it was! With the crowd the heat was stifling; then there was the extortion of the soldiers; and to crown it all, I was tortured with worry for my baby there.[23]

The openly declared concern regarding her child is unique in classical texts, illustrating the dilemma of her decision to follow her vocation or to be a mother. Perpetua's baby, still breastfed and not unweaned, stays with her in the prison for several days and is then handed over to Perpetua's father. After the trial, Perpetua asks him to give her back her child but he refuses. In her words:

> But my baby had got used to being nursed at the breast and to staying with me in prison. But father refused to give him over. But as God willed, the baby had no further desire for the breast, nor did I suffer any inflammation; and so I was relieved of any anxiety for my child and of any discomfort in my breasts.[24]

One painful experience was Perpetua's separation from her family and her pagan father. Kitzler describes the dilemma like this:

> There is a recurrent theme running through Perpetua's narrative: the desire to settle the score with the world around and to disentangle herself from all its bonds. The world at large with its impositions finds its incarnation predominantly in the character of Perpetua's pagan father, who visits her in prison, imploring her to discard her faith and thus save her own life; he also attends Perpetua's trial, and can be probably traced as a projection in Perpetua's visions. It is the figure of the father who in the beginning springs on Perpetua as though he would pluck [her] eyes out, after she uncompromisingly proclaims her Christian faith to him. Following his unsuccessful attempt to persuade Perpetua to offer a sacrifice to the pagan gods, Perpetua gave thanks to the Lord and was comforted by his absence.[25]

(By the way: I wonder about the feelings of parents who are losing their children to a radical or fundamentalist movement today.)

Kitzler continues (and we feel the hidden emotion in his words):

> Perpetua's second encounter with her father is even more dramatic: he again implores Perpetua to renounce her faith not only for her own sake, but for the sake of the whole family, which has become suspect in the eyes of the authorities in the wake of Perpetua's conviction. He rounds off his arguments by falling at his daughter's feet, kissing her hands, and tearfully addressing her not as a daughter, but as a lady . . . The final meeting takes place before the fight in the amphitheatre; her father's grief reaches its climax as he falls flat on his face before his daughter, plucking his hair and beard and saying such words "as would move all creation" . . . The more desperate the father becomes . . . the more Perpetua grows in self-confidence (turning the normal gender-hierarchy upside down and gaining the position of dominance), the more quickly she disentangles herself from her social and filial bonds. Though at the beginning she views her father with understanding and sympathy, this sympathy is gradually replaced with the resolve to fulfill the requirements of her new faith (she is baptized in the prison), even at the cost of her own life, as the affinity for her new transcendent family gains the upper hand over her earthly one. Thus she comments on her father's most emotional outburst by saying laconically: "I felt sorry for his unhappy old age."[26]

Two images of God

Perpetua told four dreams to her father confessor in the weeks when she was waiting and preparing herself for the fight in the arena. Following von Franz, they show how in her unconscious she was partly still rooted in the antique symbolism and partly already in the emerging Christian symbolism.

Her instructor Saturus, also in prison, one day said to her that she could ask God and watch her dreams if God would tell her about the future. In her first dream/vision she found herself at the bottom of an iron ladder, very high and touching the heaven and so narrow that one could ascend only one after the other.

> On both sides were dangerous instruments so that one who would fall down would hang or be killed . . . But at the bottom of this ladder was a huge dragon . . . lurking for those who would try to step on the ladder. Saturus went up before me (as he also voluntarily was killed first, because he taught us . . .) and he got to the upper end and turned . . . Perpetua, I hold you, but be careful that the dragon will not bite you. And I answered: he will not harm me, in the name of Jesus Christ. And the dragon came slowly out as if he feared me, and I stepped on his head like the first step of the ladder. At the top I saw a huge garden, and in the middle a big white-haired man in the dress of a shepherd, milking sheep, and around him many thousands of people in white garments . . . he lifted his head, looked at me and said: Good, that you came, child! And he called me and gave me from the cheese, which he was milking, like a bite, and I received it with folded hands and ate. And all standing around said: Amen! And by the echo of these voices I woke up, still eating something sweet, I don't know what it was. And immediately I told this to my brother (Saturus) and we realized . . . it meant the coming passion. From now on we had no more hope on this world.[27]

Von Franz shows how the dragon still belongs to the antique symbolism of Python, the serpent of the mother goddess, whereas the garden and the shepherd are already thoroughly Christian imaginations. I can't go into details here, but it is remarkable how the age-old archetypal mother goddess agrees with the individuation process of the young Christian mother who had given away her own child. This is absolutely surprising. We may reflect the image also on the background of St. Mary, the virgin mother of Jesus, who a thousand years later was identified by the Church with the star woman in the Apocalypse – the revelation of John (John 12). There, a terrible dragon is lurking in front of the celestial woman in delivery, waiting to swallow the newborn boy. The woman, mother to be, is "clothed with the sun and the moon under her feet, and on her head a crown of twelve stars." The woman and her baby are saved by God, but Michael and his angels will fight the dragon and throw him in the abyss. Tertullian and Augustine interpreted the dragon as the pagan world, the *diabolus*, evil and the world of sins that has to be overcome, whereas in old Egypt, the dragon and snake were venerated as incarnations of Thot-Hermes, Osiris, or *Agathos daimon*: the good willing. St. Mary sets her foot on the dragon's head. In the shape of the uroboros, both sides are still and forever combined. The image of the ladder reminds von Franz of Jacob's ladder; she also amplifies it with Gnostic and monastic imaginations (the ladder of the ascetic life) of the first centuries.

The milk or cheese Perpetua gets from the divine shepherd is seen as the Eucharistic fare and nourishment the devotees will get. The shepherd himself is an archetypal symbol; he cares for his animals, brings order, and is in accordance with nature. Christ's image as the "Good Shepherd" also has a long tradition; following von Franz it represents the Self, to which all archetypal images are oriented.[28] The caring and loving shepherd has "female" aspects, opposed to the image of a harsh ruling patriarch.

In her second and third visions, *Perpetua sees her younger brother Dinocrates, who died a few years before from a carcinoma. First, he appears as the ill and wounded boy he was, coming out of a space similar to Hades, the underworld of the Greek and Roman imagination.* Perpetua feels mercy, and after this dream she starts to pray for her brother. In the next (the third) vision, *Dinocrates appears again, entirely healed. He is now able to drink fresh water out of a basin, like in paradise, and goes to play with others like children do.* The interpretation says that Dinocrates equals a pagan spirit who will be redeemed by the prayers of his sister. In the fourth and last vision, Perpetua sees what will happen in the arena: *She will be transformed into a man* (!); she has to fight with a huge Egyptian warrior (instead of the wild cow of reality); and she sees a Master of Ceremony in a beautiful white and red garment, like a pagan priest of Saturn, with a green branch with golden apples. The man declares that Perpetua will have to fight the Egyptian, who will kill her with his sword, but if she will overcome him she will get a branch with green leaves. She succeeds, puts her foot on the Egyptian's head; she gets the green branch, and she feels elevated and as if she is flying into the heights.

To tell instead the bitter ending of Perpetua and her friends: She entered the crowded stadium singing hymns in a kind of ecstasy; a wild cow ran against her and slit her white robe. Felicitas wanted to help her to cover her nakedness; the spectators were moved and voted she should be killed by the sword, not by the animal. So it happened. She even had to assist the young executioner in using his sword against her. It is, in fact, a quite sad story.

Interpretation – to better understand our time

Von Franz's study was originally published together with Jung's key work *Aion*, which means we are now in the center of Jung's interest and Jung's psychology. *Aion* was published in 1950, after the catastrophe of the World War, of the totalitarian experience, of Hitler and Stalin, the Holocaust, and the Atom bomb.[29]

I will now examine and trace the hidden meaning of this complex. Paul's message deals with a kind of virtual reality. He preached the end of time and the imminent coming of the Messiah; he set an inner world against the outer reality. The keyword of his experience and project was *resurrection*. Now everything was new for him: *It is no longer I who live, but Christ lives in me.* He worked in a world of great conflicts, of social quarrels and the pending war between Rome and Jerusalem. His alternative was redemption and the comeback, the parusie (return) of the Messiah. His teaching was radical; even if he emphasized that he made just recommendations. Seen psychologically, the "life in Christ" and expectation for the soon-to-come end of days meant living in absolute presence, in the "here and now." Nothing else counts when you are facing the apocalypse.

The Roman world had lost its soul, even if Augustus wanted to heal the wounds of the civil war and established strong systems of power. Even with poets like Ovid and Virgil, we have to imagine this world was a culture at the edge. One could sail securely from one end of the Mediterranean to the other, and Paul could claim his rights as a Roman citizen. Nevertheless, the culture had strong shadow sides: slavery, the deprivation of women, the brutal army, the cruel spectacles, and the missing perspective for the many. The extraverted culture produced its own opposite: the introverted and ascetic view of the early Christians and the longing for purity by the Pharisees, to draw just a sketch of very complex processes. What is the inner psychology, for example, of the barbaric and bloodthirsty slaughters in the public theaters? When wild animals were pushed to kill humans, this setting on stage (*Inszenierung*) seems like an unconscious acting out of a cultural complex: the self-righteous and self-deceptive overcompensation of guilt, desperation, and hopelessness. There are parallels. C. G. Jung wrote "After the Catastrophe" of Nazism, World War II, and the Holocaust: "An infernal distorted picture of man appears which is not bearable for humans. Man is tortured by this grimace (Fratze) and therefore he torments others. He is split in himself."[30] The reconstruction or reinvention of human culture became a kind of necessary unconscious collective project, not only that of the emperor in Rome. All these symptoms can be discovered, in slightly modernized form, in our times.

One aspect of the early Christian movement, as in Paul, Montanus, or Perpetua, was escapism: the longing for flight and escape from the ugly reality. When Perpetua entered the arena where she would be killed by wild beasts, she sang hymns as if in a trance. She was not the only one; on the contrary, this kind of escapism was widespread and became problematic for the pagan society with its slave system. On the other hand, Perpetua seemed to be quite conscious. Paul was absolutely convinced that the Messiah would come soon. Escapism often avoids the confrontation with reality. For the martyrs the outer realty was replaced by an inner world, but the empire reacted brutally. *The Empire Strikes Back* is the title of both a movie and computer game. I think of kids today, always on the computer or phone, their trance, their "second life," and their online relations with more or less virtual people. If this behavior is about an initiation into a new culture, what are its elements and perspective?

Martyrs testify and bear witness; they are heroes and victims with a strong shadow. Erel Shalit wrote an excellent study about this issue.[31] Some modern martyrs even commit suicide by killing many others. By contrast, Jesus was the one who was seen as the absolute victim, in the spirit of deepest devotion. He was not killed "for" our sins (to wash them up) but because of our sins. Again Paul: "We preach Christ crucified, to Jews a stumbling block and to Gentiles foolishness. But to those who are the called, both Jews and Greeks, Christ the power of God and the wisdom of God" (I Cor. 1:23). The identification with the crucified God and the longing for martyrdom for some may be a kind of restitution, a repair of their humiliated God- or Self-Image.

I have in mind three women of our time – Sophie Scholl, Etty Hillesum, and Ulrike Meinhof – who died and were honored as martyrs; two of them were murdered, and one may have been murdered or committed suicide.

Marie-Louise von Franz in her study on Perpetua mentions Sophie Scholl.

> It is about a dream which the 21 year old catholic student, Sophie Scholl, had, who because of anti-Nazistic propaganda in Munich was beheaded by axe. In the night before her death she dreamed in prison that she was carrying on a beautiful sunny day a child to its baptism in a white garment. The way to the church went up a steep mountain, but she held the child well and firmly in her arms. Immediately and unexpectedly a crevasse (a crack of a glacier) opened before her feet. She had just time to lay the child on the secure side, and she herself fell into the abyss.[32]

Von Franz continues:

> She died in reality very brave and staunch and explained her dream herself (to the chaplain of the prison) that the white garment was the idea for which she prepared the way by her death ... The steep way up to the church reminds us of the ladder in Perpetua's first vision, the heavy way of individuation. The fate of Dinocrates corresponds to that of the child which had to be baptized.[33]

There are many moving parallels. The child is the Divine Child, a strong universal symbol for resurrection.

Etty Hillesum (1914–1943) died in Auschwitz, a young woman in the Netherlands who sacrificed her life in the service of her Jewish people. She spoke about her faith with her friend, the Jungian therapist Julius Spieß, a refugee from Nazi Germany who lived in Amsterdam. Before his emigration he was Juli Neumann's (Erich Neumann's mother) chirology teacher in Berlin. Etty wrote about her happiness and thankfulness for her decision to sacrifice herself. It reads as if she lived her last weeks in a kind of permanent gratefulness, an overwhelming love. *The Thinking Heart*, her diary with dreams and inner dialogues, reminds me of Perpetua's diary.

To name the third woman in this context might be controversial. Ulrike Meinhof (1943–1976) was born in a Christian family. Her father, Werner, joined the Nazi party, but he published a booklet with Christian texts and paintings – a legacy for his daughter. As a journalist and peace-activist, Ulrike supported a leftist political party, the *Deutsche Friedensunion DFU*, for which my father was a candidate in the election campaign of 1961 for the German parliament. She visited my family during these times, together with her foster-mother, Renate Riemeck. I was eleven. Because of the erection of the Berlin Wall in 1961, the DFU didn't win a mandate. Meinhof was engaged against the US war in Vietnam and nuclear armament, and against the influence of old Nazis in the German Adenauer-Government. Later on, Meinhof became the founder of the Red Army Faction (RAF) and a terrorist. She gave up the care for her two children. In 1976 she died in prison, either by suicide or murder. Her friend and comrade in the RAF, Gudrun Ensslin, was born in a Lutheran Christian family; her father was a reverend. Both Meinhof and Ensslin began their careers in the spirit of the *Sermon of the Mount*, but they ended in murder and terrorism. Kept imprisoned by their radical views, they finally had no compassion for others. But many of the 68 Generation regarded them as martyrs.

Drawing a coherent picture of our time seems quite impossible. It is unfair to compare Meinhof and Perpetua. Nevertheless, they held their fanaticism in common. They took a clear position in political and moral challenges. They realized, to use Jung's words, that "The world's anima is in prison." Nevertheless, again drawing on Jung,

> Enormous destructive power is given in the hands of man. Now the question is whether the will to use it shall be bound by the spirit of love and wisdom . . . If one understands and feels that already in this life he is attached to the limitless then wishes and attitudes change.

To speak with Paul:

> It is no longer I who live, but Christ lives in me.
> But now abide faith, love, hope; but the greatest of these is love.

Acknowledgments

I have to thank for their advice and help especially Hortense Reintjens-Anwari (Cologne) and Murray Stein (Zurich) for their ideas and support, and my wife, Beate, and Tom Singer (San Francisco) for their encouragement. Tamar Kron (Jerusalem) gave me important information about Martin Buber and Erich Neumann's not-yet-published analysis of the development of Jewish religion. Of course, all errors go on my account.

Notes

1 M.-L. Von Franz, *Passio perpetuae. Das Schicksal einer Frau zwischen zwei Gottesbildern*, Zürich: Daimon Verlag, 1982, p. 191. (Ursprünglich ["originally"] in C. G. Jung, *Aion. Untersuchungen zur Symbolgeschichte*, Zürich: Rascher Verlag, 1951).

2 E. Nestle and K. Aland, *Novum Testamentum Graece et Latine*, 25th Ed, Stuttgart: Württembergische Bibelanstalt, 1963.

3 All biblical translations from the American Standard Bible. Biblical quotations are cited in the text by book, chapter, and verse.

4 A. Badiou, *Paulus. Die Begründung des Universalismus* (Saint Paul—la foundation de l'universalisme, 1977), Zürich-Berlin, diaphanes, 2009.

5 C. G. Jung, "Answer to Job" (1952), *Psychology and Religion: East and West*, in *The Collected Works of C. G. Jung*, Vol. 11, trans. R. F. C. Hull, Princeton, NJ: Princeton University Press, 1969. (Hereafter references to Jung's *Collected Works* appear as CW and volume number.)

6 A. Jaffé, *Der Mythos von Sinn im Werk von C. G. Jung*, Zürich: Daimon, 1983; Jörg Rasche, *Prometheus. Der Kampf zwischen Sohn und Vater*, Zürich: Kreuz Verlag, 1988.

7 W. Giegerich, *Dreaming the Myth Onwards: C. G. Jung on Christianity and Hegel*, New Orleans, LA: Spring Journal Books, 2013.

8 J. Rasche, "The Jewish Anima," in Joerg Rasche and Tom Singer (eds.), *Europe's Many Souls: Exploring Cultural Complexes and Identities*, New Orleans, LA: Spring Journal Books, 2016; and "Europe and Islam," in Rasche and Singer (eds.), *Europe's Many Souls*.

9 L. Hadjifoti, *Saint Paul: His Life and Work*, Athens: Editions M. Toubis, 2004, S.95.

10 P. Lapide, *Paulus zwischen Damaskus und Qumran. Fehldeutungen und Übersetzungsfehler*, Gütersloh: Gütersloher Verlagshaus, 1993; and *Ist die Bibel richtig übersetzt?* Gütersloh: Gütersloher Verlagshaus (Random House), 2004.

11 J. Neusner, *Judentum in frühchristlicher Zeit*, Stuttgart: Calwer Verlag, 1988.

12 G. Scholem, *Zur Kabbala und ihrer Symbolik*, Frankfurt am Main: Suhrkamp Taschenbuch, 1981. (Originally published Zürich, Rhein-Verlag, 1960.)

13 Lapide, *Paulus zwischen Damaskus und Qumran*.

14 Tamar Kron, personal communication, 2017.

15 Tertullien, *De Baptismo*, chapter 17:5.

16 Von Franz, *Passio perpetuae*, p. 191.

17 A. Posener, *Maria*, Reinbeck bei Hamburg, Rowohlt Tb, 1919, p. 76.

18 C. G. Jung, *Psychologische Typen*, CW 6, Olten und Freiburg, Walter, ¶¶12 ff.

19 Posener, *Maria*, p. 83.

20 V. Beane Rutter, *Saffron Offering and Blood Sacrifice*, in V. Beane Rutter and T. Singer (eds.), *Ancient Greece, Modern Psyche: Archetypes in the Making*, New Orleans, LA: Spring Journal Books, 2011, p. 72.

21 In the following paragraphs I will follow especially Marie-Louise von Franz and Peter Kitzler. See Von Franz, *Passio perpetuae*; and Peter Kitzler, "Passio Perpetuae and Acta Perpetuae: Between Tradition and Innovation," *Listy filologické*, 2007, vol. 130, no. 1–2, pp. 1–19.

22 Kitzler, "Passio Perpetuae and Acta Perpetuae," 2007, 2 f.

23 Translation and quote after Kitzler, "Passio Perpetuae and Acta Perpetuae," p. 7.

24 Ibid.

25 Ibid., p. 8.

26 Ibid.

27 Author's own translation, after Von Franz, *Passio perpetuae*, p. 21.

28 Von Franz, *Passio perpetuae*, p. 52.

29 C. G. Jung, *Aion. Untersuchungen zur Symbolgeschichte*, Zürich: Rascher Verlag, 1951.

30 C. G. Jung, "Nach der Katastophe," *Zivilisation im Übergang*, CW 10, Olten und Freiburg, Walter, ¶493.

31 E. Shalit, *The Hero and His Shadow: Psychopolitical Aspects of Myth and Reality*, Carmel, CA: Fisher King Press, 2011, Kindle edition.

32 Von Franz, *Passio perpetuae*, p. 65.

33 Ibid.

7

DANCING THE DANCE ON

Eve Jackson

Embodiment

One of the most memorable pieces of advice I have received concerning practicing as an analyst came from Raphael López-Pedraza: "Don't lose your body!"[1] It was addressed to a roomful of largely intuitive Jungians, many of whom had not yet *found* their body in Lopez's sense, which I take to mean being present in the experience of the living body.

Our whole civilization has lost the experience of embodiment. We became dissociated from nature and, in so doing, lost touch with the most intimate and personal expression of nature, the immediacy of our own physicality. We came to relate to nature and to our own now reified bodies through a fantasy of control. Entire industries are devoted to helping us make the body as we want it. This dissociation is the work of the aggressive dragon-slaying modern ego, which is now busy blindly destroying the physical world it depends on, the body of the great mother herself.

So it comes about that we can read a book or stare at a computer screen without noticing that we are getting a headache. We can attend a conference and talk and listen for several days in an auditorium and over a glass of wine afterward, without registering what is happening with us physically. We can go through years of analysis without developing extensive somatic consciousness.

Jung, of course, included the body in his work at least theoretically, considering it as much a part of the whole human being as is the psyche. At one point in his seminar on Nietzsche's Zarathustra, where he develops this theme of psyche/soma, he discusses the effect on the digestion of metaphysical ideas, suggesting that we should test such an idea by "try[ing] it out for a month or so, whether it upsets your stomach or not."[2] The implication that it might take a month for our consciousness to connect the mind with the gut is an admission of serious somatic dissociation.

The very term *psychosomatic*, being applied almost exclusively to disease, indicates that we only become aware that psyche and soma are connected when something goes badly wrong. This disconnect is at its most extreme in the case of the intuitive, who, on the other hand, can readily connect with the imagination, the focus of Jung's interest, so it is not surprising that somatic awareness was not really integrated into the practice of analytical psychology. In the last twenty to thirty years, more analysts have been seeking ways to bring body and image together – to give one outstanding example, there is Robert Boznak's technique for working with dreams.[3] This union, however, remains beyond the reach of many analysts.

We have to go back a long way to find cultural ancestors who still naturally experienced the living body, permeated with soul and spirit, back beyond the body as machine (Descartes), the body opposed to spirit (Christianity), the body as the prison of the soul, and the body as a potential threat that must be dominated (Socrates/Plato), beyond the reified body – we must go back all the way to Homer.

When we get there, guided by scholarship, we get a glimpse of another way of being: According to Michael Clarke's *Flesh and Spirit in the Songs of Homer*, Homeric man does not *have* a body or a mind:

> rather his thought and consciousness are as inseparable a part of his bodily life as are movement and metabolism . . . the ongoing process of thought is perceived as if it were precisely identified with the palpable inhalation of the breath, and the half-imagined mingling of breath with blood and bodily fluids in the soft, warm, flowing substances that make up what is behind the chest wall.[4]

Notice that this being-in-the-body also involved more *fluidity*, as there had not yet been that *separatio*, thanks to which this "fluid realm of direct experience has come to be seen as a secondary, derivative dimension, a consequence of events unfolding in the 'realer' world of quantifiable and measurable scientific facts."[5]

In addition, sense perception in Homer has an effect on what is perceived and at the same time changes the perceiver. There is no claim to detachment.[6] So the Homeric figures were closer to what David Abram calls "the body's silent conversation with things."[7] Losing our body is also losing our intimate connection with the environment.

Eventually the phenomenologists Husserl and Merleau-Ponty developed a view and a language in which we can talk of this (for most of us unconscious) connection as intersubjective reality and the interplay between the senses and the sense objects. At the same time, various forms of bodywork that have developed in the West in the last century can help us to open to this primordial experience.[8] It is also hidden in the notion, still alive in parts of southern Europe, of the effects of the "evil eye," the look that can kill. In the East the flowing aliveness of the body and its embeddedness in the environment was never altogether lost but kept alive in the practice of various disciplines that are as much spiritual as physical. My own discovery of the body as lived experience came through practices drawn from the Chinese and

Tibetan traditions, *taiji*,[9] qigong, and body-based meditation, on which I enlarge a little in this chapter. The numbered images accompanying this chapter can be found at the Archive for Research in Archetypal Symbolism (ARAS) at https://aras.org/ancient-greece-modern-psyche.

Dance

Dance derives from a time when the body was sacred, when the whole human being could be experienced as part of nature through which divine energy flowed. It has undoubtedly been a universal human activity from the beginnings of our species; perhaps it is the earliest art form, an active participation in the dynamic movement of life. The psychologist Wolfgang Köhler reported that the anthropoid apes in his laboratory in Tenerife performed round dances with gay abandon, and in the forest, apes have been observed "dancing" and shouting in defiance of thunder-storms. They apparently have a penchant for costume as well, and entwine themselves with vines and twigs.[10]

Artifacts and texts from ancient Greece reveal that dance was widespread throughout its history – in the cults of the gods (Figure 7.1), in festivities, in rites of passage such as preparation for marriage or for war (Figure 7.2). In some cases, dancers wore masks and imitated animals (Figure 7.3) and possibly embodied activities of immortals or fell into ecstatic abandonment to divine spontaneity. Many dances were already ancient by the classical period. Some of these dances have been passed on from generation to generation (Figure 7.4) from prehistoric times to the present, not unchanging but in unbroken continuity, as they were carried to new places with migrant populations. To give a more recent example, when Greeks from the Black Sea came as refugees to mainland Greece at the time of the exchange of populations with Turkey in 1923, they brought with them their characteristic dances.[11] In Greece today, many small children who have only recently learned to walk already copy dance steps and grow up with traditional dances in their bodies. These dances have never had to be "recovered"; they have simply gone on being widely danced, century after century.

FIGURE 7.1   Dancers from frieze of sanctuary propylaeum, 340 BCE, Samothrace
(https://aras.org/ancient-greece-modern-psyche)

FIGURE 7.2   Warrior dance, vase from Walters Art Gallery, Baltimore (from Lawler, *The Dance in Ancient Greece*)
(https://aras.org/ancient-greece-modern-psyche)

FIGURE 7.3   Bull-masked dancers, vase, British Museum (also from Lawler, *The Dance in Ancient Greece*)
(https://aras.org/ancient-greece-modern-psyche)

FIGURE 7.4 Painting by Theophilos (1873–1934), Theophilos Museum, Mytilene (https://aras.org/ancient-greece-modern-psyche)

Songs, even tunes, have been changed and substituted over time, and steps always vary, even from village to village. Very likely what has changed least is the rhythm, the pulse of the dance. Some of the complex rhythms still danced perpetuate meters from ancient poetry.

Rhythmos is measured time. We can speak of biorhythms (for example, the heartbeat), and then there are rhythms found and played by a drummer, which may or may not coincide with natural rhythms of the body and can actually affect them. Lucian, writing in the second century CE, suggests that dancing was inspired by the rhythmic movement of the planets.[12]

Rhythmizo means "arrange in due order, adjust." In a shared dance, rhythm helps us to synchronize our steps, to move together in conscious collectivity and create a new level of flow, to tune ourselves to each other and to a particular mood or archetypal constellation. In Günter Grass's novel *The Tin Drum*, there is a spectacular scene in which Oskar, the midget drummer, takes up position underneath the podium at a Nazi rally. As the Nazi officers march forward in step to the band on the rostrum, Oskar loudly beats out a Viennese waltz. Most of the musicians are irresistibly drawn into his rhythm, leading to the total confusion of the marchers and onlookers. It is not easy to be militaristic in waltz time.[13]

Various dances still performed in Greece survive from the dances of ancient cults. To give a few examples, some women's dances from Cappadocia are thought to come from the Artemis cult. There is a much-debased and bowdlerized Dionysian rite in Ilia (Eleia), in the northeastern Peloponnese, that goes by the name of *Gennitsari*. *Serra*, from the Black Sea area, is thought to be the ancient Pyrrhic dance. *Boules*, danced in Naoussa in Greek Macedonia, especially during carnival, is believed to come from a Persephone/Hades ritual. There is a short book on this subject by Dora Stratou, the great twentieth-century teacher of traditional Greek dance.[14]

Probably the most commonly performed type of Greek dance, in its many forms, is the *syrtos* ("dragged dance"). Originally it was danced around an altar in a broken circle. Such a dance normally moves in an anti-clockwise direction, with the dancers facing partly inward and moving to their right. A broken as opposed to a closed circle has the advantage that the dancers at either end are free to add movements and improvise, and the leader can change the direction of the moving line, so it snakes away from the original circle. In this type of dance, the improvising leader is perhaps also being led.

The crane dance

One particular dance called *Tsakonikos* (Figure 7.5) typically moves in a spiral and sometimes in snaking loops. Danced in a part of the eastern Peloponnese, the Tsakonikos is thought to have come from Minoan Crete. Undoubtedly people moved between Crete and the Peloponnese in ancient times, as the historical connections between the Minoans and Mycenaeans imply, and there have been many displacements since that time. There are other theories as to the dance's origins, however. Some say it is a warrior dance, but this does not strike me as likely. Another theory is that it was adapted by Theseus to the Apollo story and represented the struggle of Apollo with the Python. If so, what remains celebrates the Python rather than Apollo's killing of it. Then there is a theory that it is a more recent dance local to the area. But we know that spiral dances are ancient. These dances have been picked up by the neo-pagans. Starhawk wrote a book entitled *The Spiral Dance* in 1979,[15] which describes numerous witchcraft rituals. It contains two brief descriptions of dances performed in a spiral, which are not dissimilar to Tsakonikos, although she does not tell us where they came from.

FIGURE 7.5 Tsakonikos

(https://aras.org/ancient-greece-modern-psyche)

The theory I favor is that Tsakonikos is, in fact, from the so-called crane dance mentioned by Plutarch in his *Life of Theseus* (Figure 7.6):[16]

> On his voyage from Crete, Theseus put in at Delos, and having sacrificed to the god and dedicated in his temple the image of Aphrodite which he had received from Ariadne, he danced with his youths a dance which they say is still performed by the Delians, being an imitation of the Labyrinth, and concerning certain rhythmic involutions and evolutions. This kind of dance, as Dicaearchus tells us, is called by the Delians The Crane, and Theseus danced it round the altar called keraton, which is constructed of horns ("*kerata*") taken entirely from the left side of the head.

It seems likely that this is the same dance as the one referred to in the *Iliad*, in the description of the pictures wrought on the shield made for Achilles by Hephaestus.

> Next [Hephaestus] depicted a dancing-floor like the one that Daedalus designed in the spacious town of Cnossus for Ariadne of the lovely locks. Youths and marriageable maidens were dancing on it with their hands on one another's wrists . . . [T]hey ran lightly round, circling as smoothly on their accomplished feet as the wheel of a potter when he sits and works it with his hands to see if it will spin. And there they ran in lines to meet each other.[17]

Notice some of the words in these two descriptions: *circling, involutions and evolutions, labyrinth, Daedalus.*

One question that arises is how (in Homer's description) this circling becomes lines that "meet each other." Kerényi argues, reasonably, that this is a description

FIGURE 7.6   "Crane dance," François vase, sixth century BCE, National Archeology
Museum, Florence

(https://aras.org/ancient-greece-modern-psyche)

of a spiral dance. He also adds that according to a scholiast, Daedalus taught Theseus
the dance. Following Kerényi's reasoning, Homer's account could well be a description of the Tsakonikos. After winding in to the center, there is a turn, and those
now going out pass close to those who are still coming in (Figure 7.7).

FIGURE 7.7   "Opposed snake" vase, Romania, fifth millennium BCE (Gimbutas) – the
lines correspond to the movement of the dancers in Tsakonikos, some
going toward the center, others outward

(https://aras.org/ancient-greece-modern-psyche)

There is another ancient hint that Daedalus worked with spirals. It comes from
a lost play by Sophocles, referred to in the *Epitome* of Pseudo-Apollodorus:[18]

> After the death of Icarus Daedalus made his way safely to Camicus in Sicily.
> And Minos pursued Daedalus, and in every country that he searched he car-
> ried a spiral shell and promised to give a great reward to him who should pass
> a thread through the shell, believing that by that means he should discover
> Daedalus. And having come to Camicus in Sicily, to the court of Cocalus,
> with whom Daedalus was concealed, he showed the spiral shell. Cocalus
> took it and promised to thread it, and gave it to Daedalus and Daedalus
> fastened a thread to an ant, and, having bored a hole in the spiral shell,
> allowed the ant to pass through it. But when Minos found the thread passed
> through the shell, he perceived that Daedalus was with Cocalus, and at once
> demanded his surrender. [Actually, Cocalus tricks Minos and kills him.]

The name of the dance – "the crane dance" – is a puzzle. Cranes do, indeed,
dance. They do a mating dance, but they don't go around in a line; rather it's a

couples' dance (Figure 7.8), in which the two birds dance opposite each other. Most commentators have tried to find some association with the crane, perhaps the relationship between the migration season of cranes and particular rituals. But an alternative etymology is offered by Lillian B. Lawler in her book *The Dance in Ancient Greece*.[19] She relates the Ancient Greek word for crane, *geranos*, to a homonym from the root *-ger*, meaning to wind, "as of rivers and serpents."

FIGURE 7.8 Cranes' mating dance

(https://aras.org/ancient-greece-modern-psyche)

She goes on to say that

> [l]ike so many other old maze dances, it probably originated as an imitation of the winding path of a serpent. [I]nscriptions [found on Delos] indicate that the dancers carried *rhymoi* – a word over which there has been great controversy. It actually seems to mean "ropes"; and it is highly possible that in the classical period, at least, the dancers may have carried a long rope-like or garland-like object suggestive of a serpent. The ritual carrying of a large snake (or a replica of one) in a dance is not without parallel. [Compare the Chinese dragon dance.] As we have noted, the Minoan Cretans seem to have had similar dances; and from them the Delian dance may well have stemmed. As performed by Theseus and his companions in the legend, the *geranos* is clearly a winding maze or "snake dance."

This seems linguistically plausible to me. In Modern Greek, the verb *gerno* means to bend or bow. Presumably also *ger* is a variant of *gyr* as in *gyros*; in Ancient Greek, it means a circle or circuit, from which we have *gyrate* and *gyroscope* in English. There are other examples of related words where the letters *epsilon* and *ypsilon* replace one another. In fact, the name given to the crane, *geranos*, may be connected, without it necessarily being the immediate inspiration for the dance name. It probably comes from the same root, referring to the snaking way in which the bird "cranes" its neck and also makes leaping gyrations while "dancing" with a partner.

Now to the question of the rope. Although I am unfamiliar with the linguistic arguments, the interpretation offered of the word *rhymoi* as rope may be connected to a root that means to pull or drag (compare the word *syrtos* for a dance in which the dancers are pulled along by the leader). In the late eighteenth century, a book was published containing the correspondence of Madame Elisabeth Chénier, the Greek mother of the French pre-Romantic poet André Chénier. She came from the privileged Greek population in Constantinople (present-day Istanbul). The collection contains a letter from a Monsieur Guys on modern Greek dances, as well as Madame Chénier's response. One particular dance is referred to as the *Candiote*, meaning it comes from Crete (Candia) or perhaps specifically from the place now known as Heraklion (Candia), near Minoan Knossos. In the letter, Monsieur Guys says he has seen this dance himself, along with another similar dance, sometimes led by a girl holding a silken rope. Madame Chénier responds:

Daedalus composed this dance in order to preserve the memory of his ingenious building and to help Ariadne to remember and learn all the twistings of the Labyrinth.[20]

When they dance the Candiot with a rope, it is, I believe, in memory of the ball of thread which Ariadne gave Theseus, by virtue of which, having conquered the Minotaur, he was able to get out of the Labyrinth.

Of course the ball of thread is itself another image of the winding and unwinding process and, indeed, the thread itself and the "silken rope" have been twined in a spiral, like the twisted thread of the Fates, which spins the winding path of our lives. These are all variations on a theme.

So the terms *labyrinth, winding maze, circling, twisting, involutions and evolutions, snake, rope and spiral, labyrinth* all describe movements performed by a line of coordinated human bodies in a complex, fluid style.

Labyrinth

Karl Kerényi worked for many years on the theme of the labyrinth and in 1950 published a monograph entitled *Labyrinth-Studien*[21] dedicated to C. G. Jung. Kerényi finds that the nexus – *spiral, dance, labyrinth* – emerges not only in the Minoan culture (Figure 7.9), but also in other traditions spread across the world (Figure 7.10). Particularly striking is the spiral dance associated with the sacrificed vegetation maiden Hainuwele in Indonesia, but Layard, who also explored this motif, found examples in Vanuatu and Southern India,[22] and the spiral motif, generally, and spiral dances, in particular, are extremely widespread.

FIGURE 7.9 Coin from Knossos, second century BCE (Kerényi, from Labyrinth–Studien)
(https://aras.org/ancient-greece-modern-psyche)

FIGURE 7.10 Labyrinth from Mesopotamia (Kerényi, from Labyrinth-Studien)
(https://aras.org/ancient-greece-modern-psyche)

A fourth element Kerényi finds associated with *labyrinth, spiral,* and *dance* is the *underworld*. In the Greek myth Theseus and his companions are going into the labyrinth to their death, but through the intervention of Ariadne with her thread they reemerge into light and life. In the Greek story, they are sacrificial victims, but one can also see this as a version of an initiation rite, not altogether unlike that of Eleusis. In Jungian terms, we describe the labyrinth experience as denoting a process of being drawn into the unconscious, a letting go of the ego position, followed by a reemergence. The Greeks – perhaps due to having more developed egos – came to regard the labyrinth as a place of terror and as a prison, but it did not necessarily have such connotations for the Minoans.

(This is not to deny that there may really have been human sacrifices in Minoan Crete.)

In his book on Dionysos, Kerényi identifies Ariadne, whom Homer describes with an epithet he normally reserves for goddesses (*euplokamos*, "of the lovely locks") as the "mistress of the labyrinth" to whom offerings of honey were made, as recorded on a tablet found in Knossos.[23]

> In the history of civilization, honey offerings and dances go hand in hand as forms of myth and cult, even when they survive in a mature high culture. The intervals in the Knossion [labyrinth design found on the floor of a corridor at Knossos], which, if it was a dance figure, must originally have been rounded, were the paths of the dancers who honored the "mistress of the labyrinth" with their movements. The dancing ground, on which the figure of the dance was drawn, represented the great realm of the mistress . . . Even in [the Theseus] story, which has become so human, Ariadne discloses a close relationship, such as only the Minoan "mistress of the labyrinth" could have had, to both aspects of the labyrinth: the home of the Minotaur and the scene of the winding and unwinding dance.[24]

This would mean that Ariadne, along with her mother Pasiphaë, who "shines on all," is the lunar consort and mother of the bull god, the Cretan Dionysos, later transformed into a Cretan Zeus. She is a kind of Persephone, and the labyrinth is her realm.

Kerényi believes that when the symbol of the spiral was truly alive the reference to the labyrinth and underworld was implicit, and that even when it served as decoration, often in the form of the curling or straight-line meander design, it also had an inherent value as an auspicious or protective sign, much as the cross became a sign of a more differentiated consciousness, with tension between the opposites, for Christians. Marija Gimbutas, in her book *The Language of the Goddess*, devotes two chapters to the abundant spiral imagery on artifacts from Neolithic Europe, indicating that this symbolism goes back to at least the fifth millennium BCE (Figure 7.11).[25]

FIGURE 7.11   Figurine, fifth millennium BCE, Volos Museum (Gimbutas, from *The Language of the Goddess*)

(https://aras.org/ancient-greece-modern-psyche)

Kerényi comes to the conclusion that "any investigation of the labyrinth has to start from the dance."[26] In other words, the dance came first as a ritual, and constructed labyrinths were a later development. He also notes that the labyrinth design found on the floor of a corridor at the palace of Knossos "leads towards the most important source of the palace's light: a courtyard framed in 7 columns"[27] and points out that there is nothing in the legend of Theseus to suggest that in entering the labyrinth the hero broke open the gate that is mentioned. The meander and spiral lines point to an open labyrinth that – if one turned at the centre – was a passage to the light.[28]

The dance Tsakonikos involves precisely this turn at the center, as do many mazes.

Spiral

Beyond the specific cultural nexus I've referred to thus far, there is another vast context in which the spiral can be observed, and that is in the natural world. Kerényi only touches briefly on this in his *Labyrinth-Studien*, mentioning, interestingly, that "today we believe we know – those ancient artists and dancers didn't guess this – that the embryo and seed carry immortality in spiral formations."[29] He can only be referring to DNA, so I assume that even before Crick and Watson its spiral form had been detected.

Kerényi mentions in passing what the anthropologist Jeremy Narby discovered in his work with Amazonian shamans.[30] He found a correspondence between the twisting ayahuasca visions (Figure 7.12) and the double helix of DNA and suspected that both referred to the same underlying truth. The spiral is at the heart of life, its formation, its perpetuation. It comes into view in what we call the unconscious – what we may see as a deeper form of consciousness than our familiar ego-centered conscious. It is a symbol of the mysterious source of all things and of deathless transformation.

FIGURE 7.12   Painting by Ayahuascero, Peru (Narby, from *The Cosmic Serpent*)

(https://aras.org/ancient-greece-modern-psyche)

But the ancient Minoans didn't need twentieth-century microscope technology to see DNA, or, for that matter, telescopes to see spiral galaxies. They could see the spirals all around them – in swirling water, in trees, in germinating seeds, in flowers, and most particularly in the tendrils of the two Dionysian plants – the ivy and the vine. For some reason the Minoans didn't portray the vine in their artwork, but natural spiraling forms were a favorite motif, whether octopi (Figure 7.13), curling locks, or stylized plants (Figure 7.14). They saw the spiral everywhere and depicted it with great fluidity, and it is one of the elements that accounts for the extraordinary vitality and exuberance of their work (Figure 7.15). The design on the enigmatic Phaistos disk is also in spiral form (Figure 7.16). This mysterious object covered in hieroglyphs was unearthed at the Minoan palace of Phaistos and has been the subject of numerous interpretations.

FIGURE 7.13   Minoan vase with octopus

(https://aras.org/ancient-greece-modern-psyche)

FIGURE 7.14 "Prince of the lily" fresco, Knossos
(https://aras.org/ancient-greece-modern-psyche)

FIGURE 7.15 Kamares ware bowl
(https://aras.org/ancient-greece-modern-psyche)

FIGURE 7.16 Disk of Phaistos
(https://aras.org/ancient-greece-modern-psyche)

There are, of course, different forms of spiral: not only two-dimensional spirals, single, or continuous as the meander design; but also three-dimensional spirals, such as the helix and the vortex, and spirals based on the golden section (as often found in nature). And the fluid undulations of the snake, with its spiraling twists and coils, also belong to the spiral image. Indeed, Jung points out that spiral rotation is often represented by a snake.[31] So those who see in the "crane dance" rope a snake and those who see it as a winding/unwinding ball of thread are not at odds with each other, although they may be talking about slightly different versions of the dance. The serpent – that spirit of nature – was also sacred in Minoan Crete (Figure 7.17) and in many other traditions until the solar dragon-slayers came along, the gods and heroes who fought and killed the serpent of darkness.

FIGURE 7.17 Minoan priestess figurine, Knossos
(https://aras.org/ancient-greece-modern-psyche)

A spiraling force is mercurial, as the caduceus shows. It can flip over; a twisting stream of cigarette smoke can become a vortex ring. It is also dynamic, in that a single spiral is always asymmetrical, compared to, say, the generally stable form of the mandala, so it calls up its opposite to create a dynamic balance. The yin-yang symbol can be seen as a two-dimensional representation of two complementary spiraling forces forming a vortex sphere (Figure 7.18). Jill Purce, in her book *The Mystic Spiral*, has written an extensive exploration of the forms and symbolism of the spiral.[32]

FIGURE 7.18 Spherical vortex
(https://aras.org/ancient-greece-modern-psyche)

At the level of the body, the rotating spiral channels and the coiled Kundalini, the Shakti power, are well attested to and resemble the snakes of the caduceus. I can also report from personal experience that in the process of consciously feeling my way into the body through taiji and meditation I have found the dynamic spiraling process subtly and powerfully at work throughout the body. Blockages don't so much dissolve as *unwind*. But this process is not something one *does*. Simple awareness allows it to happen in the same way that becoming conscious of psychic elements facilitates an autonomous response from the unconscious.

The rotation of the energy center in the belly, known in the Chinese tradition as the *dantian*, sends out spiraling energy through the legs and arms. This is what gives immense strength to the soft movements of taiji. The taiji master's movements are manifestations of a whirling force field, which is integrated with the field of the world around him or her. The mind and senses extend indefinitely beyond the skin. The famous "unbendable arm" of the Aikido master is powered by the spiraling flow of energy from the *dantian* down through the feet into the earth.[33] The helical screw is immensely stronger than the straight nail, hence this internal spiral movement roots the practitioner in the ground. This downward force sends an equal and opposite force up through the body, sustaining the position of the arm. Achieving this function takes many of years of subtle psychophysical work. One can also see the spiraling force powered by the belly in the *raq sharqi* (belly dance) and the spiraling around a central axis in the whirling or turning of the Mevlevi Dervishes. The adept experiences the process as being whirled rather than whirling; the ego yields up its control. The whole ritual, incidentally, is a reflection of celestial motion.

We also encounter the spiral in our psychic processes. Jung gives us a picture painted by a female analysand depicting an embroidered handkerchief seen in a dream (Figure 7.19).[34] He tells us only that "The dreamer had no notion of what was going on in her, namely the beginning of a new orientation, nor would she have understood it consciously." The curved spiral, here closer to the center, is an older form, according to Kerényi, than the rectilinear. It seems obvious that it is primal. The Catalan architect Gaudi is often quoted as saying that there are no straight lines or sharp corners in nature; perhaps this is not absolutely true, but sustained straight lines are generally a product of ego consciousness. In the dream image the dreamer is moving away from the square construction of the ego/handkerchief into the more natural spiraling movement of the psyche, from which, we are told, a "new orientation" emerged.[35]

A common complaint in our work is that the frustrated analysand is just going around in circles. There is talk of quitting, as things are going nowhere, and we encourage the thought that the process might be spiral rather than circular. In the natural run of things, one is, in fact, going in spirals anyway, due to the dimension of time, as one does the round of the complexes. Driven by the tyrannical animus, then caught by the paralyzing mother, whisked away by the *puer aeternus*, down into the pit again: it all feels so familiar. But we never return quite to the same place, never put the same foot in the same river twice; that's why we often don't see the return coming. This is just the working of time. Then consciousness adds a further dimension, so that each time around one is surprised by new insights, sometimes costly or painful, on and on, until one begins to see that all these situations are connected, are different aspects of one thing. Then, again, the

FIGURE 7.19 Handkerchief dream image from Jung, "Concerning mandala symbolism," CW 9i

(https://aras.org/ancient-greece-modern-psyche)

development of the functions of consciousness proceeds by the way of the snake, from superior to inferior, via the second and third functions.

What we usually mean by a labyrinth is not quite the same as a spiral. The spiral has an unimpeded natural momentum, whereas the labyrinth (for example, the maze in Chartres cathedral [Figure 7.20]) generally involves the snaky line doubling back on itself. It is more complex. From a distance we can see the pattern, but when we are in it we feel at the mercy of unexpected checks and turns. We get to the center just as surely if we follow the path, but it doesn't feel like we will; there are moments of hesitation. Such movements could be woven into an intricate dance. Tsakonikos can be danced in a looping fashion as well as a spiral, so one can imagine a combination of the two.

FIGURE 7.20   Diagram of maze in Chartres Cathedral
(https://aras.org/ancient-greece-modern-psyche)

The labyrinth also evolves into something that presents us with choices, fork-ing paths, crossroads, conscious decisions. It is no longer enough to just follow the way the road leads, and if the ego can't decide, or gets it wrong, we need the help of Ariadne or Mercurius. A woman who had just left a destructive relationship dreamt that she was wandering about in the streets of London and asked a man for directions to where she was going. He pointed back along the road she had just come from. Indeed, she was not yet finished with the relationship and had to go back into it before she could come out of it fully.

The subtitle of Kerényi's book on Dionysos, in which he talks about the Cretan labyrinth, is *Archetypal Image of Indestructible Life*. The symbol of the spiral points toward the archetype behind that image, toward the eternal dynamism of life-and-death-and-life, expanding to infinity and contracting to infinity. It points to the life force, spinning the universe into – and out of – being. It is this the dance imitates.

In going into the center of the spiral, the dancers of the "crane dance," or winding dance, were being led toward the source of "life-and-death," toward the mistress of the labyrinth. If done in a prepared and serious way, as an initiation into the great mystery, in such an encounter the old ego position might be at least momentarily dissolved, so the dancer could emerge again into the light renewed and transformed, with a "new orientation."

In the dance Tsakonikos, we start in a broken circle and snake around to create a spiral, which then unwinds. There is a turning point at the center and we pass each other going in opposite directions, some still going in, while others are on their way out. It is an ancient imitation of the infinitely powerful but fluid forces of nature that surround us and propel us from within, and human bodies have been performing it on and on since the Stone Age, through classical antiquity, Christianity, and into modernity.

In Santorini we ended the conference by performing this dance together.

Notes

1   At a seminar on Dionysos in London in the late 1990s.
2   Jung, *Nietzsche's Zarathustra: Notes on the Seminar Given in 1934–1939*, Vol. 2, Princeton, NJ: Princeton University Press, 1988, Part I, p. 355.
3   Technique described in Robert Boznak's book *Embodiment: Creative Imagination in Medicine, Art and Travel*, London and New York: Routledge, 2007.
4   Michael Clark, *Flesh and Spirit in the Songs of Homer*, Oxford: Oxford University Press, 1999, p 115; quoted in Iain McGilchrist, *The Master and His Emissary: The Divided Brain and the Making of the Western World*, New Haven, CT and London: Yale University Press, 2009, pp. 74–5.
5   David Abram, *The Spell of the Sensuous*, New York: Vintage, 1997, p. 34.
6   McGilchrist, *The Master and His Emissary*, pp. 265–6.
7   Abrams, *The Spell of the Sensuous*, p. 49.
8   To give a few examples, the Alexander technique, the Feldenkrais Method, and the many forms of therapy that have developed out of the work of psychoanalyst Wilhelm Reich.

9   This is the official, internationally recognized Pinyin romanization of the word written in the older Wade-Giles system as *t'ai chi*, and commonly written *tai chi*.

10 Steven Lonsdale, *Animals and the Origins of Dance*, New York: Thames & Hudson, 1982.

11 Until that date there were extensive Greek populations in Asia Minor (Turkey), mainly in Constantinople (Istanbul), and along the coasts of the Mediterranean and the Black Sea. In 1922, the Greek government foolishly decided to invade Turkey in an attempt to win more territory, resulting in the total destruction of the Greek city of Smyrna on the Mediterranean coast of Asia Minor and an eventual treaty that required the expulsion of the Turkish population from Greece and of the Greek population from Turkey.

12 Lucian, *On the Dance*, referenced by Lillian Lawler, *The Dance in Ancient Greece*, London: Black, 1964, p. 12.

13 Günter Grass, *The Tin Drum*, Fawcett edition, New York: Pantheon Books, 1966, pp. 112–13.

14 Dora Stratou, *Greek Dances: Our Living Link with Antiquity*, trans. Amy Mims–Argyraki, Athens, 1966.

15 Starhawk, *The Spiral Dance: A Rebirth of the Ancient Religion of the Goddess,* New York: Harper & Row, 1999.

16 Plutarch, *Life of Theseus*, Book XXI, trans. Bernadotte Perrin, Cambridge, MA: Harvard University Press, The Loeb Classical Library, 1914, p. 45.

17 Homer, *Iliad*, trans E.V. Rieu, Harmondsworth, UK: Penguin, 1950, Book 18, p. 352.

18 The Library of Apollodorus, *Epitome*, E.1.12–E.1.15.

19 Lawler, *The Dance in Ancient Greece,* pp. 47–8.

20 Elisabeth Santi Chenier, *Lettres Grecques de Madame Chenier*, Paris: Charavay, 1879, pp. 161–2. Available online: https://archive.org/details/lettresgrecquesd00ch.

21 Karl Kerényi, *Labyrinth-Studien*, Zurich: Rhein-Verlag, 1950.

22 Mentioned in Kerényi, *Labyrinth-Studien*, p. 24.

23 Karl Kerényi, *Dionysos: Archetypal Image of Indestructible Life*, Princeton, NJ: Princeton University Press, 1976, Ch. III.

24 Ibid., pp. 98–9.

25 Marija Gimbutas, *The Language of the Goddess*, London: Thames & Hudson, 1989.

26 Kerényi, *Labyrinth-Studien*, p. 37.

27 Kerényi, *Dionysos*, p. 95.

28 Ibid., p. 94.

29 Kerényi, *Labyrinth-Studien*, p. 49.

30 Jeremy Narby, *The Cosmic Serpent: DNA and the Origins of Knowledge*, London: Victor Gollancz, 1998. First published in French as *Le Serpent Cosmique*, Geneva: Georg Editeur, 1995.

31 C. G. Jung, "The philosophical tree," *Alchemical Studies*, in *The Collected Works of C. G. Jung*, Vol. 13, ¶349 and note. Hereafter references to Jung's *Collected Works* will be referred to by CW and volume and paragraph number.

32 Jill Purce, *The Mystic Spiral: Journey of the Soul*, New York: Thames and Hudson, 1974.

33 As a demonstration of his level of attainment, the master stands, holding his arm up, while somebody attempts to push the arm down. Although the arm is relaxed, it cannot be forced to bend. This appears to be impossible or a trick to those who think only in terms of muscle power.

34 Jung, "Concerning mandala symbolism," *The Archetypes and the Collective Unconscious*, CW 9i, ¶649 and figure 4.

35 For more on the spiraling process of analysis, see Jung, "Introduction to the religious and psychological problems of alchemy," *Psychology and Alchemy*, CW 12, ¶34.

8

THE JUDGMENT OF ELECTRA

Introduction

Craig San Roque

> He sits down in drinking camps. He gets lazy. He gets lost in town. He learns
> ganja culture, his mind changes, he kills women, he forgets jukurrpa, (cultural law),
> kurunpa, (his spirit) slides away, he loses power, he lies down. Karnka Crow sucks
> his blood. There he is lying there, sick. Walawaru the Eagle comes again and lifts
> him up high in the sky. Eagle says, "This is your life. Use your brain. A man can
> choose. Which way will you go?" "I will stick with you," says the man.
>
> *(The Life of a Man, from* Eagle and Crow, *by Andrew Spencer Japaljarri, Alice*
> *Springs, 2015.[1] Quoted in* Trouble, *by Kieran Finnane[2])*

The place where I live, Alice Springs, is in the center of Australia's Aboriginal
countries. It is here that the world's perhaps oldest-living continuous culture exists
uneasily alongside immigrant peoples of mostly northern ancestries. British law and
Christian religion reached remote Central Australia, in a seriously affecting manner, during the 1870s, bringing law, food, language, and attitudes of the European
sensibility of place, purpose, and progress. Migrations continue to pervade; and
now peoples from many different ethnic nations live in Central Australia, interspersed among the twelve or so local "tribes" whose languages and cultural law are
the bedrock of the life and memory of our desert landform.

The history of the world seems to be a history of migrations, beginning with the
long walk out of Africa. Survival, extinction, migration, and invasion is the human
way of things. Some live, some die. I am thinking about the way people die by
crime, and the way differing peoples handle such crimes through the establishment
of law and customs of punishment, retribution, and the settlement of discontent.

The story of Eagle and Crow negotiating for the life of the man is told by Andrew
Spencer Japaljarri, an indigenous Central Australian man renowned for his skills as a
mediator in cultural and customary law conflicts and who, in his teaching paintings,

such as *Eagle and Crow*, drew on traditional Warlpiri stories to illuminate contemporary social challenges facing Aboriginal and Australian people. The dilemma faced by the man in his encounters with Eagle and Crow might give you an idea of the existential tensions, even borderline disorders, with which we live in Australia. In Japaljarri's terms, the Crow stands for willful self-destruction and mindless abnegation of responsibility for family and culture. The Eagle embodies a clear view and the resolve of the man to try to think for himself in new conditions, while still following the ground of his indigenous culture. At a certain point, however, a person might worry that traditional culture and law may not serve well in new times. The tension, even grief, in this realization can be quite disturbing to balance of mind.

The Central Australian indigenous culture has embedded within it laws that set out the basis for handling offenses against human life. This law operates (and has done so for a very, very long time) upon a system of negotiated physical "bloodletting" as acts of reprisal and reparation. The peoples of the Mediterranean had and may still have similar systems. Some of that system is depicted in the acts of Orestes: his crime, his pursuit, arrest, and trial, as is revealed in the theatre of Aeschylus's trilogy, *Agamemnon*, *The Libation Bearers*, and *The Eumenides*.

This brief introduction to a selection from my performance work, *The judgment of Electra*, is not the place to detail how ancient Mycenaean/Grecian law and present indigenous Australian customary law works. There may be similarities or affinities in those customs. Suffice it to say that I have for twenty-five years been involved in, and witness to, how such matters proceed locally.[3]

There have been occasions when Australian Aboriginal men and women have challenged the authority of the British crown to intervene in or supersede indigenous law practices, especially where it concerns punishment, retribution, or settlement of offenses inflicted upon Aboriginal people by Aboriginal people. Some of this history and present confusion is highlighted in Kieran Finnane's book *Trouble: On Trial in Central Australia*.[4] Her insightful book is an account of several significant cases brought to trial in Alice Springs Supreme Court over the last few years. Those cases include murder, manslaughter, or deliberate injury resulting in death. The cases involve black-on-black, black-on-white, and white-on-black offenses.

All cases also involve significant degrees of intoxication, as well as conflict and confusion in cultural law and in moral values and heart-wrenching uncertainty in the community about how to respond to such bewildering and tragic events. Bewilderment is mixed up with community accusations of racism, prejudice, fear. Strident oppositional schizoid thinking is a part of our town's troubled mental and emotional atmosphere. Magical thinking and sorcery is sometimes invoked as the cause of death, though the facts clearly point to excessive intoxication and ungoverned rage. Escalating accusations of sorcery become justifications for further acts of murder, yet so much takes place in an ordinary kind of way.

> Trouble erupts on days that are like other days in almost every respect until those moments from which there is no turning back. This is part of what

I've realised as I've been going into court, that the context of most crime, even the most serious, is ordinary, which is not to say untroubling ... Up close, as women and men die or are injured at the hands of another, categories and generalities disappear ... This goes for the complex matter of consideration of Aboriginal law too, by which I mean a cultural setting far broader than, and in the twenty-first century necessarily excluding, the tribal corporal punishment which those words conjure.[5]

Psychologically speaking, the complex and "ordinary" local mix includes dissociation, denial, intoxication, impulsive actions and reactions, intense episodes of communal anger, depression and anxiety – with minimization of personal culpability. We experience volatile violence, often inflicted on close family members, and we experience suicides of young men and women who are kin to us. It is for this reason that I sometimes think that our people here, both black and white, are caught up in a plague of collective, enculturated borderline disorders. This is a condition of psychic and social anguish that may well be a consequence of the strange ruptures of realities that took place as the white men, first on horses and then in trucks, pressed ever farther into the indigenous world. This is a condition of merciless, confusing, reciprocal traumatization, depicted starkly in the 2017 Central Australian film *Sweet Country*.[6]

Kieran Finnane's accounts in *Trouble* reveal how, in some cases, the Aboriginal justice process is distorted by a way of thinking that seeks either to deflect responsibility or to invoke spirits or spiritual powers as explanations for assaults, accidents, manslaughter, or retribution. In the story of Orestes and his family, I also see the invocation of traditional law and ancestral spiritual powers to explain and justify abductions, sacrificial killing of young women, and crimes against family and kin – crimes that the Greek Erinyes, as guardians of maternal law, consider to be the worst of human acts. I write this as someone who is caught up in a similar contentious process. My interest is neither detached nor academic. I am not attempting here a scholarly analysis of ancient Greek law. Writing *Electra* is a device to help me focus on local problems of bicultural justice that defeat most of us, including magistrates and lawyers.

Australia has its share of immigrants from Sicily, Greece, the Balkans, Lebanon, Syria, Vietnam, Somalia, Sudan, Ireland, all regions where interfamily confrontations, transgenerational trauma, and cultural justice follow patterns that might be familiar to Japaljarri and the Aboriginal customary law that he and his kin follow and negotiate. The disorder, the borderline conflicts, the confusions, the choices, the potentials, all combine to compose the picture of disturbed reality behind Japaljarri's story and painting of *Eagle and Crow: The Life of a Man*.

The issues turned over into the hard light of day by Kieran Finnane's *Trouble* are neither abstract nor dissociated from the harsh light of our local reality. It is hard to live in and live with the clash of ancient Australia and the modern politick, a form of bureaucratic organization designed to govern compliant peoples who understand the social contract. Japaljarri's kin are not compliant and are perhaps puzzled by the contemporary Australian social contract and are resistant to its laws. It is harder still to think clearly and take useful action when one's feelings are caught up in a mostly unconscious mess of cultural complexes.

In short, it is difficult to grasp the complexity of the struggles between indigenous lore/law and Australian/British lore/law. It is distressing to live with the corrupted ferocity of the blunt ideas and bewildered acts of lawlessness committed by mixed-up black and white persons, many of whom are drunk when bad things happen.

Finnane's accounts, her laying bare of genuine conflicts of understanding in law, justice, and retribution, led me to Athens 500 BCE. I turned to history for guidance. I turned to Aeschylus's drama of the arrest and trial of Orestes. The Greek trilogy, *The Oresteia*, highlights contention between custodians of two customary laws of that time. The human condition in Aeschylus is not quite the same as the Australian situation; nevertheless, there is some subliminal resonance.

Aeschylus's drama turns around a series of intra-family and transgenerational crimes. The tragedy crystallizes around incidents of the Trojan War and interpretations of justice as understood in Aeschylus's times by Athenian law, mixed in with magical thinking and attribution of cause to spiritual powers/divinities. The pre-Athenian and probably pre-Mycenaean maternal family law opposed the slaughter of women and children and the spilling of the blood of one's own kin. The Erinyes, in their incarnation as Furies of retribution, accuse both Agamemnon and Orestes of offending the most ancient forms of good order, in particular the murder or desecration of mothers and daughters. The Mycenaean warrior kings and priests have their own view of what is right. They have their own interests, tending toward the interests of the fathers and sons – and colonizing empire.

As a meditation on the Central Australian condition and, perhaps, the ancient and modern conflicts and atrocities elsewhere, and inspired by Kieran Finnane's court reporting, I began to rewrite the Athenian saga of the family of Atreus as a theatre work according to my own interests. It has become twelve tales awaiting a full performance, perhaps once again in the Alice Springs rock quarry where *Persephone's Dog* was performed.

Synopsis

In the original knotted cluster of mythic tales and theatre works about Orestes/ Electra and their ancestry there are variations at every turn around who did what to whom and how. I have followed a line that suits my purpose.[7] This synopsis of my version gives a context for the text of *The judgment of Electra*.[8]

1. Orestes (according to a custom described by Homer) pours his blood into a pit at the grave of his father, Agamemnon, invoking the ghost to appear. Agamemnon's ghost urges Orestes to vengeance. Electra is present. The story unfolds.
2. Orestes has been arrested for the murder of his mother. He appears at the "supreme court" (in Athens). The trial takes place in a dreamlike manner.

The Erinyes are present. Various segments of the story are told by those who took part in this generational saga – Orestes, Electra, Helen, Clytemnestra, and others – partly as though giving evidence, partly in dissociated reverie. Aided by Pythia of Delphi, Themis as an original creation being (now an aged woman in a wheelchair) tells an historical contexting narrative. They tell of a catastrophic flood and the fate of the survivors, ancestors of Electra and Orestes. Themis, according to myth, set in place laws of "good order" to govern human behavior. Generations continue. Specific crimes break the order. The grandfathers of Orestes and Electra, the two brothers Atreus and Thyestes, commit further crimes against each other. In revenge, Atreus deceives Thyestes into unwittingly eating his own children. Thyestes, in disgust, goes into exile. He then has an incestuous relationship with his daughter, Pelopia. She becomes pregnant. She abandons her infant son and suicides. (Some say she "married" Atreus and the suicide took place when she later discovered the identity of her son as Aegisthus.)

3. The sons of Atreus – Agamemnon and Menelaus – marry twin sisters, Clytemnestra and Helen. Helen betrays her husband Menelaus, fleeing to Troy with her lover, Paris. This provokes the war with Troy. The Greek commander Agamemnon is compelled by "religious" customary law to sacrifice his daughter Iphygenia to further the war. The rest is history. Ten years later Agamemnon returns.

4. In the background is the convoluted story of Aegithus. You have to know this. This part of the story is usually cut from the record. Aegisthus is the incestuous son of Pelopia and Thyestes, remember? Thyestes unwittingly ate his two sons, cooked up by his brother Atreus. In true mythic pattern the baby boy is found by goatherds who bring him up, suckled by a goat/*aigos* – from which his name is derived. At adolescence, they hand him over to the local warlord/king, Atreus, who is, in fact, his uncle, though no one acknowledges this.

5. A strange triangular relationship develops between Aegisthus and Atreus (now his foster father) and Thyestes (his biological father). Atreus commissions Aegisthus to assassinate Thyestes. Their true identities are discovered (in true tragic fashion), and the delinquent Aegisthus, turning the tables, murders Uncle Atreus instead of his own father. If you are losing the plot on this, do not worry, even a psychoanalyst would have trouble writing it up as a case history.

6. In due course and perhaps with the intention of revenge, Aegisthus becomes the consort/lover of Clytemnestra while her husband is away in Troy. Aegisthus and Agamemnon are cousins in a rather distorted way. Aegisthus and Clytemnestra conspire to assassinate Agamemnon on his return from the war, which they carry out. Electra witnesses that murder. The boy Orestes, Clytemnestra and Agamemnon's son, is spirited away for safety. (Some say by Apollo in disguise.)

7. Orestes returns home as a young man to fulfill his obligation to male/Mycenaean customary law. He executes his mother and her partner in crime, Aegisthus. Orestes is pursued by the vengeful Furies/Erinyes, protectors of

maternal wellbeing. In Aeschylus's story, Orestes, in high paranoia, turns himself in at Delphi, seeking asylum from the Furies. Apollo sends him to the goddess Athena, in Athens, to be brought to account.

8. In Aeschylus's play, Athena highlights the contradictory pressures to which Orestes is expected to conform. Seeking a fair resolution to a long and cruel family saga, Athena establishes a jury of twelve citizens, perhaps for the first time in that city – the birthplace of "democracy." In my version, Electra takes the place of the divine Athena. Electra pleads her brother's case. At Athena's quietly internal bidding, Electra finds a mind of her own and a discernment by which to judge the case, freeing herself from the paralyzing compulsion to follow contradictory cultural laws. She, like Aeschylus's Athena, makes a judgment for compassion and balance.

A comment on family trouble

To my mind, Electra's plea parallels the man in Japaljarri's story of Eagle and Crow. The man realizes after many trials that he has to think for himself; he can no longer blame others or excuse crimes committed by himself or his family. In Central Australia this Greek-like contentious confusion is with us. Many are fully aware of the balancing procedures needed to seek due settlement for crime. Indigenous custodians of custom sought for many years, especially through the 1990s, for a balanced compromise of the two laws. The judiciary of Australia, for a while sympathetic, were unable to engage in compromise or make significant negotiations based on recognition of how indigenous law might operate with satisfactory reconciliation outcomes, albeit in difficult contemporary circumstances. Finnane writes to this matter in *Trouble*.

Recent events in Australia are turning around a proposed revision of the Australian Constitution that would recognize and acknowledge the prior existence of the indigenous people. Events indicate a political ambivalence, with political representatives unable, so far, to acknowledge and negotiate the reality of indigenous custom, or adequately to recognize, in the Constitution, the originality of indigenous peoples. This is no simple matter. In my experience the inconstant and ragged failure to recognize and manage the difference consciously has led to oppositional defiance and underground aberrations of violence, such as that revealed in the case stories in *Trouble*.

Furthermore, as Finnane shows, a relentless mania of drunkenness makes clear judgment very hard for us all, in this Central Australia, the intoxicated state . . .

In my version, Electra embodies Athena's role in Aeschylus's *Eumenides*.[9] Electra thinks for herself; she shakes off the domination of cultural magical thinking; she rejects (courteously) the attribution of cause to the influence of cultural divinities. It is Electra, in remorse and in recognition of generational trauma, who calls for the citizens to judge the crimes that plague our own city, crimes committed by family members. A daughter of the murdered, sister of the accused, pleads the case for balance. Would that things could be so.

THE JUDGMENT OF ELECTRA

Recitation

1 Electra remembers / assassination by the pool

Electra. When my father came home from the war, my mother met him at
the door.

She took him inside. She took away his sword. She removed his clothing.

She took him to the pool. The pool we used for a bath. She washed him.

A man came out of the dark. He threw a net over my father. Together; they
stabbed him.

My young brother saw our father enter that door. He was then ten years old.

At that moment a man took my brother by the hand, saying, "Boy do not go
into the house. They will hurt you." He took the boy away to a safe place,
saying – "There will come a time when a son must avenge his father.
This is the law. Remember this."

Ten years later, at the age of twenty, my brother returned. In disguise, he came
to the door.

I met him. I let him in, knowing murder is on the way. My mother welcomes
the stranger.

I am standing in the shadow. They are standing by the pool. I see my brother,
turning to our mother. He says – "Forgive me mother." I see the knife.
Her blood spurts like milk, like pus.

Like blood from an old, old wound. He leaves her for dead.

You see that? I see that . . . night after night. My father caught in the net.

His head pulled back; the knife. My mother's blood. Again, again . . .

2 Clytemnestra's ghost

(Electra turns to her mother's ghost suspended before her.)

Electra. Look now, look now, our mother's ghost. Her nightmare speaks . . .

Clytemnestra. I dreamed I gave birth to a snake. I wrapped it. I gave it my breast to suck. I screamed in my sleep. Night after night.[10] For God's sake, I want only to be forgiven.

Electra. My brother . . . see him there, walking through town. Old ladies see him.
They call. "For God's sake boy, you cannot kill your own mother."

Electra. At the wake of the dead, after the funeral, there are times when the clan explodes. Mad men, mad women, driven mad by grief, rain rocks down upon their heads.
Look there. Look there . . . my mother's spirit again, speak.

Clytemnestra. See this wound and say – whose was the knife? Listen you powers of the deep earth, and understand. The man who killed me . . . Let him not escape.

Electra. My brother said – "When my father died. There came a man.
He took care of me. He instructed me in law. He gave me a knife."
And this – listen to this – my brother said . . .

"There are in my skull two countries. In the one, these furious mothers. A warm dark music here. It suckles me. My sorry mother, wronged and murdered, requires right action.
I ask no exception to that rule."

"There are in my skull two countries . . .
Here (my brother said), sharp-edged men call for retribution. Two laws at war in my skull."
So said my brother Oreste.

Electra pauses. – she gazes into the line of ghosts of the women in her family.
Her mother Clytemnestra, her sister Iphygenia, Helen, Aerope, Pelopia, the daughter of Thyestes.

I see a long line of ghosts. Look, that poor young mother hanging there. Pelopia.
How many murders flowed into your womb . . . How many flowed out?
Look there; look there . . . long lines of family trouble.

3 This gray-eyed woman

Electra. When all is said and done, in this judgment, I turn to the women.
You who care for my mother's pain, you who would execute my brother.
This is not his fault. He is caught in a net. He is pulled down by this family,
     by generations; their killing, their cruelty, their crime.

Call the ghosts of our family. Bring them all in. Let them all stand trial for
     this ghastly thing.
Yet – who is to judge this thing? No holy book, no heavenly gods have the
     brain to judge this thing. If this man is to be judged, he must be judged
     by the people who live with these crimes.
We, who live in the shame of these crimes.

*Electra waits for a response from the people. Nothing. No one speaks. No one comes
forward. Electra turns as though to leave – she pauses, listening to a voice.*

I heard a voice speaking to me. It was as though a gray-eyed woman were
     whispering in my ear – "Electra. Go back; go back before the crimes
     of your ancestors. Find the mind of your own. Do not ask anything of
     them. Reach in. Find your sharp heart. Unknot all this. Decide this case
     Electra. Decide as you, today, think to decide."

4 The judgment

Electra. *Assuming composure for the judgment, indicating the family gathered, the
living and the dead.*

Here my father. Here my mother. Here my sister . . . My brother.
The quality of mercy is upon my mind.
And I, Electra, said to the women, custodians of their own and old law.

"How many of you sit in your cave beneath this hill?" And they said –
     "Twelve."
And I said – "I acknowledge you. Your sorrow, dear ladies for the loss of the
     order you set in place so long ago. Jealousy, ladies for the blue-eyed gods
     who came and took away so much, ruined your cave beneath the hill,
     cut up the rocks . . ."

"Hunger, dear mothers; for you scratch through rubbish for your food.
Loss, grandmothers; of all the gifts you brought mankind.
Grief, dear mothers; for all the young girls.
Confusion ladies – worst of all – this confusion."

To you all I say; today. "Select twelve people from the streets. Let them hear
   the account.
Let them judge this man. Let those who live in the shame of this crime decide . . ."

What now you say, what now, who is this girl speaking to us?

I say; "It is not for me to judge . . . and not for ancestral blood-hungry gods.
Who are they to judge our present time?"

Here are twelve people from town. You; the people who live with these
   crimes,
you cast the stone. Look at this man. My brother. Consider the history.
Consider the crime. Consider the facts of our family.

Take up a black stone for his execution. Or take up a white stone for his release.
And you dear ladies, should there be doubt; you will have the casting vote.
(Will you be kindly or will you kill again?)

In the beginning you set out good order. The payment of blood for blood.
This I believed. Then men came from the north with new laws to serve men
   and money.
I believed their mysterious voice, so the blood of war could run its course.
This I believed . . .

5 A mind of her own

Now this, I tell you, this – Electra has found the mind of her own.
This I say. This. "Murder has become the mother of my new mind."
I shall put it to work and sharply. Oresti, brother, speak.

And he said; "For the killing of my mother I am guilty. To my hungry angry
   mother I say this – And to him, my angry bloodied father I say this – All
   of us have been under a spell.
For this I am sorry. Execute Oresti if you will . . ."

"To my sister I say – whether I live or die,
set something clean and new in the body of your sons.
May they never again take up arms against a woman."

Electra. *Turning to the people.*
Cast now your vote. For execution – cast the black stone. For release, cast
   the white.

If the verdict is death – prepare to continue the same old story.
If the verdict is release, prepare to reorganize the governance of this city.

The casting and counting. Electra considers the verdict.

There are six and six. We hang in the balance. Ladies; you decide.
From the shadows came two women. They said to me, "Electra your spirit
   has been so hurt.
Your soul has been so twisted." They laid their hands upon me. They made
   me straight.
They said, "There comes a time when nurture is the only move to make.
To slay this man does nothing for that nurture. The quality of mercy falls as
   gentle rain.
From mercy we take our lead. Oresti is freed."

And when I heard those words from the two women who came from the
   shadow,
I say those same words again; to you. "Our spirits have been so hurt. Our
   souls have been so twisted. There comes a time when nurture is the only
   move to make. Let us become straight."

Would that this our fractured land would heal. Would that we could gather
   the children.
Would that all women could sit down tonight, beneath this hill and not be
   afraid . . .

Electra concludes – she bows and turns into the dark.
End

Notes

1 Craig San Roque, "Eagle and Crow: Andrew Spencer Japaljarri," *Alice Springs News*, December 8, 2015, www.alicespringsnews.com.au/2015/12/08/eagle-and-crow-andrew-spencer-japaljarri. By permission of Craig San Roque as collaborator with Andrew Spencer Japaljarri on the painting and original poster work from which the quote is taken.
2 Kieran Finnane, *Trouble: On Trial in Central Australia*, Brisbane, Australia: University of Queensland Press, 2016, p. 257.
3 Craig San Roque, "Arresting Orestes," in Thomas Singer (ed.), *The Vision Thing: Myth, Politics, and Psyche in the World*, New York: Routledge, 2000, pp. 105–22.
4 Finnane, *Trouble*, p. 257.
5 Ibid.
6 *Sweet Country*, directed by Warwick Thornton, screenplay by David Tranter and Steven McGregor, 2018. See *Sweet Country* (2017 Film) on Wikipedia (en.wikipedia.org/wiki/Sw#655CB3).
7 Electra has been the subject of plays by Euripides, Sophocles, Eugene O'Neill, and Jean Paul Sartre, among others, and a 1962 film by Michael Cacoyannis with Irene Papas as Electra. Each artist has presented a variation on the character, actions, and

circumstances of Electra, within the overall pattern of the House of Atreus, just as I have done here.

8 *The judgment of Electra*, distilling the final three tales of the ten, was first presented in the Olive Pink Gardens by firelight at night, as part of the Alice Springs Writers' Festival, May 2017, with Farida Khwaja as Electra. There are some local references that will be apparent to Alice Springs people, especially Electra's plea to the women who sit beneath the hill. This is a reference to the Athens Acropolis cave associated with the Aeschylus's *Eumenides* and also to Akeyulerre Hill (Billy Goat Hill), a site dear to indigenous women at the Akeyulerre Healing Centre. See www.akeyulerre. org.au.webloc.

9 Jules Cashford, personal communication, March 10, 2018, about the *Erinyes* becoming named as *Eumenides*:

> The Greek texts all say that the name "Eumenides" only came after the judgement of Athena – when the fearful law of blood was relented – and then the "furious" became the "kindly." This also registers in language the transformation of consciousness that must have happened to make such a change in law possible. (I remember it at school, thinking that "things can be changed, then.")

In the Erinyes' metamorphosis into Eumenides, there were instructive shifts in terms, from words connoting darkness to words connoting light. Until the Erinyes became Eumenides, they were described as children of Night (see Aeschylus's *Eumenides* ll.72–3).

The name *Eumenides*, which signifies "the well-meaning" or "soothed goddesses," is a mere euphemism, because people dreaded to call these fearful goddesses by their real name, and it was said to have been first given them after the acquittal of Orestes by the court of the Areopagus, when the anger of the Erinyes had been soothed.

10 Clytemnestra's words in italics are from Aeschylus's play.

9

GETTING A GRIP ON *PROTEUS*

Tracking telos from three snake dreams in Aeschylus's *Oresteia* to his lost satyr play

Craig E. Stephenson

This essay is dedicated to Dr. D. J. Conacher, Trinity College, University of Toronto, and to Virginia Beane Rutter; in memoriam, our Humanitas. With thanks to Ruth Padel, Professor in Poetry, King's College London.[1]

In Aeschylus's tragic trilogy *The Oresteia*, the action is propelled forward by a succession of three dreams.[2] Returning from exile to revenge his father King Agamemnon's death, Orestes plots how to kill his mother. Hearing the Chorus describe Queen Clytaemestra's dream of suckling a snake (in *The Libation Bearers*), he claims to apprehend the meaning, saying, "See, I divine it" (l.542), and the Chorus agrees with his interpretation of the dream as prophesying his own return. But something is left out of his interpretation, something Orestes only experiences later after he has murdered his mother. Her snake resurrects in a second dream, a hallucinatory nightmare that only Orestes can see and from which he flees in terror. In the third dream (in *The Eumenides*), the snake materializes into outer reality for all Athenians to witness. This incarnation of the dream allows Aeschylus to dramatize the collective's response to the dream's demands.

Literary dreams such as these three can share both the teleological meaningfulness and the enigmatic nature of real dreams. Of course, the essential difference is that they do so by the dramatist's design. For psychoanalyst George Devereux, literary dreams are "in part meant to be consciously understandable for theatregoers more or less familiar with traditional systems of dream interpretation," and yet a well-designed literary dream can still "impinge like the blow of a sledge-hammer on the audience's unconscious, compelling each . . . inner self to participate in the dream experience."[3] Hence, a literary dream can both feed the audience's need for meaning and exacerbate its susceptibility so it can readily experience the uncanny and the numinous. The challenge for the writer is to model his literary dreams on real dreams in such a way that they partake of both conscious meaningfulness and unconscious depth. Too much hidden meaning and the audience has every right to accuse the writer of malice and ill will. Too contrived and interpretable and the audience becomes conscious of the device and loses touch with the action it was supposed to serve.

The principles of Jungian dream analysis can shed light on the teleological significances of this three-part chain of dreams in the *Oresteia* and suggest why Aeschylus's literary dreams still "impinge like the blow of a sledge-hammer" on a twenty-first-century audience. Can they also contribute to the current debate about Aeschylus's *Proteus*, the lost satyr play that followed the tragic trilogy in 458 BCE? In his essay "Individual Dream Symbolism in Relation to Alchemy," Jung identifies the satyr play as

> a mystery performance, from which we may assume that its purpose, as eve-rywhere, was to re-establish man's connection with his natural ancestry and thus with the source of life, much as the obscene stories, ασχρολογα, told by Athenian ladies at the mysteries of Eleusis, were thought to promote the earth's fertility.[4]

The Greek tragic paradigm

In her seminal work, *In and Out of the Mind: Greek Images of the Tragic Self*, Ruth Padel explores Greek conceptions of human innerness and the way in which Greek tragedy shaped Western notions of self. She analyzes fifth-century Greek tragedy's biological and daimonological metaphors for what constitutes mind (incorporating both consciousness and darkness) and what it might have felt like for the Greeks to go out of their minds. Two points are particularly relevant for the *Oresteia*. One concerns the primacy of the image in fifth-century Athens:[5]

> before Aristotle, scientists treat an image (the universe governed by justice, for example) as sufficient explanation of the phenomenon (that there is regu-larity and balance in the large-scale changes of the world). The image is not a vehicle for explanation. The image *is* the explanation.[6]

This distinction will be important for understanding the Athenians' final collective response to the manifestation of the Furies as snake.

At the same time, Padel emphasizes that tragedy is only *one* paradigm of the collective Athenian psyche.[7] It explores a specific territory: the causes and results of things going wrong. Its center of attention is inside a human mind as it suffers. In the *Oresteia*, the center of attention is inside Orestes' mind, a mind that will go mad because it exists in a universe in which one god opposes another: Apollo demands vengeance for the death of Agamemnon; the Erinyes counter-demand vengeance should Clytaemestra be killed. This multiplicity of gods and their contradictory demands cause Orestes' mind to become deranged.[8]

The prospective snake-as-dream in the three-part cycle of plays takes place within this tragic paradigm. But in the year 458 BCE, Aeschylus wrote and produced

a fourth play, one that moved the audience into a different dramatic convention
and a different paradigm. To what end and with what effect?

Three snake dreams in the *Oresteia*

Clytaemestra's dream

Clytaemestra's dream in *The Libation Bearers* is the most accessible of the dream
experiences in Aeschylus's trilogy. The account of Clytaemestra's dream is offered
by the Chorus of foreign serving-women as an explanation for the libation rite
that they have been ordered to perform at the tomb of Agamemnon. Clytaemestra
has told the Chorus that she dreamed of giving "birth to a snake" (l. 527) that
"drew in blood along with the milk" (l. 533) when she "gave it her breast to suck"
(l. 531). Subsequently:

> She woke screaming out of her sleep, shaky with fear,
> as torches kindled all about the house, out of
> the blind dark that had been on them, to comfort the queen.
> So now she sends these mourning offerings to be poured
> and hopes they are medicinal for her disease.
>
> *(ll. 535–9)*

Orestes immediately interprets the dream as a foreshadowing of his plan of
vengeance: he is the serpent that will bite its mother. Classicist H. D. F. Kitto
notes a further meaning to the dream and its synchronization with Orestes' return
to Argos: it shows that "the bold act of Orestes [is] also one in which the unseen
powers of the universe are involved."[9] So Kitto finds in the dream the tacit presence of the gods. Devereux is much more inclined to characterize Kitto's "unseen
powers" as internal, personal forces; hence, "not the dream but its interpretation
makes it self-fulfilling . . . Orestes interprets the dream, out loud, in a particular
way so as to make it come true in that particular way."[10] Devereux's notion of an
internalized self-fulfilling prophecy set in motion by the interpreter's word may be
more appealing to a twenty-first-century mind than Kitto's reminder that prophecy implies the presence of the gods. Neither critic, however, seems conscious
enough of Clytaemestra's presence in the dream. Their observations have more to
do with the dream's foreshadowing of dramatic action than with the unconscious
expressiveness of the dream itself and what it reveals about the dreamer.

Clytaemestra's dream is, of course, disturbing. It is explicitly maternal, in contrast to her character in the play. Listen to how the citizens of Argos criticize her:
"That is how she's used her power – the waiting, hopeful woman who plans like
a man" (ll. 10–11). Aeschylus's knowledge of dream psychology is nowhere more
evident than in the devising of this dream for his aggressive, axe-wielding queen,
a dream that reveals her repressed femininity. The appropriateness of this maternal
dream-imagery can be appreciated by contrasting Aeschylus's version with the

account of the same dream in Stesichorus's *Oresteia*, in which "she [Clytaemestra] dreamed there came a serpent with a bloodied crest and out of it (the crest) appears a Pleisthenid king."[11] Here, the serpent is clearly the murdered Agamemnon, and Orestes as avenger comes out of his bloodied skull like Athena from the head of Zeus. The dream expresses Clytaemestra's fear of a patriarchy that comes seeking revenge. Aeschylus retains the image of the revenging serpent, but his snake symbolizes a fate to which the viperine Clytaemestra herself gives birth; thus, his dream is much more rooted in the psyche of the dreamer, and the fate that is prophesied is one to which she is bound by blood and milk.

In a Freudian interpretation, Devereux suggests that Clytaemestra's dream reflects a twofold guilt: first, the sense of her failure as a wife; and second, more importantly, the sense of her failure as a mother. Devereux argues that the dream reflects her inhibited maternal instincts and the super-ego's need to confess and atone. In Clytaemestra's case, Devereux finds it telling that she should dream of nursing her newborn child-serpent, seeing as the Nurse reveals that Clytaemestra did not nurse her children:

> . . . darling Orestes! I wore out my life
> for him. I took him from his mother, brought him up.
> There were times when he screamed at night and woke me from my rest; I
>   had to do many hard tasks, and now
> useless; a baby is like a beast, it does not think
> but you have to nurse it, do you not, the way it wants.
>
>   *(ll. 749–54)*

Now, if we believe this spontaneous expression of the Nurse's maternal woe upon hearing the false news of Orestes' death, then Clytaemestra's baring of her breast before the vengeful Orestes becomes an appalling deceit:

> Hold, my son. Oh take pity, child, before this breast
> where many a time, a drowsing baby, you would feed
> and with soft gums sucked in the milk that made you strong.
>
>   *(ll. 896–8)*

That the Nurse, alone on stage, should lie is unreasonable; that Clytaemestra would be capable of such guile should not surprise any audience that has witnessed her ironic declamations. Her dream, then, becomes an unconscious compensatory wish: "she does in the dream what she failed to do in reality."[12] But the giving of her breast to the dream serpent is no more successful than the libation rite that she orders to be performed at Agamemnon's tomb. The self-punitive aspect of the dream becomes in this way prophetic; Clytaemestra bears a serpent that, like an unweaned baby, bites the breast and draws blood.

Devereux, as a Freudian, feels compelled to de-emphasize the prophetic aspect of Clytaemestra's dream in deference to her past guilt. Jung would designate the function of Clytaemestra's dream as "reductive."

> A reductive dream tends . . . to disintegrate, to dissolve, to devalue, even
> to destroy and demolish . . . does more than anything else to undermine
> effectively a position that is too high, and to reduce the individual to human
> nullity and to dependence on physiological, historical, and phylogenetic
> conditions. Every appearance of false grandeur and importance melts away
> before the reductive imagery of the dream which analyzes the conscious
> attitude with pitiless criticism and brings up devastating material contain-
> ing a complete inventory of the most painful weaknesses . . . Everything in
> it . . . is retrospective and can be traced back to a past which the dreamer
> imagined long since buried.[13]

It is misleading to differentiate, as Devereux does, between Clytaemestra's compensatory id-desire for maternity and the punishing response of her super-ego.
Rather, her dream functions as a *simultaneous* negative compensation; that is to say,
it has a negative but nonetheless vital significance for her consciousness. It offers to
consciousness the symbol of the snake.

In Jungian terms, the serpent might represent "a sort of secret attraction to the
missing inner double which one fears and loves."[14] It arouses fear because it is
unknown, and it attracts because it connotes Aesculapian healing, the possibility
of becoming whole:

> The snake of Asklepios was to glitter in a wolf-like nocturnal world and
> yet with its cold body symbolize as it were the warm light of life: a para-
> dox . . . the limits between chthonic darkness and solar radiance are effaced
> in a way that is almost terrifying.[15]

The ambiguity of Greek snake-power is reflected in the double meaning of
pharmakon, which denotes both a "healing drug" and "poison."[16] The temples
dedicated to Hermes, to Asklepios, and also to the chthonic mother goddesses
always had a central pit, cave, or grotto where the chthonic god – often in the
form of a snake – was housed and placated with gifts.[17] The Greeks propitiated
household snakes with bowls of milk, not because they were necessarily loyal
houseguests like dogs or rat-catchers like cats, but because they were uninvited,
unavoidable, and unpredictable cohabitants. The Greeks lived with the daily question of whether and where the household snake might appear. Would it grant a
boon with its forked tongue (associated in Aesculapian dreams with a healing) or
strike with its venomous fangs?

Clytaemestra's giving birth to a snake shows just how extensively she has
rejected her inner life in order to maintain her "outward eminence" as queen.
She gives birth to – externalizes creatively – something absolutely foreign and
nonhuman. She decides to nurture it with her breastmilk, and perhaps because it
has been starved for so long, it is not propitiated but instead bites, drawing blood
with the milk. But if it is venomous, as Devereux argues,[18] then it is venomous only to Clytaemestra as Queen. It seeks integration through the neglected,

instinctual nurturance of the breast, but it will be a painful integration in which the Queen may die.

Of course, the dream is concurrent with the threatening return of Orestes, to whom she gave birth some twenty years ago and whom she has neglected; this is a meaningful coincidence that the playwright would not want us to forget. The dream is both reductive and prophetic: Clytaemestra's psyche is reflected through dream-images of a neglected instinctual life seeking redress, and it is symbolized in such a way that Clytaemestra's future is unconsciously but prophetically anticipated.

Orestes' dream

What Orestes finds in Clytaemestra's dream is a portent: a symbol with which he can identify as the avenging son in a family of vipers. What he finds in the last moments of *The Libation Bearers* is a frightening personal psychic reality that threatens to overwhelm him. Orestes has a "bad dream":

> they come like Gorgons, they
> wear robes of black, and they are wreathed in a tangle of snakes.
>
> *(ll. 1048–50)*

Orestes is awake, but this does not mean that what he experiences is not a dream. Jung observed that "we are quite probably dreaming all the time but consciousness makes so much noise that we no longer hear the dream when awake."[19] In Orestes' case, the Furies simply demand to be heard. They are not experienced as fancies of affliction. By overwhelming consciousness, they become more "clear" and "real" than the "noises" of Orestes' waking life (ll. 1053–4). And admitting that they exist only in his mind does little to diminish their power:

> You cannot see them, but I see them. I am driven
> from this place. I can stay here no longer.
>
> *(ll. 1061–2)*

If this appearance of the Furies can be called a "dream," then, in Jung's terms,[20] it is a "spontaneous self-portrayal, in symbolic form, of the actual situation in the unconscious" of Orestes.

Like Oedipus, Orestes is a tragic figure, doomed to a fate that binds him to his parents. Exiled as a child, he returns to Argos where the claims of both parents threaten to tear him apart. Agamemnon, the father, is omnipresent in *The Libation Bearers*, even though he never speaks a line. His physical presence is established in the first lines of the play and in the use of the tomb as a set piece;[21] his psychic presence is conjured by Orestes, Electra, and the Chorus. Apollo as his Olympian representative compels Orestes to avenge his father's murder, arguing that there is nothing to fear because mothers are not genuine parents.

Clytaemestra, the mother, argues that the blood-tie of mother and son must be honored above the marriage bond; hence, matricide would be a greater crime than Clytaemestra's murdering of her husband. If Orestes violates his maternal blood-tie by killing Clytaemestra, she threatens him with her Furies. If he does not kill her, then he disobeys an imperative from Apollo and will be punished by his father's deities. His heroic quest is incestuously confined to his parents, a quest as double bind that promises no golden fleece and no foreign princess, only madness. As Kitto observes, "Nothing could more forcibly express the bankruptcy of the cosmic and social system of Justice which we have been contemplating."[22]

Orestes' dream shows how disastrously one-sided is his choice to enact vengeance. Having identified himself solely with the claim of his far-from-positive father, he finds himself locked in a dyad in which he is cast as the dream serpent-slayer and in which his mother becomes the viper-dragon that must be slain. As in her dream, Clytaemestra offers her breast to the aggressor, and the infantile quester falters, caught in the grip of an incestuous inertia. Only Pylades' appeal to the authority of the Olympian fathers frees Orestes from Clytaemestra's maternal but deceitful supplication (ll. 900–3). Then, Orestes lops off the head of Clytaemestra (and the head of that other snake [Aegisthus] with one clean stroke), to paraphrase the Chorus's summary of the action. But, like the Hydra, a "tangle of snakes" (l. 1049) emerges dreamlike in the place of Clytaemestra's severed head.

Orestes' snakes are as foreign or alienated as Clytaemestra's. Originally contained in the physical symbol of his mother, the snakes in Orestes' dream are wronged by his one-sidedness and then unleashed by his patriarchal sword. His infantile hero-ego cannot keep them at bay, and so Orestes flees fearfully from the stage in search of Apollo for protection from the reality of his dream life.

The dream of the Furies

Aeschylus's dream-realities become progressively more imposing as the trilogy unfolds. Clytaemestra's dream woke her from sleep. Orestes' dream invaded his waking life. But nothing matches the dream of the Furies at the beginning of *The Eumenides*. Here, dream and conventional reality seem, at first, strangely inverted. The dead Clytaemestra appears on the stage as a dream-figure and participates in a Homeric dream convention in which the dreamers are told by their dream-figure that they are asleep:

> You would sleep, then? And what use are you, if you sleep?
> It is because of you I go dishonored thus
> among the rest of the dead . . . Hear me.
> It is my life depends upon this spoken plea.
> Think then, O goddesses beneath the ground. For I,
> the dream of Clytaemestra, call upon your name.
>
> *(ll. 94–116)*

Clytaemestra's remarks show that she is a dream-figure and that she is trying to wake the Erinyes out of a sleep induced by Apollo. Critic R. G. van Lieshout calls this the only "passive dream" in Greek tragedy – that is to say, the only dream in which a tragedian has used the epic formula of the dream-visitor appearing to the passive dreamer.[23] In terms of the drama it provides something unique: a partially narrated, partially enacted dream-hunt for an imagined Orestes, in which Clytaemestra's castigations serve as stage directions:

> Oh whimper then, but your man has got away . . .
> You moan, you sleep. Get on your feet quickly, will you? . . .
> The beast you are after is a dream, but like the hound
> whose thought of hunting has no lapse, you bay him on.
>
> *(ll. 118, 124, 131–2)*

The Erinyes that invisibly hounded Orestes in the last moments of *The Libation Bearers* are now visible as the Chorus, although they have not yet been awakened. In a collective dream, they haunt an imagined Orestes, and simultaneously they dream of the ghost of Clytaemestra who haunts them, chiding them for dreaming of Orestes (and of her). Their dream sets up a curious conundrum of "boxes within boxes": Devereux writes, "If the Erinyes had not dreamed of Clytaemestra's ghost, her ghost would have remained unoperational. If Clytaemestra's double had not intruded (Super-ego-like) into the Erinyes's dream, the Erinyes would have remained inactive, since Apollo had put them to sleep."[24]

Devereux compares this situation to a painting in which "a man holds a mirror in which he sees himself holding a mirror," and he dismisses the ontology implicit in both the painting and the play as "a priori nonsensical." Critic Wendy Doniger O'Flaherty suggests, however, that Devereux's "grumpy" indictment misses the ontological point: "What is troubling," she says, "is not that [Aeschylus's] dreams expand in ever-widening circles [as Devereux's painting does] but that they twist in upon themselves [like a Möbius strip]," as if the two sides of mind actually have only one surface. "A Möbius strip is a one-sided surface formed by holding one end of a rectangle fixed, rotating the opposite end through 180 degrees and then attaching it to the first end. This form has two sides, but only one surface: it bends in on itself forever," like the ouroboros.[25]

The opening of *The Eumenides* is disturbing because it is no longer possible for the audience to differentiate dreamer from dream, consciousness from the unconscious. What was inside is now outside; what was dead is again alive; what was male – the Apollonian demand for heroic vengeance – is suddenly shadowy and female, the thirst for bloody revenge. The snake as resident god inside the Greek home, as daemon inside the male Greek mind, manifests itself in the outer world. Progressively, through Aeschylus's three plays, the Erinyes as chthonic goddesses have acquired a presence as compelling as Apollo's, and their dream presence has gained an ontological status equal to that of conventional reality.

The three snake dreams have accumulated such power through the course of the trilogy that, amazingly, the chthonic rivals the Olympian. Even the decision of the Athenian court reflects this surprising deadlock of primacy: listening to the testimony of Apollo versus the Furies, the jury of Athenian citizens splits their vote, six to six.

Four conclusions

What happens to Orestes?

Each of the three plays of the *Oresteia* has been structured around a main event that occurs two-thirds of the way through the play: the murder of Agamemnon, the murder of Clytaemestra, and the moment when the court of Athens must convict or acquit Orestes. The remaining third of each tragedy is then devoted to exploring the consequences of that event and its implications for the future of the principal character. But by the end of the third play, who is the principal character?

In a curious way, by the time the court reaches its verdict, Orestes is no longer of primary importance to the trilogy that bears his name. The verdict frees him to return safely to reclaim Argos. He is "off the hook," though it may be harder for a modern audience than a classical Athenian one to feel that justice has been well served by Athena's patriarchal legal arguments and decisive tie-breaking vote. Significantly, Orestes bids everyone "farewell" and gratefully slips away, relieved and eager to depart.

In other tragic renderings of Orestes' story, in Euripides' *Orestes*, for example, the young hero remains forever in his "dark hurt." Trapped somewhere between Argos and Athens, he is recognized as polluted and contaminating, and the people threaten him with death by stoning.[26] And in *Iphigeneia Among the Taurians*, Euripides imagines an Orestes who completes the journey to Athens to find:

> At first no host received me willingly.
> I was hated by the gods. Some had respect and pity,
> and set a table for me as their guest:
> a separate table, alone, under the same roof as them.
> By their silence they built up the feeling
> I couldn't be spoken to
> so I was apart from them in food and drink.
> Each had pleasure of Bacchus
> filling an equal amount for all, but into private cups.
> I didn't think it right to question them, my hosts.
> I was my mother's killer. I hurt in silence,
> pretending not to notice. I cried.
>
> *(ll. 947–60)*

Euripides portrays Orestes' world as bankrupt. This is a setting that we are more familiar with, through the writings of Kafka and Beckett: an ironic place of futility and alienation and suffering in which the only answer is silence.

In Aeschylus's trilogy, the god Apollo incites Orestes to kill Clytaemestra. Orestes names Apollo "in chief" as "the spell that charmed me to such daring" (ll. 1029–30). And it is also Apollo and the Olympian fathers whom Pylades invokes in the moment when Orestes finally faces his mother. Likewise, Athena, sister to Apollo, retells the story of being born from the head of Zeus in order to support Apollo's patrilineal argument during the trial that men beget and women merely bear, that the masculine naturally supersedes the claims of all "other" principles. Athena is hardly impartial, then, and her bias eventually gives Orestes the benefit of the jury's deadlock.

A Jungian perspective opens this question further, for Jung would have characterized Orestes' dilemma as being caught between the moral tension of two equally valid positions: one identified with Apollo and consciousness, one with the Furies and dreams and the unconscious. Orestes endures this torture until he can lay it at the feet of the goddess Athena. Orestes remains bound within a legacy of punitive madness, weighed down by the ontological weight of both his actions and his dreaming, until Athena tips the balance of justice in his favor (Erinyes do not instruct murder for murder).[27] But can one imagine other dramatis personae being constellated in this tension? For instance, could Athenians have considered the possibility of, not Olympian Athena, but the Titaness Themis appearing *apò mēkhanês theós* to preside over the trial? Or, would they have noticed that, curiously, in the first two lines of *The Libation Bearers*, Orestes thought to invoke not Apollo but Hermes, the bridge-maker and intermediary between the chthonic and Olympian worlds:

> Hermes! God below the earth, protector of my father's power,
> become my saviour, fight beside me as I ask you now.
>
> *(ll. 1–2)*

Of course, neither Themis nor Hermes appears within the classical Athenian tragic paradigm of this trilogy, but it is interesting to note their absence.

When Orestes leaves Athens, his personal dilemma is not so much resolved as passed on to Athena, now as a collective problem, in which she and the citizens that bear her name are implicated. To the audience in the year 458 BCE who watched twelve Athenian forefathers as jurors cast their votes, the question in the last moments of the play must have struck suddenly very close to home: how to protect Athenians from the consequences of Athena's having ruled in favor of Apollo and the patriarchal, against the chthonic and the feminine?

What happens to the snakes within the tragic paradigm of the trilogy?

Athena is caught in an impossible dilemma as she is left by Apollo to face the primal outrage of the Erinyes. The angry Chorus of the daughters of Night accuses her and the younger generation of Olympian gods of having "ridden down the laws of the elder time." In retaliation, they threaten to lay their curse on the land. Athena invokes both Zeus and Persuasion: she firmly threatens the Erinyes with Zeus's thunderbolts, and she also offers them refuge from their sense of exile, an underground place (appropriately for their snake-likeness) within the city, beside the house of the founding King Erechtheus. On the one hand, if they accept, they are forbidden from inciting rage between Athenian citizens and are only permitted to manifest their terrifying bloodthirst in the context of war wherein Athenian males can direct their fury outward in defense of the polis. On the other hand, Athena welcomes them as "guests of the state" and even employs the metaphor of land-holding, proposing that the Furies will be incorporated into the city (and into Athenian collective consciousness) "in all justice, with full privilege." Finally, Athena takes up the magical power of words to affect the divine, propitiating the dreadful Erinyes by addressing them as "these Kindly Spirits" (l. 993).

Jung recognized the possible value of apotropaic thinking, of how with a word or a mandala image one might construct "a *sulcus primigenius*, a magic furrow around the *temenos* of the innermost personality in order to prevent an outflowing or to guard by apotropaic means against distracting influences from outside."[28] But Jung could also express dissatisfaction with apotropaism as a dangerously hubristic attempt to grapple with irrational powers housed within the unconscious. In this regard, he writes about the clever but ineffective use of mere euphemism, "giving a bad thing a good name in order to avert its disfavor," "disposing of these things with a 'nothing but' explanation,"[29] constructing a "convenient rationalistic conceit . . . [for] banishing the mysterious gods with a word."[30] Athena's word-strategy draws a magic ring around the Furies as she attempts to contain their threat, and once contained, she then wisely and persuasively integrates them as "Kindly Spirits" into the Athenian *imaginaire*.

The three-day Athenian festival of Dionysus called Anthesteria or the "Older Dionysia" included the "most polluted day" of the Athenian year when, it was said, "All Athenians are Oresteioi."[31] If the audience at the "Great Dionysia" watching the original production of the *Oresteia* in the year 458 BCE experienced catharsis, it must have been in part through this identification with Orestes and his dramatic deliverance from the transgenerational curse on the house of Atreus, but also, and more fearfully, through witnessing the deliverance of its own polis from the curses threatened by the Furies. Aeschylus led his audience through a teleological progression from chaos to justice and on a larger, more expansive ordering of its cosmology. Philosophically, he was privileging the increasing ontological claim of the snake dreams, so that, by the third play, the Athenian jurors and the Athenian audience could see what earlier Clytaemestra and Orestes could only describe as dreamt. Psychologically, he was resolving the blood conflict, not by expelling the threatening foreign element from the city but by incorporating it so that, at the end of the trilogy, the final procession leads the propitiated ancient daughters of Night to a subterranean hold deep within Athens.

And yet the theatrical experience Aeschylus devised over fifteen centuries ago didn't end with that moment. In the fifth-century BCE theatre festival of the

Greater Dionysia, the trilogy of tragic plays was always followed on the same day by a fourth piece, a satyr play.

Satyr plays: stepping outside the Greek tragic paradigm

With so few satyr plays remaining extant (Euripides' *Cyclops* is the only complete surviving specimen), scholars, reluctant to speculate, have traditionally downplayed their significance. As a result, Wikipedia (accessed May 1, 2017) resorts to classifying the plays as "tragi-comic," which confines them to the Aristotelean binary. However, recent scholarship carefully differentiates the satyr play from both tragedy and comedy and suggests crucial functions that satyr plays may have performed in the Dionysian festivals in early fifth-century BCE Athens.

François Lissarrague and Mark Griffith have catalogued the distinctive features of the genre. The satyr settings are more often rural or exotic; that is to say, the plays are set in liminal territories, far from the cities and royal palaces of tragedy and comedy. Comedies parody tragedy, make reference to present reality, including current-day political figures, and address the audience directly (that is to say, drawing attention to comedy's artfulness). However, satyr plays hold to the tragic trajectory, including complete respect for the fiction enacted on the stage. The humor of satyr plays resides only in the additional presence of the satyrs, in taking the well-known tragic story and introducing into it a group of satyrs who react to the situation in their own peculiar fashion. Griffith puts it succinctly: "Take one myth, add satyrs, observe the result. The revisioning of myth is through this specific filter. The joke is the incongruity."[32] The satyrs are performed as

> subhuman yet wholly "daimonic," and physically gifted beyond the capabilities of human beings . . . the Athenians seemed to find them strangely good to think with, and to "play" with: an unusual and intriguing kind of *mimesis*. *This was not a marginal activity.*[33]

For their satyr plays, writers employed the same legendary heroes and dramatic circumstances as in their tragedies, and their main characters retained a serious composure. The shift in tone derived only from the commentary of the Chorus, which could sound wild, undignified, naïve, greedy, cowardly, drunken, or playful. The Chorus members were typically costumed with horse ears, *perizoma* (shorts) with attached *phalloi*, and long bushy horse tails. Their elderly Chorus leader, often a Papposilenos or Old Silenus, was iconically ugly and jovial, tipsy and inappropriately (for an old man) priapic. It was this undifferentiated libidinal lack of deportment, the regressive erotics and giddiness of a lewd but harmless adolescent horde, more than human but at the same time less socialized, that countered the otherwise elevated tone. For instance, in Euripides' *Cyclops*, Odysseus must (once again) save his men, trapped in the cave, from being devoured by Polyphemos; the subversive tone is established by the addition of a band of satyrs who are enslaved to the giant and who tend his sheep; they have no fear of being devoured themselves, so they demonstrate no particular empathy with the Greeks but like to drink wine and sing songs. They are relieved to be freed eventually from their toil for Polyphemos, but the outcome feels inconsequential. The effect is not so much comic relief as dialectic distance, one foot in and one foot out of the tragic paradigm. As Lissarrague observes using a metaphor from music, the chosen tragic strain or leitmotif established in a tragic trilogy is performed a fourth time but now in a different key.[34]

Getting a grip on the lost Proteus

Aeschylus was an acknowledged master of the satyr play, but the play that followed the *Oresteia* is lost. Only two lines survive:

> A wretched, miserable pigeon, trying to feed
> After its ribs have been smashed by the fans winnowing the grain.
>
> *(fragment 20, p. 165)*

The content for this metaphor is not clear.

It is known that the cast of characters included Proteus and his daughter Eido/ Eidothea, Menelaus and Helen, and a Papposilenos and his Chorus of satyrs. Possibly, the play depicted Menelaus on his journey back from Troy, as recounted by Homer in Book 4 of the *Odyssey*, in which Menelaus (traveling presumably with Helen) finds himself stranded in Egypt on the island of Pharos and forces Proteus to reveal which gods have run him aground. The other possibility is that Aeschylus dramatized an anecdote from the sixth-century poet Stesichorus's poem *Palinode*, in which Menelaus, on his journey home and shipwrecked in Egypt, finds Helen waiting for him there. Either way, there is textual evidence to suggest that Aeschylus foreshadows his satyr play about Menelaus and shape-shifters by emphasizing in the first play of the trilogy, *Agamemnon*, the importance of Menelaus's journeying back (ll. 674–80).

Since the satyr play is entitled *Proteus*, Aeschylus surely cast the old man of the sea as the essential catalyst to whatever expansive revelation confronts Menelaus in Egypt. The liminal Proteus resides on the remote island of Pharos, one day's journey from the Nile. His daughter reveals to Menelaus that her father rises each day from the sea and naps among the coastal rocks, surrounded by his seal-subjects. Anyone wishing to know the future should try to catch hold of him at that time. Proteus has the power to assume every possible shape – lion, snake, boar, or water – in order to escape the necessity of prophesying, but if he is held fast until he tires, he will resume his appearance and answer truthfully. If Aeschylus followed the Homeric anecdote, then his Menelaus would have held his grip on Proteus as he writhed and roared and hissed and dissolved until the shape-shifter exhausted himself, and then he could pose his question. Proteus would have revealed that Menelaus had hubristically neglected to make offerings to Zeus and the other gods before setting sail from Troy, so that he must now sacrifice a hekatomb in Egypt before they will grant him his homeward journey. Proteus would also have revealed to Menelaus the murder of his brother Agamemnon and have mentioned the possibility that the house of Atreus may still be put to right by Orestes.

But Aeschylus could also have placed Proteus at the center of his satyr play in order to set the entire *Oresteia* on its ear. For according to Stesichorus, before Helen was abducted, Hermes secretly brought her to Proteus for safekeeping (or when Paris and Helen stopped in Egypt, Proteus kept Helen there), thereby protecting the sanctity of her marriage to Menelaus, while Zeus sent Paris on his way to Troy with a phantom. Only during his difficult journey back from Troy does Menelaus fortuitously discover Helen waiting for him in Egypt. Euripides took this detail from Stesichorus for his play *Helen*, and it is also picked up and discussed by Herodotus (*Histories*, Book 2). The story throws into question the entire significance of the history of Helen and the Trojan war: the difficult gathering of the Greek army, the launching of the battleships with the blood sacrifice of Iphigenia, the long years of siege, and the brutal sacking of the city, to say nothing of the revenge murders of Agamemnon and Clytaemestra.

We can then add to this mythic shift the humanoid presence of Pappasilenos and the Chorus of satyrs, who perhaps articulate with drinking and song and dance (but inadvertently, without empathy, without identification and cathartic release) the incongruity and pitiless expansiveness of the subject matter that was the tragic *Oresteia*. Just as important, Aeschylus's satyr play reinserted Dionysus into the center of the theatrical experience by making even more explicit the actors as players, not as comedians drawing attention to the unreal artifice of the stage, but as liminal beings honoring the god by giving themselves over to performing Otherness as if possessed. An Athenian male citizen performing as a Chorus member in Aeschylus's *Oresteia* would have played, in one day, four roles: a male elder of Argos, an Asian serving-woman, a Fury, and then a satyr.

If there is a telos-like progression from three to four plays, then perhaps it is implicit in the movement from the three snake dreams in the trilogy to the shape-shifting Proteus (or even the shape-shifting Helen) of the fourth play. In the tragic paradigm of the trilogy, the ontological division between the snakes in the mind and the Furies outside the mind dissolves when inner and outer are suddenly revealed to be a single surface, bending in on itself. Then, like an ouroboric snake, the satyr play advances on the *Oresteia*, devouring its own story.

Notes

1 The following is a list of works and personal correspondences that I don't cite but that I found inspirational and worthy of imitation: Desmond Conacher, *Aeschylus's Oresteia*, Toronto: University of Toronto Press, 1987, as well as personal correspondence on September 5, 1985; Nicole Loraux, *The Divided City: On Memory and Forgetting in Ancient Athens*, trans. Corrine Pache, New York: Zone Books, 2006; Tom Robinson, personal correspondence, December 16, 1997; and Pierre Voelke, *Un Théâtre de la Marge: Aspects figuratifs et configurationnels du drame satyrique dans l'Athènes Classique*, Bari: Levante Editori, 2001.

2 All textual quotations from David Grene and Richard Lattimore (eds), *Greek Tragedies: Aeschylus II*, Chicago, IL: University of Chicago Press, 1960. Third edition edited by Mark Griffith and Glenn W. Most, Chicago, IL: University of Chicago Press, 2013. Quotations are referenced by line number in the text.

3 George Devereux, *Dreams in Greek Tragedies*, Oxford: Basil Blackwell, 1976, pp. xxvii–xxviii.

4 C. G. Jung, "Individual Dream Symbolism in Relation to Alchemy" (1936), *Psychology and Alchemy*, CW 12, trans. R. F. C. Hull, Princeton, NJ: Princeton University Press, 1968, ¶105. (Hereafter references to Jung's *Collected Works* appear as CW and volume number.)

5 Ruth Padel, *In and Out of the Mind: Greek Images of the Tragic Self*, Princeton, NJ: Princeton University Press, 1992, p. 34.

6 Anne Carson also describes the experience of the Greek philosopher Simonides who lived on the brink of this time when pressure was placed on poetry to justify its claim to special wisdom: "Simonides was a forerunner of what is called the Greek 'enlightenment,' that intense period of fifth-century intellectualism when the sophists launched their critique of poetic wisdom and set about devising a science of dialectic to replace poetic teaching." See Anne Carson, "Simonides and the Art of Negative Attention," *Brick*, Winter 1996, No. 53, pp. 4–7.

7 It is important to be specific: "Classical Greek Tragedy" should perhaps more correctly be designated from the earliest surviving tragedy in 472 BCE to the latest in 405 BCE. Aeschylus began producing tragedies very early in the fifth century and had his first victory in the dramatic contests in 484 BCE. See J. R. Green, *Theatre in Ancient Greek Society*, London: Routledge, 1994, p. 1.

8 Aeschylus, as a writer of fifth-century Greek tragedy, works with a specific vocabulary when he portrays this dilemma, as Ruth Padel explains: "It is obvious now, but it wasn't always, that Greek culture and language, and specifically the Athenian culture that these tragedies reflect, is male, and therefore reflects male views of everything: of self, of language, of contrasts like nature and culture, self and other, male and female, outer and inner; and also of mind . . . For the Greek male worldview, anything female, dead, or wild is easily perceived as 'other'" (Padel, *In and Out of the Mind*, p. 9). This is not to dismiss Greek tragedy as merely "patriarchal" and therefore suspect, but we must be mindful that the vocabulary of Greek tragedy and its attendant imagery will be skewed in a very specific way. Jung once suggested that "the theatre [is] an institution for working out private complexes in public" (*Symbols of Transformation*, CW 5, 1912/1956, ¶48). Using the conventions of Greek theatre, Greek men of the fifth century were looking at what they experience as "alien" within themselves. Using the conventions of Greek tragedy specifically, they explore the notion of suffering in the mind. And according to collective perceptions of the female in Greek culture, the mind suffers like a woman. In imagery that informs all Greek tragedies, the mind – like a woman in Greek society, like female sexuality as viewed by the male – is acted upon, invaded, violated, victimized by the outside world and especially by divinity. In *Mysterium Coniunctionis*, Jung considered it necessary to include a parenthetical rider for the reader of his explorations of medieval alchemy: "I am speaking here only of masculine psychology, which alone can be compared with that of the alchemists" (CW 14, 1955/1963, ¶128). A similar rider should be borne in mind as one enters the realm of Aeschylus's *Oresteia*.

9 H. D. F. Kitto, *Greek Tragedy*, London: Methuen, 1939, p. 79.

10 Devereux, *Dreams in Greek Tragedies*, p. 203.

11 Ibid., p. 172.

12 Ibid., p. 213.

13 C. G. Jung, "On the Nature of Dreams" (1945/1949), *The Structure and Dynamics of the Psyche*, CW 8, 1968, ¶¶496–7.

14 Marie Louise von Franz, *Puer Aeternus*, Santa Monica, CA: Sigo, 1970, p. 78.

15 Karl Kerényi, *Asklepios: Archetypal Image of the Physician's Existence*, London: Thames and Hudson, 1960, p. 17.

16 Padel, *In and Out of the Mind*, p. 145.

17 Anne Maguire, "The Crowned Serpent," in J. F. Zavala et al., *Contributions to Jungian Psychology*, Valencia: Victor Orenga, 1990.

18 Devereux, *Dreams in Greek Tragedies,* p. 197.

19 C G. Jung, *Children's Dreams: Notes from the Seminar Given in 1936–1940*, Princeton, NJ: Princeton University Press, Philemon Foundation, 2010, p. 3.

20 Jung, "On the Nature of Dreams," CW 8, ¶505.

21 Jan Kott, *The Eating of the Gods*, New York: Random House, 1970, p. 250.

22 Kitto, *Greek Tragedy*, p. 86.

23 R. G. van Lieshout, *Greeks on Dreams*, Utrecht: Hes, 1980, p. 12.

24 Devereux, *Dreams in Greek Tragedies*, p. 156.

25 Wendy Doniger O'Flaherty, *Dreams, Illusion and Other Realities*, Chicago, IL: University of Chicago Press, 1984, pp. 240–1, 251.

26 Padel, *In and Out of the Mind*, pp. 177–8.

27 Ibid., p. 178.

28 C. G. Jung, "Introduction to the Religious and Psychology Problems of Alchemy" (1935/43), *Alchemical Studies*, CW 13, 1968, ¶36).

29 C. G. Jung, "The Relations between the Ego and the Unconscious" (1928), *Two Essays on Analytical Psychology*, 1969, CW 7, ¶400.

30 Jung, *Symbols of Transformation*, CW 5, ¶576.

31 Padel, *In and Out of the Mind*, p. 182.

32 François Lissarrague, "Why Satyrs Are Good to Represent," pp. 228–36, in John Winkler and Froma Zeitlin (eds), *Nothing to Do with Dionysos*, Princeton, NJ: Princeton University Press, 1990, pp. 235–6.

33 Mark Griffith, *Greek Satyr Plays: Five Studies*, Berkeley, CA: California Classical Studies, 2015, p. 10, italics mine.

34 Lissarrague, "Why Satyrs Are Good to Represent," p. 42.

10

READING JOCASTA

Tamar Kron

Note to reader: In this chapter the author interweaves analytic and subjective reflections with an imaginative account of Jocasta's life, drawn from her novel, Theban Nights.

Jocasta: the destiny of a mother's "fantasy of *tikkun*"

Oedipus's mother is identified in Jungian writings with the Sphinx, the monstrous great mother who seduces her son-lover only to destroy and devour him. My novel *Theban Nights*, a work in progress, is an imaginative attempt to give voice to this denied and rejected mother who dared to disobey the patriarchal oracle. Jocasta, in my narrative, begins her individuation with the wish for a child, which transforms her from a young, obedient, and unaware object to a mature subject fighting for the rights of motherhood. She is empowered by what I call "the fantasy of *tikkun*." *Tikkun*, in the *Kabbalah*, an ancient form of Jewish mysticism, means rectification of the world, the human effort to bring order and peace; the bringing of repair, in the sense of reconciliation between opposites either in ourselves or in the world.

Tikkun in this case, the case of Jocasta, involves getting a love-child from an unloving husband, then losing the child and trying to heal the wounded mother–son relationship. But, tragically, the healing is concretized. When concealment and denial fail, Jocasta acts at last out of her own free choice; instead of waiting for Oedipus to discover the truth, she chooses to end her life with the sick and dying people of Thebes. The analyst of our postmodern time has to take into consideration the impact of archetypes not only on the symbolic level, but also in their chthonic-concrete expression. Thus, contemporary families with single mothers, either actually or psychologically, may enact the archetypal relationship of Jocasta and Oedipus. Wounds of rejection, abandonment, and past traumas can arouse "the fantasy of *Tikkun*," which cannot be realized.

Introducing Jocasta

Allow me to introduce you to the mythological heroine Jocasta, wife and mother of the famous Oedipus, King of Thebes. The well-known myth of Oedipus was, of course, a fertile subject for the ancient Greek poets and for playwrights like Aeschylus, Euripides, and Sophocles.[1] In *Oedipus Rex*, the tragedy written by Sophocles around 429 BCE, Oedipus is the protagonist and his wife-mother Jocasta is a secondary character. His life story and the agonies he suffers are described in full, whereas Jocasta's travails before her marriage to Oedipus are not recounted. We learn only that she married King Laius and bore him a child, and that Laius, fearful that he was doomed to perish by the hand of the child, as predicted by the oracle, orders him killed. Instead, however, the baby is handed over to a shepherd who takes him to Corinth. And the tale resumes when Oedipus, having unwittingly slain Laius and solved the riddle of the Sphinx, is given Laius's widowed Queen Jocasta as his prize. At this point Jocasta disappears from the scene again until Oedipus learns the terrible truth. The catastrophe is handled differently by the various playwrights and poets, as I will explain later.

It is interesting to note that Sigmund Freud attended a wildly successful modern production of Sophocles' tragedy in turn-of-the-century Vienna, and it was this performance and his reactions to it that gave rise to his theory of the Oedipus complex. At the time he had been immersed in self-analysis, as he writes in *The Interpretation of Dreams* and in his letter to Wilhelm Fliess in October 1897:[2]

> A single idea of general value dawned on me. I have found, in my own case too, [the phenomenon of] being in love with my mother and jealous of my father, and I now consider it a universal event in early childhood, even if not so early as in children who have been made hysterical. If this is so, we can understand the gripping power of Oedipus Rex, in spite of all the objections that reason raises against the presupposition of fate; and we can understand why the later "drama of fate" was bound to fail so miserably . . . the Greek legend seizes upon a compulsion which everyone recognizes because he senses its existence within himself. Everyone in the audience was once a budding Oedipus in fantasy and each recoils in horror from the dream fulfillment here transplanted into reality, with the full quantity of repression which separates his infantile state from his present one.

Jocasta and Oedipus, her son-husband, had an afterlife too, as described by Homer in *The Odyssey*, the section where Odysseus encounters various characters on his way through Hades:

> And I saw the mother of Oedipodes, fair Epicaste, who wrought a monstrous deed in ignorance of mind, in that she wedded her own son, and he, when he had slain his own father, wedded her, and straightway the gods made these things known among men.[3]

And their afterlife continues in literature, psychological theory, and ideology to this day. The character of Jocasta, however, has remained for the most part secondary and latent, and yet she exerts an intense magnetic force that I will explore here.

Almost thirty years ago I found myself sitting in the Freud Center Library of the Hebrew University of Jerusalem, trying to write something about Jocasta. At the time I was a lecturer in the Department of Clinical Psychology with a psychoanalytic orientation – long before I became a Jungian – and I was working as a therapist in the open ward of a psychiatric hospital. I had a nine-year-old son and a one-year-old daughter by then and had spent the last few months of my recent pregnancy in the high-risk pregnancy unit, away from home and my young son and away from my work. But I would have paid any price to have my baby. In the high-risk pregnancy unit, I was surrounded by women like me, women who persevered, day after day, with the fervor of pilgrims and never a heretical thought or doubt as to their divine calling. Time lost its ordinary meaning for us. It crept slowly ahead in a single direction – the expected birth. And all of us in the unit were dressed alike in uniform pink pajamas.

The women I treated at the psychiatric hospital also wore pink pajamas, but they were suffering from postpartum depression and an inability to connect with the children they had borne. It was then that I began to write my first book, *Women in Pink*, which dealt with the patients under my care.[4]

But what was it about maternity and the vulnerable womb that I was trying so hard to understand in the character of Jocasta? As I sat in the library, reading through the few articles I was able to find on the subject, I felt thwarted. The so-called Jocasta complex, I discovered, is the converse of the Laius complex, as explained by the psychoanalyst Georges Devereux: it is a "complex of the parent which manifests itself in seductive behavior, particularly on the part of the mother, who is genitally aroused by nursing."[5]

I found this theory pejorative in a misogynistic way, and the other articles I was able to find at the time, a handful at most, seemed to regard mothers in general as the mothers of an individual protagonist and primary subject of research, not as people in their own right. A mother might be a good enough mother, a powerful great mother, a terrible dark unconscious mother, but never a subject as such. The material on Jocasta was so dull I gave up trying to understand what she represented to me in terms of my experience as a therapist and as a mother myself and ended my search. I forgot all about her. That is, until she returned full force, like the return of the repressed.

Around that time I had a young patient who was hospitalized some months after giving birth to her first child. One Friday as I helped her prepare for a home visit, she kept asking questions about my children, and I felt a sort of guilty satisfaction when she compared herself unfavorably to me. I was the good, successful mother; she was the bad, unnatural mother. That night I had a dream:

> *I was rushing down a main street in Jerusalem and noticed that it was deserted and that all the shops were closed. Just then I saw my patient walking toward me. Tamar,*

she said, how come we're meeting today? It's Saturday. And I answered, Because I
promised you. Suddenly I noticed that she was wearing my clothes, my favorite long
blue skirt, my white blouse, and a sweater my mother knitted for me. I woke up,
moved by the dream and a little bewildered.

Later I analyzed it in various ways: As a countertransference dream, in which the
patient represents me and I represent my personal mother; as a projective identification dream, in which the patient interferes with my private life while I take on
her sufferings; and as a Buberian Dialogue dream, which presents the possibility of
a real I and Thou meeting between us.

It was not "the royal road to the unconscious," as Freud held dreams to be,
but an interchange between my Self and the patient in a dialogical dimension. If
I interpreted the dream from the outside I would remain in an I–It rather than
an I–Thou relationship with her and would miss the chance to help her break out
of her isolation. The next time I met with her, she told me she had dreamed she
was sick in the head and retarded. Instead of interpreting the dream for her I talked
about motherhood, about the feelings of inadequacy and isolation many mothers
have, myself included. We spoke about her feeling that something had been taken
away from her and had made her unfit for life. I listened without expectations. As
she grappled with her ambivalence and her own "good–bad" mother polarity, she
was no longer alone in the process and neither was I.

This insight led me to Buber's legacy – the curative force of the therapeutic
encounter.[6] Through Buber I became more and more involved with Jungian psychology and began my training as a Jungian analyst. During my studies in analytical
psychology, I took a course with Erich Neumann's student Devorah Kochinsky on
Neumann's book, *The Origins and History of Consciousness*.[7] In her class each student
chose a chapter of the book to summarize and present to the group. I chose to
compare Freud's exposition of the Oedipus complex and its development in his
An Outline of Psychoanalysis[8] with Neumann's chapter "The Slaying of the Mother"
in *Origins*.[9] I found Neumann's account of the hero's struggle with the sphinx,
the dragon, and the Great Mother far more illuminating than Freud's ideas. But
although Neumann speaks of the sphinx in the guise of the terrible mother as she
appears in Sophocles' *Oedipus Rex*, he never mentions Jocasta by name and I forgot
about her again. And then, in wake of my work as a therapist in the psychiatric
hospital, she floated back to consciousness and I began to wonder why she had
been so largely ignored in the literature of depth psychology, even by Von Franz
and Neumann.

My work at the hospital had led me to write a comparative study of the dreams
presented by women during pregnancy, after birth, and in a state of postpartum
depression. I began reading more analytical works about the feminine, in general, and maternal subjectivity, in particular. Jocasta floated back yet again. I felt
compelled to treat her as a literary and psychological personage this time, not a
mythical character, to imagine her fully as a woman who must undergo a process of
individuation through pregnancy, the loss of her child, and her reunion with him.

She was too remote to communicate her life experience and what she had learned from it, so I would have to enter into a dialogue with her. And ten years ago, I did.

I read everything I could find about life in ancient Greece. The contradictions and ambiguities I found in this greatly admired civilization astounded me. In a secondhand bookstore in the United States I happened on a large dusty volume called *The Topography of Thebes from the Bronze to Modern Times*, by Sarantis Symenongolou, filled with maps and sketches of ancient palaces, graves, and other archaeological proofs of prosperous reigns that coincided with the years when King Oedipus is said to have ruled.[10] This was Jocasta's city, founded by her ancestors Cadmus and Harmonia. Here the mysterious sphinx accosted all who entered. I had to see for myself and so I took a trip to Thebes, called *Thiva* in modern Greek.

In Thebes

And there I was. I unpacked and sat down on the narrow balcony of my hotel room overlooking the main street of the town. A summer breeze ruffled the white curtains behind me, and the live Greek music at the taverna across the way went on until three in the morning. By that time my eyes were drooping but I couldn't sleep. And when I opened my eyes, I saw her by the light of the street lamp, a slender figure with tangled black hair, draped in white.

Theban Nights, Jocasta scene 1

Here I am, she said.

I looked for you all day long, I answered. I found a street named after you, and streets named after all the who's who of Thebes: Antigone, Electra, Pindar, Creon, and Oedipus. There's even a Laius Street.

Why were you searching for me? She asked with surprise.

I've been thinking about you for years. I tried to write a scholarly article about you, but it was so dull and dry I gave up. Then I tried writing a story about you, but the publisher rejected it. He said it was too crammed full of information and your voice was muffled by it. So I thought I'd come here and just listen. Tell me who you are.

I am Jocasta, Queen of Thebes, wife and mother of Oedipus.

The sun is about to rise. I look at her face in the light of dawn.

Once I was beautiful, she says. Oedipus fell in love with me. But now I'm old. I had better leave before the sun rises – I don't want anyone to recognize me.

When will I see you again? I ask.

Come to my palace in the afternoon. I'll be waiting for you. I'll tell you what I can.

Afternoon

It was very hot in Thebes that afternoon. I sat on a little hilltop. Not a soul was in the streets. The young man at the reception desk had said, "You look for antiquities?

Walk around and you find them everywhere." And find them I did, ancient ruins, just out there, unfenced and unmarked, shattered columns, crumbled walls, ancient stone blocks with enormous blood-red poppies growing between them. The museum was closed for renovations. The stone fountain where Oedipus supposedly washed his hands after killing his father is crowned with arches and three sculpted lion heads. Acanthus plants, the spiny leaves of which are imitated in Corinthian capitols, were lovingly cultivated here a long time ago, but now they droop around the dirty fountain.

Where will I find Jocasta? I sit down on a column beside an especially deep pit. The sun begins to set. And there she is, standing before me. Her hair is piled on top of her head and held in place by a golden clasp. Her eyes look bright and thoughtful.

Theban Nights, Jocasta scene 2

How do you see me now in the light of day? she asks.

I see you have suffered, but you have also known happiness. And you are regal and very lovely.

She looks like a marble statue in the rosy twilight hour.

I spent my girlhood in the gynaikonitis where all the women of the household lived. My little brother Creon, my loving playmate, lived with us until one day without warning Father moved him into the andron. He's too old to play with girls, said Father. It's time for him to learn to be a man. And then he was gone. I caught sight of him at a distance, wearing an oversize chiton. I spent my days learning how to cook and weave and embroider, how to wind the peplos just so, with the pleats hanging down from the waist. Girls and even women were not allowed out of the house except on special occasions, festivals and ceremonies and the like. Sometimes I would sit on the roof for hours, gazing over the walls of Thebes at the fields beyond. I had a nursemaid, a dear Phoenician slave named Taliopa. She would tell me bedtime stories, the myths of Thebes, about my ancestors, Aphrodite, goddess of love, and Ares, the god of war, and the alarming fate their daughter Harmonia passed on to my grandmother Autonoe and her sisters, Agave, Ino, and Semele, each of whom lost a child through tragic circumstances. Taliopa slept on the floor beside my bed at night, and whenever I cried out from a nightmare about Ascalpus, the ill-omened screech owl snatching my doll away, she would rock me in her arms and comfort me.

"Well," she would say, "Next time run after Ascalpus – make him bring dolly back. Opa! Here she is, my darling. Nasty Ascalpus has mussed her little peplos. Let's smooth it out. Now hold her tight. Lie down and sleep."

But I couldn't stop crying. He was so dark and ugly, circling overhead and hiding the light with his wings. So we'd get up and lay flowers on Hestia's altar.

And I had nightmares about another winged creature, too, part woman, part lion, who would try to catch me with her sharp talons. I wanted to scream, but I couldn't make a sound; I couldn't breathe. That was the worst nightmare of all. What it betokened, Taliopa wouldn't say.

Mother was acting strange. She had stopped weaving. We could hear music and laughter coming from the andron, but Mother wasn't invited to greet the guests at the banquets anymore. She grew thinner and thinner. Taliopa sent for the pharmica who came to the courtyard in disguise and brewed a potion for Mother, the blood of a young she-goat with crushed cat-claws and sacred ashes from Aphrodite's shrine, which she smeared all over Mother's naked body. But nothing helped. She became so ill she no longer left her room and only sprawled on the couch with her eyes closed.

When I began to bleed each month Taliopa took me to the Temple of Artemis for my dedication to the goddess, holy Artemis, the she-bear, protector of cubs. Poor Mother struggled out of bed and came with us – she wouldn't have missed that for anything.

Not long afterward she sent for Father. He came to our quarters and looked me over. Pretty girl, he said. Mother lowered her eyes. You'll make a fine bride, Jocasta. I've already spoken to your husband to be.

Who is he, Father? Who, Mother? Is he going to take me away? Father just laughed and left us standing there.

Please Mother, tell me. Who is he? Who will I marry?

Your cousin Laius, the King of Thebes, and you will be his queen.

Oh please, by the gods! Don't let him take me away; I beseech you!

She closed her eyes and bowed her head.

Again we went to the temple of Artemis, and this time we sacrificed locks of my hair and my childhood toys: a ball, a hoop, my doll.

That night Taliopa woke me up. I had been crying out in my sleep again, the dream about Ascalpus the owl, screeching and hooting with laughter as he flew over my head. Taliopa wrapped her warm arms around me. "Don't leave me, Taliopa," I said as she rocked me the way she used to when I was a child. "I'll ask Father to let you go to Laius's house with me. Please don't leave!"

The morning of the wedding I kneeled at Mother's feet in front of the hearth and Mother beseeched Hestia to watch over me always. Then I dipped in the nuptial bath and the attendant prayed to Aphrodite and sprinkled water over my naked body to arouse my desire; and then she dressed me in a splendid robe, plaited my hair, and adorned me with jewels. Finally, Mother wrapped the red wedding shawl around me and led me to the andron. Laius, behold your virgin consort, Father said. May Aphrodite bless you with vigor tonight!

How old were you then? I ask Jocasta.

I don't really know, but I must have been fourteen or so. He was at least ten years older. He'd been away from Thebes for a long time, so I had never laid eyes on him before.

And I never saw Mother again until she died. Taliopa stayed with Mother in her gynaikonitis because she was so sick.

The only thing I remember about my wedding night is Laius's heavy body on my back and the pain when he penetrated me from behind. But after that whenever he took me to bed at night he would caress me. I liked the feeling on my as yet undeveloped body. The moon waxed and the moon waned, but the bleeding came each month. I wanted a baby with all my heart. I longed to give Laius a child so he would be pleased with me. I prayed to Artemis. My body was changing. Laius came less often to my bed. He called for me only to join him in the public feasts and then he would stay in the andron with his friends.

But I was lonely and alone. One night I had a terrifying dream. A large black bird was circling overhead, shedding its feathers over me, and finally it plummeted to the ground, and I knew, my mother was dead. In the morning Laius came to bring me the news.

For the first time since the wedding I walked through the gates of my childhood home. The faithful Taliopa came out to meet me and led me to Mother's room. She was lying on the couch with her eyes closed. She suffered horribly in her last days, Taliopa said. She no longer knew where she was.

Did she not call for me, Taliopa? I asked.

Taliopa looked down.

Mother had forgotten me.

No, no, never, Jocasta! Taliopa cried. But you are Queen of Thebes now and she did not dare trouble you. You belong to Laius.

Creon came and tried to comfort me. The closeness of our childhood was restored. In anguish I told him how deeply I longed for a child.

Why has Laius stopped coming to your bed? He is duty-bound to sire an heir with you, his queen, his wife. Creon raised his voice.

He desires young boys, not me, I sobbed. But I will be strong. I will entreat our Lady Artemis and she will intercede on my behalf.

Yes, Jocasta, I say, you turned to the dispassionate goddess Artemis and began to have a will of your own.

She seems younger suddenly. Less care-worn. She smiles at me, a sidelong smile. I continued to beg, I supplicated, but Laius only recoiled. He was cursed, he said, on account of a sin he had committed, and I could never bear his child. Taliopa came to live with me. Creon arranged it. She finally told me about the curse on Laius. On his way to the Nemean games, he abducted young Chrysippus, son of Pelops, the King of Pisa, who had sheltered him in his exile. And after Laius raped him Chrysippus killed himself out of shame.

I was horrified but I refused to accept my fate. With Taliopa's help, I would defy the curse.

Written in Jerusalem

After Thebes

I wrote about Jocasta when I returned from my trip to Thebes. Why was I so determined to bring her to life, to put words in her mouth? After a time, I lost direction again and stopped writing, but sometime later I had the first in a series of dreams about an abandoned child entrusted to my care, and I knew I had to keep writing.

When I was finally able to revisit Jocasta, I wrote a scene in which Jocasta dresses as a boy and, with the help of a palace slave who gets Laius drunk, enters his chamber and effectively rapes her husband in order to become pregnant, much as Lot's daughters raped their father in the biblical story. And again, using a biblical motif, the story of Judah and his daughter-in-law Tamar this time, I had Jocasta ask Laius in his drunken delirium for a memento of their coupling. He gives her his signet ring.

So what kind of man is Laius? One who is afraid of the natural processes of life, afraid of maturation, of siring a son who might kill him. He is a persona, not a real father-king. Jocasta sees the child she bears as belonging to her, not Laius, who never intended for her to conceive. The child is to be her compensation for Laius, but what a tragic compensation Oedipus turns out to be. Compensation that is concrete and violent rather than symbolic is inevitably tragic.

Theban Nights, Jocasta scene 3

Jocasta is pregnant, no longer alone. She will give birth. The pregnancy begins to show.

Whore! Laius pummels her head, her belly. I will have you put to death; I mean it! he threatens.

He is about to kick her in the belly when she presents him with the signet ring.

Laius, in the name of Artemis, I implore you! Look at the ring! Is it yours or not?

Mine, is it? Maybe someone stole it from my room at your behest.

I have stolen nothing. You gave the ring to me yourself five months ago. You didn't recognize me because I came to you disguised as a boy.

What have you done, Jocasta! Liar! Deceiver! Your fate is sealed, whore!

I was the boy the slave master brought to your chamber five months ago, and I asked you for your signet ring as a sign of your love. Yes, Laius. I was the boy. You penetrated me in your drunkenness and sewed your seed. A child grows inside my womb, your son, your heir.

What have you done to me? I am doomed . . .

Why doomed? The child will preserve your name and carry on the reign of the house of Labdacus.

By Apollo, I am a cursed man, and my curse will fall upon you, too.

What is the curse, Laius? Tell me!

How should I tell you? Better that you never know, he moans.

She feels a stirring of compassion for him and opens her arms, but he pushes her away and leaves.

And every night the sphinx returns to Jocasta and lies heavy on her chest. She sends Taliopa with a message to Creon. Your sister Jocasta will soon give birth, and

Laius threatens to kill the child. Help her, she begs you, in your mother's name! Save the baby's life! She will send the newborn to you directly, and you must hand him over to the shepherd who will take him somewhere far away.

A servant presses a poultice of artemisia leaves to Jocasta's belly to relieve the throes of labor. The baby is born into the waiting hands of Taliopa, who cuts the cord and lays him on Jocasta's breasts. Jocasta kisses the tiny hands and feet.

When Laius comes to take the child from her, Jocasta shields him with her body. No, Laius! You will not kill him! Not my son! she proclaims.

I command you, Jocasta, turn him over to me at once! It is our fate; it is the will of the gods!

Let me suckle him tonight, one night, to be his mother. Grant me this.

One night and no more!

Suddenly he leers at the infant and grabs it from her arms. Squeezing the tiny feet together he pierces them with the gold pin from her chiton. The baby screams in pain and blood drips from its wounded heels.

Now his feet will never catch me! He flings the infant back to her and stamps off.

All night long Jocasta feels the baby on her breasts. She suckles him. His smell, his touch envelope her. She knows that he will live. She knows he will return to her one day. She must believe it.

In the morning she kisses him again and again and wraps him in a sheepskin. Taliopa delivers the sleeping baby to Creon's chambers.

Written in Dor Beach

Dream of the hyena

Here I am, at the seaside cottage on the coast, still struggling with Jocasta. Last night I tried to describe how she feels when the baby has been sent away. How she imagines him, exposed on a mountain peak, devoured by wild dogs. Toward morning I had this dream:

> *I'm sitting and writing in a fairly large, unfamiliar room. Then a hyena enters. It looks more like a big dog, but I know it's a hyena, with black fur spotted white. I'm not afraid. I pat it on the back and feel the fur. The hyena pays no attention to me and crawls under the round table in the corner of the room. It stands very still. Then I woke up.*

I researched "spotted hyena" and found that it's the sole species of the *Crocuta* genus, also known as a "laughing hyena," and it really does look like the hyena in my dream. Spotted hyena society is matriarchal. The females are larger than the males and dominate them.

Suddenly I realized that Jocasta – and my identification with her as I wrote – is present in the world of archetypes, gods, incest, and maybe that's what the hyena represents, a world that lurks under the table, threatening my conscious self.

And returning to Jocasta, I know that she is haunted now. She imagines the baby and wishes she had died with him. She tears her clothes, her shawls and belts, her peploi and himations. She stops bathing herself and combing her hair; she refuses food except for a crust of bread with a bite of cheese. No more meat or wine. She stops offering sacrifices on the altar of Hestia. She leaves her room only at night to wander the long corridors of the palace. The sentinels let her pass. The Queen of Thebes is deranged, haunted by ghosts, the ghosts of her grandmother Autonoe and her sisters, all of whom lost their sons. Jocasta envisions them, like her, tearing their hair out and screaming. And the baby on the icy mountain peak, parched and blue with cold, freezing to death and swallowed by the hungry earth. Again and again she recalls the scene of Laius seizing her baby, dangling him by his tiny red feet, and piercing them with the golden pin of her peplos.

Theban Nights, Jocasta scene 4

Fifteen years go by, fifteen times summer, autumn, winter, and spring. And toward the end of the sixteenth summer when the corn is ripe, for the first time since she bore her son and lost him, Jocasta leaves the palace grounds. She joins the women of Thebes in a procession to the Temple of Demeter to celebrate the rite of the mother and daughter who are one, the festival of the Thesmophoria. Jocasta, wearing a long dark mantle, walks among them, carrying the laws of Demeter on her head and offerings for the goddess on her shoulder. At sunset they arrive on a hilltop where each woman in turn casts a live piglet into the Megaron, together with a clay phallus and cakes in the shape of men and serpents. All of these will rot in the pit and will later be mixed with seed to fertilize the earth. After the ceremony the women lie down to sleep in the temple courtyard and Jocasta dreams that she is in a dark cave where she meets the gods of Fear and Death, Phobos and Thanatos, who say to her, Soon death will come to your door again, bearing the mystery of the father who is the son.

On the second day the women eat nothing but sesame cakes with honey, and sitting barefoot on mats of grass, their hair unkempt and dressed in rags, they mourn with Demeter over her daughter Persephone who is held captive by Hades in the underworld. Jocasta weeps and vows to the goddess that she will abstain from meat and wine and intercourse until her son's return.

The third day, the day of the beautiful birth when Demeter is reunited with Persephone, is filled with ribaldry and merriment around a giant bonfire. The women are dressed in white, their hair combed and faces shining. The priestess throws herbs into the fire and then they all feast on roast piglet and drink quantities of wine, all but Jocasta, that is, for she has made a sacred vow to the goddess to abstain from meat and wine and intercourse until her son's return. Yet although she has drunk only water, she too is seized with frenzy.

And suddenly it's over, and as the procession goes down the hill Creon's chariot appears in the distance and Jocasta's heart stands still. What word of her son has he brought her?

My sister, my queen, he says. Your husband, Laius, is dead. Slain at the cross-roads by a band of robbers who disappeared without a trace.

For two nights Jocasta stands vigil over the corpse of Laius, her husband, her king, washed with fragrant water, anointed with oil, adorned with a wreath, a coin in his mouth, boat fare for his journey to the world of the dead. Dead. Dead are her eyes, dead and dry. She tears at her hair with the other mourners but feels no grief for this stranger who begot a son in her womb; no pity for her husband who was killed by a band of brigands on the road. An ignoble end of life. His soul has departed like a little breath of wind.

Before dawn of the third day, Jocasta lights the hearth fire and offers Hestia a sacrifice of renewal. Laius has no heir to offer a funerary sacrifice on his behalf. Creon has taken charge of the kingdom.

All winter long Jocasta abides in her room as befitting the widow of the king, but when the swallows return and the west winds blow, the courtyard of the gynaikonitis blooms with life again. The ladies set up their looms in the sunshine; they weave and sew and prepare a feast; they dance and play their drums and cymbals, flutes, and pipes. But at night Jocasta's sleep is still troubled by Phobos and Thanatos and the dreams that tell her death is on the way, bringing the secret: from the mother's womb came the son, and into her womb the father will return, the father who is the son.

It is not for us to question fate or the ways of the gods, says Taliopa when Jocasta tells her the dream. Come child, she says. Spring is here. You must ask the priestess of Demeter to release you from your vow of abstinence. And so she does, and Jocasta feasts and drinks her fill of new wine night after night and joins the women in their maniacal dances until she falls exhausted on her bed.

But one morning Creon arrives with fateful news: the sphinx is perched on the city gates and swoops down on all men who leave or enter Thebes. Jocasta whispers in his ear: is she here to punish us for abandoning the baby to die on the mountaintop?

Creon shudders. What could I do? I pledged my help, dear sister, and so I called on a shepherd to take the infant there, but a pack of wolves descended on his flock and the shepherd fled. Neither of us is guilty of the infant's death and the father who willed it is now in Hades.

Death fills the streets of the kingdom. The cruel sphinx has devoured many men, and no one dares to walk abroad. Plague and famine spread. Taliopa dies and with her dies the hope of new life in Jocasta's breast. Death has come as in her nightmare, but what of the mysterious message about the father who is the son?

As she stands vigil over Taliopa, Creon arrives. Tomorrow, he announces, I will send out a proclamation that whosoever answers the riddle of the sphinx shall wed Jocasta and rule over Thebes.

Jocasta hangs her head. As you wish, she says. My kingdom shall be his prize and my body his reward.

Written in Santorini

Reflection

I haven't written in a long, long time and I know why. Jocasta is about to be reunited with Oedipus, and I fear I'll sink into a depression when I pick up the story.

I am daunted by what comes next, the encounter between Jocasta and Oedipus and the awakening of her erotic love for him.

During my stay at the 2017 Ancient Greece, Modern Psyche conference in Santorini I had two more recurrent dreams about a child in my care.

> In the first, I'm looking after a blue-eyed baby girl with a bright round face. I take her for a walk on the beach, but she is cranky and starts to cry. Later on we play – maybe she's a little older by then – and in the afternoon I bring her home but her dark-haired father is waiting in a black car, looking furious, and says that he kept calling and calling but I didn't answer. I apologize and say we were busy and I didn't hear the phone ring.
>
> In the second dream, I'm looking after an infant wrapped in a big blanket that is in fact the blanket on my bed here in Santorini. Some children ask me, "How are you going to nurse the baby?" and I say, "Don't worry, I'll bottle feed him." It isn't clear when the mother is due back, but when she comes I return the baby to her and help her bathe him, and hold the towel for her when she takes him out of the tub, and then wrap him in a little blanket and put him in her arms and say, "I'll leave you alone now and let you two get acquainted."

Eroticism is emotional and passionate – not sexualized and instinctually procreative – and there is a big difference between them. Erotic feelings are *normally* experienced by nursing mothers because the baby is an extension of the mother's body and so may arouse what Freud termed *autoeroticism*. It is the intimacy between mother and baby, not just the nursing per se, that is erotic. The baby's very dependency may arouse a mingling of maternal and erotic feelings, and this in Neumann's view is a positive phenomenon as opposed to the negative mother's pathological rejection of the child and the physical aversion she experiences toward it.

As the child grows up the mother's feelings undergo a transformation. Negative feelings come into play alongside positive expressions of child-rearing – annoyance, anger, disappointment, and so on. As the child grows and develops, so does his or her distance from the mother, and the erotic component of the relationship is changed. But if a child is given up by the mother at birth, an idealized image often develops along with fantasies about what might have been and about reuniting with the child one day.

Miriam

A patient of mine comes to mind. I'll call her Miriam. She sought therapy because of the overwhelming guilt she felt when her son came out of the closet and abandoned his wife and children. At the age of sixteen, Miriam fell in love with a married man who wooed her passionately but abandoned her once she became pregnant. When the baby was born, she did her best to care for him on her own, but she felt so helpless she put him in an institution. A few years later he was taken in by a foster family.

Miriam married subsequently and gave birth to two daughters, one after the other. Her husband refused to allow the boy into their home, or even to let her meet him. He demanded that she give him up formally for adoption and threatened to divorce her if she refused. Miriam was too concerned about her daughters' future to oppose him.

When the boy was eight years old, Miriam's relationship with her husband ended in divorce. A few months later she brought her son home, and he immediately became the center of the family and of Miriam's life. His sisters had their father to go to, but for him, Miriam was everything. She felt a strong need to compensate him for all the years they'd spent apart from each other. His sisters had their own bedroom, but he slept in his mother's room until he was fourteen years old. Miriam pampered him endlessly. She would soap him up in the shower and take him out for dinner and a movie when the girls were with their father. Sometimes she and the boy would spend a weekend at a beachfront hotel where they shared a room as usual. But at some point, Miriam began to realize that he was too old to sleep in her bed, and she tried to change their arrangement. Her son reacted to this with outbursts of rage, and Miriam sought psychological help. Finally, she was able to move him out of her room, but the strange intimacy between them persisted.

The boy graduated from high school and did his army service. He entered a relationship with a female soldier on his base, and they married shortly after meeting. The relationship between the bride and her mother-in-law was rather cool and distant, but Miriam doted on her grandchildren – in compensation, she believed, for the empty years without her son.

But then her son broke the news to her that he was gay and had decided to leave his family and move in with his lover. Miriam was devastated. In tears she confessed that she had willfully ignored the signs of his sexual orientation. "Everything's ruined! Everything I tried to create is ruined!" She could not bring herself to acknowledge that it was brave of him to come out of the closet and to live according to his true nature. She was terrified that he wouldn't be allowed to see his children anymore and that she wouldn't either, and even after she was told where the law stands on the issue, the nightmare scenario continued to torment her. Anger at him for destroying her fantasy was overlaid with guilt. She had pampered him too much. She should not have let him sleep in her bed. She had given in to his every whim.

The love and intimacy that seemed to compensate for the cruelty of their separation had turned against them – like Oedipus and Jocasta, they had become a couple: physically, a grown woman with a grown man, but emotionally, a mother and child.

The course of Miriam's treatment was extremely frustrating. She was so locked into her guilt, she could not begin to address her feelings of disappointment and anger.

Thoughts of suicide assailed her. The relationship with her daughters, never particularly close or warm, was all but cut off now, and she had no desire to see them, no impulse to speak to them on any subject. She dropped out of therapy several times but would return a week or two later. It took many hours of therapy to reach beyond the guilt, anger, and disappointment to the profound underlying grief she still felt for the loss of her son in his early years.

Genetic sexual attraction, as it is now termed, is not uncommon between blood relatives who have been separated for a long time. Family members who meet in adulthood may recognize in each other a romantic ideal of perfect love. The sense of recognition and kinship, of having found a true soulmate, has been observed in a surprising study by Maurice Greenberg and Roland Littlewood published in 1995 in the *British Journal of Medical Psychology* showing that 50 percent of those who sought post-adoptive counseling "experienced strong sexual feelings in reunions."[11] The same has been found by Raie Goodwach in Australia, who studied feelings of sexual attraction among reunited mothers and sons who had been separated immediately after birth.[12]

Santorini again

I've decided to stay on in Santorini for a few days after the conference. I'm sitting on the terrace of the Simon taverna under a sun umbrella. Greek music fills the air. I look out at the blue Aegean Sea surrounding this island, Santorini. *Thera*, the ancients called it, founded by Theras, the last known descendant of Oedipus. But what I am seeing before my eyes now is not this beautiful lagoon but the dusty ruins of Thebes, where I met you, Jocasta. You spoke to me about the birth of your son and your depression when he was taken from you, but you haven't told me yet about how you waited with mingled fear and expectation for the man who was to become your husband. As I think about Jocasta and my apprehensions about her reunion with Oedipus, I take out my laptop and start to write.

Theban Nights, Jocasta scene 5

At the time I didn't know he was the one who had been foretold in my dream by Phobos and Thanatos: "from the mother's womb came the son and into her womb the father will return, the father who is the son."

On hot summer nights I bathed in the fountain of the palace courtyard. My white breasts floated like half-moons on the water. What will the man who defeated the sphinx say when he sees my naked body? I thought. And what will I see? Will he be young or old? Slender or stout? Tender or cruel?

I heard male voices coming into the gynaikonitis. A servant quickly pinned my fine white peplos and combed my hair. Standing in the corridor were Creon and a young man.

Queen Jocasta, said Creon, Here is Oedipus who has saved Thebes from the devouring sphinx. He will wed you and take the throne. Young though he may be, he is wiser than many a graybeard. The nuptials will take place three days from now and he shall be crowned.

Looking down I saw the young man's sandals, covered with the dust of the road; moving closer, step by step, I was seized with a fierce longing to throw myself at his feet, to touch them.

I don't remember the wedding itself, but it was nothing like the lavish feast and the loud procession that followed my wedding to Laius. After all the guests had left, my new young husband and I knelt together before Hestia's altar and prayed:

> O Hestia, fair goddess of the hearth
> you who are the heart of every home
> and guardian of the gates
> we pray that all who enter here
> may be under your protection and
> we ask your blessings
> that we may live
> our lives in joy and love

Then we bathed in the fountain, and I caressed each fold of the skin on his feet. They were smooth and unblemished.

The ways of the palace were changed. The gynaikonitis was wedded to the andron, music filled the courtyard from morning till night. My king and I would regale our visitors together, and I would ride with him in the chariot, my face uncovered, as he wished. The agora bustled with all manner of goods and crafts, and whenever we set off to bring offerings to the gods, the cheering crowds would follow our procession.

Those were my happiest years, she sighs. But, of course, there was tragedy ahead. I bore my husband two sons, Eteocles and Polynices, and two daughters, Antigone and Ismene.

And then the plague spread through the city, and Oedipus felt impelled to consult the oracle. I knew what was coming; I had known all along.

Jocasta and Tikkun: a final thought

I open my eyes and for a moment I don't know where I am. The Simon taverna is almost empty now. I too know what happens next. Before Oedipus returns from Delphi with the terrible knowledge given by the oracle, Jocasta flees from the palace and enters the temple. There she mingles with the plague-stricken Thebans and dies as a common woman among her subjects. Like a true heroine she wrestles with her fate as best she can; she defies the curse.

Jocasta's attempt at *tikkun* is concrete and violent rather than symbolic and, thus, inevitably tragic. Though she defied the curse, she could not overcome it. Harmonia had passed down the necklace of misfortune to her, and Cadmus the Phoenician, the legendary founder of Thebes, had passed the curse of the dragon to his descendants. But he also introduced the alphabet to Europe, the alphabet that brought about a transition from orality to civilizing literacy and consciousness, and this has enabled us to preserve and ponder the myths of our progenitors.

Tikkun requires creative effort, and for me, the process of writing Jocasta's untold story was a *tikkun* of her presentation in literature. The possibility of encountering Jocasta as I have is the great transformational gift of analytical psychology.

Notes

1 Sophocles, *Oedipus the King*, in D. Grene and R. Lattimore (eds), *The Complete Greek Tragedies*, 2nd ed., Chicago, IL: University of Chicago Press, 1991; and Euripides, *Phoenissae*, trans. and ed. E. P. Coleridge, Perseus Collection. Available: www.perseus. tufts.edu/hopper/text?doc=Perseus%3atext%3a1999.01.0118.
2 S. Freud, *The Interpretation of Dreams*, trans. A. A. Brill. New York: McMillan, 1913; J. M. Masson (ed.), *The Complete Letters of Sigmund Freud to Wilhelm Fliess, 1887–1904*, Cambridge, MA: Harvard University Press, 1985.
3 Homer, *The Odyssey*, trans. Barry B. Powell, Oxford, UK: Oxford University Press, 2014.
4 T. Kron, *Women in Pink* (in Hebrew), Tel-Aviv, Am-Oved, 1989; and "The dialogical dimension in therapists' dreams about their patients," *Israel Journal of Psychiatry and Related Subjects*, 1991, vol. 28, pp. 1–12.
5 G. Devereux, *Dreams in Greek Tragedy: An Ethno-Psycho-Analytical Study*, Berkeley, CA: University of California Press, 1976.
6 Martin Buber, *I and Thou*, Mansfield Centre, CT: Martino Publishing, 2010. The first edition of the book was published in German 1923 and the first edition in English appeared in 1937.
7 E. Neumann, *The Origins and History of Consciousness*, with a foreword by C. G. Jung, trans. R. F. C. Hull, Princeton, NJ: Princeton University Press, 1949/1954.
8 S. Freud, *An Outline of Psychoanalysis*, trans. and ed. James Strachey, Eastford, CT: Martino Publishing, 2011. Reprint of 1949 London edition.
9 E. Neuman, "The slaying of the mother," in *The Origins and History of Consciousness*, pp. 152–169, Princeton, NJ: Princeton University Press, 1949/1954.
10 S. Symeonoglou, *The Topography of Thebes from the Bronze Age to Modern Times*, Princeton, NJ: Princeton University Press, 1985.
11 M. Greenberg and R. Littlewood, "Post-adoption incest and phenotypic matching: Experience, personal meanings and biosocial implications," *British Journal of Medical Psychology*, 1995, vol. 68 (pt. 1), pp. 29–44.
12 R. Goodwach, "Jocasta and the Oedipus myth: The adoption-reunion context for feelings of sexual attraction," *Australasian Journal of Psychotherapy*, 2004, vol. 23, no. 2, pp. 46–65.

11

GREEK NIHILISM AND THE PSYCHOLOGY OF DECADENCE

Evangelos Tsempelis

A thick cloud had formed at the top of the hill where our conference's building stood overlooking, in a spectacular way, the Aegean Sea and the island of Caldera. In late August, this weather was quite unbecoming for this setting. Yet that ominous cloud, in a curious way, stood as a perfect depiction of a certain mood that I recognized as forming in my inner climate that day. As the time for me to take the floor approached, I sensed a growing sense of resistance taking hold of me. Part of me did not want to be there; part of me wanted to flee. The occasion in itself carried some striking connotations: a newly qualified analyst from Athens flying from Zurich, where I had been residing over the past eight years, to attend a conference on Ancient Greece, Modern Psyche, held in Santorini. Something about this itinerary caused a sense of existential vertigo. As a child and a young man, I had spent many summers at a nearby island. During that time Santorini stood at the end of a very long ferry-line cruise from Piraeus. That weekend, it had taken a mere two and a half hours from Zurich to fly to the airport in Thira.

Descending from the airplane, I was struck by the beauty and the intensity of the light. And even though that experience had been a familiar one – I had spent my youth marveling in the Cycladic elements – as a consequence of my years of absence, I had become increasingly forgetful of this benevolent intensity. But to say this, I realize, is to already speak a half-truth. I can see now how that light had always revealed in its unforgiving intensity some other dimension of life that had burdened my heart. You only needed to look at the landscape to catch an insight into this dimension. Under the blazing sun lie landscapes of islandic barren rock sculptured by the elements of wind, sun, volcanic force, and time, endless time, into formations that create a patchwork of earth and sea. Gentle reader, do not get fooled by this attempt at lyrical language. Yes, there is beauty here. Our poets have sung it in words of unparalleled force. Foreigners from all corners of the world flock to Greece in charter flights and on boat cruises to experience it and capture it on film. On my way to the conference center, I heard the taxi driver complain about the havoc that is created every afternoon when these humongous ships dock, unleashing throngs of tourists who rush to ascend the hill that rises from the sea level to the blue sky. Once on top, they marvel at the spectacular views and, as it occurred to me that day, consume it insatiably with their camera devices. That appetite is also met by the local population of shop owners who provide an abundance of all kinds of products and memorabilia. To be looking at this from a certain point of view, mine that day, is to see revealed in one's eyes a certain wasteland.

Dutch disease

That wasteland, which this unforgiving light reveals, is my country. That wasteland is, in certain ways, me. To tell its story and to understand it has been a life-long effort. It is also what set me on the path to becoming an analyst – not so much out of choice as out of despair. And, as one might expect, there is no linear, fully intelligible way to talk about this. So here is what comes to my mind as I ponder this predicament in a kind of free association. Developmental economists, of all people, talk about a certain phenomenon that they have named "Dutch disease." They have come up with this term to describe a certain predicament that countries rich in natural resources in the Third World face. It represents a certain kind of financial vicious circle whereby a country exports its natural wealth in minerals in order to import consumables and services from the developed world. The exports are natural resources requiring minimum processing and human innovation. The imports are the reverse, goods and services developed by virtue of advancements in innovation and technology. This exchange keeps the countries rich in natural resources trapped in a situation of stagnation, inflation, and poverty; in order to keep up with their needs for consumables, they have to increasingly dig into their resources and deplete their earth. Whatever they receive they essentially have to repay for imports, with a certain markup, which stands for a permanent gap in development and innovation separating an advanced industrialized world from a world of poor nations and people.

Greece is certainly not a Third World country. Even during the devastating financial crisis that has lasted ten long years, the country still remains part of the richest grouping of countries comprising the eurozone. Greece is a member of the Euro-Atlantic institutions. Since its foundation as a modern nation-state in the early nineteenth century, it has consistently been on the winning side as a solid member of alliances with the most powerful Western nations. Moreover, for the thirty years preceding the crisis, the country had experienced an unprecedented period of stability and wealth. Those thirty years of a *Belle Époque*, called in Greek Μεταπολίτευση, comprise the period between the dismal years of a military junta, which ended in 1974, and the eruption of the crisis in 2008. Together with a wiping out of 25 percent of the national gross product, this crisis radically reversed what had been an established way of living for the majority of Greeks, causing the demise of the middle class and the proletarianization of political life, with its corollary, the rise of populism, fascism, xenophobia, and Euroscepticism.

It is hard to convey to an outside observer what all of this represents in actual terms – what it means to live and/or to be a citizen of this country at such an ominous time. At this point, everyone is accustomed to stories about the financial crisis, and in some way we have collectively been desensitized to news about other people's suffering and plight. Over the past ten years, I learned to decipher the inner language of this plight by means of witnessing the suffering it brought to members of family, to friends, and to acquaintances. More than 500,000 Greeks, mostly the better educated, fled the country – their wasteland – to secure a better future for themselves and their families. In such a time as ours, when more than 300,000 people have perished in the civil war in Syria, when more than 3 million refugees have fled to Turkey from the warzone farther east, it is practically impossible to speak with some sense of dignity about the "drama" of a generation of educated people who migrated from one European country to another.[1] Nor is it any easier to speak with any sense of measured accuracy about the true proportions of the tragedy that pertains to generations of young and older people experiencing such a sudden reversal of fortune when their country, ours, has received the largest ever bailout package of foreign assistance from its partners – more than 200 billion euros – which has kept the country solvent and the banks open. Yet, here too there is suffering; here too there is a categorical imperative to understand even if we do not have readily available terms of language to speak to what is at stake. In my regular visits to Greece over the past years, in addition to the usual signs – closed and deserted shops, increased numbers of homeless on the streets of Athens – I also began to notice more subtle symptoms of the crisis in the new type of obesity that seems to have spread through society, the somber and tired faces of passersby on the street, the unkempt gray and dark attire, which at times appears to be a national dress code, as well as the missing teeth, ever more apparent now in people's occasional smiles.

This is partially the reason that I wanted to flee that summer day at the conference in Santorini. I had heard remarkably eloquent, highly educated presenters, analysts from all over the world, speak about Greek myth and its pertinence for collective psyche. The more I heard these impressive presentations, woven in rich references and psychological insight, the more I felt like I was stripped of language. Here I was their colleague, who had spent more than ten years learning my Jungian references, in Greece, my home country, at a conference about Ancient Greece and Modern Psyche, about my psyche (too); here I was in Santorini, an island that I had known, an island from which my own grandmother had come, at a conference setting that carried the same family name as hers; and I had no voice or language to address this audience.

Jungians speak about the experience of being caught by a complex, evidenced by a narrowing of vision and perspective alike. A situation in which one's entire personality is being held hostage by a cluster of emotions associated with a particular set of archetypal images and experiences; a clouding of consciousness occurs and one, alas, is no longer the master of one's house. Indeed, who was I at that moment as I struggled to take hold of the powerful emotions that were forcing me to a state of inner turmoil? I remember playing a short clip from a film by Theo Angelopoulos, *Ulysses' Gaze* (Figure 11.1), where one of the actors memorably says,

> you know something, Greece is dying. We are dying as a people. We've come full circle. I don't know how many thousand years . . . among broken stones and statues . . . and we're dying. But, if Greece is to die she'd better do it quickly . . . because the agony lasts too long and makes too much noise.[2]

FIGURE 11.1 Film clip: Theo Angelopoulos, *Ulysses' Gaze*
(https://aras.org/ancient-greece-modern-psyche)

And then another one from a film adaptation by Mihalis Kakogiannis of Nikos Kazantzakis's *Zorba the Greek*, played by Anthony Quinn (Figure 11.2).[3] In that scene Zorba is depicted as the noble savage who invites his intellectual friend, dressed in Western European attire and with reserved manners akin to a civilized man, to a frenzy of free-flowing feeling, immediacy, and dance. The music accompanying this famous scene is written by Nikos Theodorakis, a composer, who occupies an epic stature in contemporary Greek culture as the man who perhaps more than anyone else has captured the national Greek psyche, having turned stanzas from some of the most renowned poets into lyrics of songs that generations of Greeks have sung – not only to express revelry in moments of joy and celebration, but also *καημός*. This special sentiment encountered in the East encompasses a mix of bittersweet feelings associated with nostalgia, regret, depth of feeling, and solace.

FIGURE 11.2 Film clip: *Zorba the Greek*
(https://aras.org/ancient-greece-modern-psyche)

My final clip was from a British film shot in the 1980s, *Shirley Valentine*.[4] It tells the story of a British working-class woman leading a life of dullness and alienation in her conventional marriage who decides to revolt by escaping to the Greek isles to discover sensuality, love, and ultimately herself (Figure 11.3). This process of self-discovery inevitably involves encounters with Greek men, who exercise on her the well-known practice of *καμάκι*, hitting on Western tourists by local Greek lads thirsty for adventure and conquest. These horny men in their broken English are subject to ridicule from a certain more sophisticated (European) perspective. But that is precisely the point of the stereotype which the film plays on. However savage in their manners, these Greek men hold a sexual potency and an immediacy of feeling, which is capable of transforming a British, middle-aged, working-class housewife into no less than a goddess of eros and sensuality. In the clip that I played that day, a Greek man at a sea-side Cycladic picturesque location naively offers in broken English to "make fuck with [her]."

In the graphic cinematographic language, which I was now depicting in the conference auditorium, I was a party to a higher truth that I could not quite grasp in my complex-struck selfhood. In that odd spot that I occupied, I can now see that I had been turned into an amalgamation of the vulgar savage, in command only of a broken and simplified language, and the intellectual who stands impotent as his praised logos does not stand much in front of an overwhelming intensity of emotion. This strange creature who had come into psychological existence was possessed by a truth that I could not see, yet one that was leading me on: *there is no place for modern (Greek) psyche in this setting of erudition and idealization of Ancient Greece*. This, of course, has nothing to do with the benevolent audience or the gentle organizers of the conference. This truth was more deeply structural, historical, and existential, speaking of a kind of ailment that was more like "Dutch disease." I had been struck by it and had been its carrier for as long as I could remember, even if I did not properly know it then. No less did I properly know this man, me, who was mumbling through his notes trying to find a face and a voice to relate to this audience.

Greek (Dutch) disease: Greece as a Western myth of humanism

As a preview, let me try to put this in simple terms: Dutch disease in Greece, as I see it, is associated with two distinct phenomena. First, the explosion of the modern tourist industry, which has since the late 1970s turned the country into a global destination. Rich in the primary resources of sun and beaches, the country and its culture have experienced a massive effect that has, on the one hand, brought income to segments of the population who had been living under conditions of hardship, while, on the other hand, brought a disruption from which local culture has not been able to recover. The commodification of beaches and sea-views has brought affluence, but also a certain desertification of the modern Greek lifeworld. What all of this constitutes and amounts to in human terms requires careful reflection. But, even beyond this, there is another whole element of Dutch disease, which is constitutive of Greek national identity, conditioning, silently and undetected, every aspect of life. The founding national myth of Greece is predicated on the notion of a continuous historical legacy extending from modernity to antiquity. Modern Greece is constituted on the notion of being the rightful heir to the legacy of Greek antiquity, which in itself occupies a central place in Western Civilization. As such, Greece is both a modern nation-state and a mythological site, an imagined land, which the West has been heavily mining first to erect its own humanistic, national, liberal democratic culture and second to suit evolving needs – whether artistic, epistemological, intellectual, existential, political, or financial – across time. From the Renaissance onward to the era of Enlightenment, European intellectuals

and artists have turned heavily to Greece to draw inspiration. This humanistic construct of Greece stands, it seems, to Modern Greece, its culture and people, in the
same proportion as primary natural resources from Third World countries stand to
the goods that these poor countries import from advanced economies, which use
knowledge and technology to process the primary resources they import into more
advanced exportable goods and services befitting a sophisticated and widely differentiated world market requiring constant innovation. If the former phenomenon
is responsible for a certain desertification of the modern Greek lifeworld, the latter
is informative of a certain ailment, which I have elsewhere described in terms of a
Greek Psychic Debt predating and conditioning the actual financial debt associated
with the current crisis.[5]

Modern Greece has built a modern nation-state in the last two hundred years.
The cornerstone for the construction of its claim to independence at the time when
the Eastern Question – how to deal with the demise of the Ottoman Empire – was
at the forefront of the foreign policy concerns of European powers in the nineteenth
century was that the Greeks were a proud, ancient people with a glorious past who
had been subjugated and oppressed by a decadent Eastern empire. Famous paintings of the time, such as Delacroix's *Massacre at Chios* depicting a military attack
by Ottoman forces in 1822, reveal the violence effected by Eastern soldiers on a
defenseless population of men, women, and children. The dark-skinned soldier,
somber and unperturbed in his military prowess, slays the naked and eroticized
bodies of white women, a symbol of Hellas in the eyes of Western contemporary
conscience in Europe of the time. The metaphor of a European white man saving a white woman from a menacing brown-skinned Turk was an integral literary
trope, a powerful imaginary construction that figured in literary works of the time.
Byron's famous poem "Giaour" (1813) is an iteration of this genre, whereby a white
Greek woman – a symbol of subjugated Hellas – is typically saved (in the case of this
poem, avenged) from the Turks by an Englishman, a Frenchman, or an American.
In addition to observing how the feminization of Greece was integral to how that
country was construed/invented as a politicized space, David Roessel also remarks
on how Lord Byron's poetry engendered such depictions, so powerfully gaining
popularity in Western Europe at the time so as to affect significantly how Greek
history and politics were subsequently perceived.[6]

Yet, although Greece as an imaginary topos was idealized, its inhabitants were
not exactly seen in the eyes of Western travelers as equivalent. Here is a stunning
quote from Lord Byron himself about modern Greeks:

> This should not surprise you, if I know this nation by local and attentive
> experience, while in Europe they judge it by inspiration. The Greeks are per-
> haps the most deprived and degraded people under the sun, uniting to their
> original vices both of those of their oppressors, and those inherent in slaves.[7]

As David Roessel poignantly argues, Modern Greece was portrayed in history and
literature as a transitional moment between a glorious classical age and a projected

hope for a resurrected future founded on classical Greek models and in resemblance to Western Europe and America.[8] In the same vein, so as to recapture the point that was made previously regarding the imaginary construction of Greece in Western minds:

> The Romantic age constructed an image of a politicized female modern Greece for the temple of Apollo. This image dominated the representations of Greece into the 20th century and was eventually transmuted by writers affiliated with modernism into another political male Greece in Dionysian frenzy.[9]

Similarly, the liberation of Greece – which became a cause for intellectuals in Europe at the time and of whom Lord Byron was an emblematic case – was associated not merely with political aims. Rather, as such, it was invested with hopes and aspirations of a political, artistic, and spiritual nature. In short, the regeneration of Greece was a matter that extended beyond the actual claim for statehood on the part of the inhabitants of a nascent Modern Greece under Ottoman rule. For leading intellectuals, like Voltaire or Byron and many others, the foundation of an independent Greece was a cause linked to the victory of reason and human rights.[10] As this same writer, who has surveyed literary references in nineteenth-century Europe, claims, the regeneration of Greece was seen and depicted as a remedy to the cultural malaise of the individual in mechanized industrial society.[11] As eighteenth- and nineteenth-century Europeans, in an age of nationalism, looked for new cultural roots and alternative cultural politics, Greece offered a twofold example of the noble savage and of high civilization.

Greece in the age of European nationalism

Ernest Gellner among others has addressed how national ideologies have defined an age of nationalism since the eighteenth century. Benedict Anderson too has argued, quite convincingly, that nations are imagined communities.[12] Modern states "manufacture" a homogenized national culture resting on references to national symbols, common ancestry, shared genealogy, and destiny. Gellner has explained that a modern economy, in order to function, requires the existence of a malleable and mobile working force that is endowed with a standardized education necessary for the demands of an industrial order. In quite dramatic language the same author has argued that at the basis of modern social order stands the professor, not the executioner.[13] Along the same lines Gellner argues that it is nationalism that engenders nations and not the other way around. Nationalism uses a preexisting cultural wealth, but it uses it both selectively and in a radically transformed fashion. It is in this manner that dead languages are revived, traditions invented, and fictitious pristine purities restored. Nationalism in that respect constitutes an imposition of a high culture on society, where previously low cultures had taken up the lives of the majority and in some cases the totality of the population.[14] Its principle lies on a belief in the congruence of polity and culture while its essence consists in the establishment of an anonymous, impersonal society, with mutually substitutable, atomized individuals, held together by a common culture. This national culture, according to the same line of thought, replaces a previous complex structure of local groups, sustained by folk cultures reproduced locally and idiosyncratically.[15]

During this remarkable historical process of reconstructing Europe's cultural and political map, Greece occupied an important position as its national liberation cause became part of "a holy battle in the struggle for the liberty of nations."[16] Yet this was on the imaginary level; on the level of politics, the realities were different. Greeks were not even a party to the treaty of 1832 between Britain, France, Russia, and Bavaria, which stipulated the terms under which a Bavarian Prince would become the first King of an independent Greek state under the auspices of Protecting Powers. As the King was a minor, Greece was ruled until 1835 by a council of regents composed of three Bavarians. The Bavarians showed little sensitivity toward the local population who had just fought a brutal war of independence and who was resentful of their rule.[17] The protectorate's new institutions were fashioned according to Western European models. The educational system was founded on French and German models.

Even the choice of Athens as the capital of the new state had little to do with the realities of the place. At the time, Athens was not much more than a small town. Yet it was associated with the ruins of the Parthenon and what those entailed in terms of the glorious classical past, thus the choice had symbolical value. A newly conceived neoclassical architectural aesthetic found expression in the new buildings that were under construction and that still today mark an era that we modern Greeks oddly associate with a bright era of burgeoning culture – a contrast to the late twentieth-century architectural chaos characterizing Athens as a hectic metropolis in late modernity. But King Otto's Bavarian rule was mostly associated with the constitutional struggle, which he vehemently opposed. Following a coup, Otto eventually had to finally concede to granting the newly independent state a proper democratic parliamentary constitution.

A researcher interested in uncovering the sociopolitical routes of the persevering malaise of clientelism of Greek political life would have no difficulty in finding routes into this founding époque, when influential chieftains from the *status quo ante* adopted democratic principles to extend their political influence. They earned votes to enter a democratic parliament in exchange for extending political favors to their electorate client base, who were none other than their former vessels. This inner perversion of democratic politics to serve interests inimical to the spirit of liberal democracy, in the name of liberal democracy, represents a legacy that we Greeks still today, arguably, struggle to work through. Would it be too exaggerated to claim that the Greek political subject, the collective imaginary entity, the *habitus* that constitutes the collective mindset of our democratic historical becoming, was infected from the outset by this legacy of dependence and inner perversion of intensions?[18] Along those lines, one could argue that it is in terms of this legacy that the long-standing refusal of Greek politicians – and a large percentage of their constituents – to accept ownership of the reforms upon which financial assistance has been granted to Greece can be understood. Therefore, we witness a curious state of affairs whereby the former pay token gestures to principles they do not espouse and the latter cast votes on the merit that those elected will not actually do what they claim to – all amounting to a culture where dissimulation is the only pervasive truth one can count on.

Greece as an imaginary topos between East and West

In Western minds, Greece after independence occupied a middle ground between East and West, a token perhaps of the perception of modern Greeks as debased. A Western romantic construction of pre-independent Greece was succeeded by subsequent constructions. The painful historical episode known in Greece as the "Disaster of Asia Minor" (*Μικρασιατική Καταστροφή*) of 1922 marked a new era in the imaginary construction of Greece in Western minds. This disaster refers to the eventual retreat of an invading "liberation" Greek army that, after marching to assume control of coastal areas in Asia Minor, where a large Greek population had resided under Ottoman rule, continued its expedition deep into the Ottoman mainland. The expedition took place in the wake of World War I and the capitulation of the Ottoman Empire to the Western Entente Allies of which Greece was also a member. The Greek military campaign to liberate "lost homelands" – part of a powerful nationalist narrative known in Greek historiography as "The Big Idea" (*Μεγάλη Ιδέα*) – was abruptly put on hold when the reformist Kemal Attatürk, the founder of modern Turkey, came to power and mounted a counteroffensive, which led not only to the defeat of the Greek forces, but also, dismally, to the eradication of the Greek population who had lived for centuries on the coast of Asia Minor. As a consequence of this catastrophe, 1.5 million Greeks were forced violently to migrate to Greece proper.

A few years earlier, at a time associated in Europe with the liberal revolutions of 1848, in Greece the government of Koletis was arbitrating power dividends with groups of militias that were blackmailing the government, demanding access to the spoils of state power under the guise of serving the Big Idea by mounting offensives to liberate areas in Thessaly and Epirus still under Ottoman influence. As a consequence, militia groups known in Greek as *Ληστές* ("Robbers") increased their power and influence while also gaining legitimacy as a part of the liberation national army. Eminent contemporary historians identify in this phenomenon the beginning of what they name as a historical proclivity on the part of modern Greeks to escape from reality.[19] Arguably, the most recent example of such proclivity was the almost fatal attempt by the populist coalition government of the radical left and extreme right parties of SYRIZA and ANEL, respectively, to bring the Greek economy to default by threatening to not comply with Greece's contractual obligations to its creditors in 2015. The two parties had just been catapulted to power over a wave of popular resentment for the conventional parties, which had ruled Greece since 1974 and which were rightfully held accountable for the bankruptcy of the country. But, I bring this historical moment in the 1840s to mark the contrast between the radicalism of liberal revolutions in Europe and the harsh realities in Greece at the time, when politics was predominated by big nationalist ideas. These, under patriotic bravado, essentially served the political ends of dubious groups and individuals who, together with the elected political elites, ruled over a population who had not yet developed the kinds of intentionalities and political self-consciousness associated with the radicalism of the 1848 movements in Europe . . .

These tough political realities hardly jibed with the prior literary idealization of Greece in Western minds. During the time of the Crimean War (1853–1856), between Russia on one side and England and France on the other, Greece, in yet another curious echo of its recent misadventures, opposed its very own creditors, England and France, and sided with Russia. Greek support of Russia was arguably an attempt to capitalize on the latter's preceding declaration of war on the Ottoman Empire perceived through the calculus of the pursuit of the Big Idea, the aspiration to liberate territories still under Ottoman rule in the north – in Thessaly and Epirus. The "Second Greek–Turkish War," which diverse groups of army officers and militia leaders undertook to carry out in the name of the Big Idea, constituted another dismal case of an escape from reality leading to a travesty for the newly founded nation. France and Britain imposed a humiliating military blockade of Piraeus in 1854 in order to force the government to abdicate its support for these irredentist groups. This Crown case of Western interference in Greece is referred to in Greek historiography as the époque of "Burglar-Rule" (Ληστοκρατεία). A Frenchman, Edmond About, Director of the French Archaeological School of Athens, published a novel in 1854 that described the thin line separating politics from robbery and anomie in Greece at the time.[20]

Changing Western conceptions of Greece: from romantic fantasy to self-discovery

Against this background, literary imagination in Western Europe marked a shift with regard to the way "Greece" was now conceived. The Asia Minor Disaster of 1922 was featured in Hemingway's writings as "a symbol of postwar chaos [resembling] that of Eliot in the wasteland."[21] And furthermore:

> If one of the metaphors of the 19th century romantic world which believed in the possibility of human progress was the revival of the Greeks and all of the minded concepts they represented in the English and American imagination, then the death of the Greeks could be used to signal the expiration of that world . . . The notion that tragedy was a familiar fact of Greek life through all the ages of history has been especially prevalent in 20th century constructions of Greece . . . [T]ragedy became a familiar element in writing about Greece only after Smyrna [an allusion to the Disaster in Asia Minor].[22]

No longer lending itself as a ground for romantic fantasy for the lofty and adventurous spirits in the West, Greece became during that time a "land where a foreigner could go to overcome personal loss or confront one's own fatalism."[23] Greece was imagined as a place offering an opportunity for Western individuals to discover themselves. Henry Miller's *Colossus of Maroussi* features prominently in this genre. As a Dionysian place, Greece was now imagined as a site where "a race knowing excess, intoxication of all kinds [resided]."[24] A theme further exemplified by Miller: "[On the Sacred Way to Eleusis] I was on the point of madness several times, I actually did start running up the hillside only to stop midway, terror-stricken, wondering what had taken possession of me."[25]

Along such an imaginary, Greece was a marvelous and unique place on earth where one could get reconnected to the elemental world, which had been dehu-manized by the material industrial culture of the West.[26] As such, writers like Lawrence Durrell and Henry Miller constructed a Greece linked to a Dionysian enjoyment of the senses. Miller in his celebration of George Katsimbalis, a literary critic and publisher of a literary journal in the 1950s, also constructed for the first time in foreign literature on Greece a larger-than-life image of the Greek intellec-tual. Arguably, this notion of an exigency for Westerners to open to the Dionysian dimension of existence bordering the risk of annihilation, as a remedy to cultural degeneration and individual nihilism, had an even older and more prominent pre-cursor in Friedrich Nietzsche and his famous opus, *The Birth of Tragedy*.

In this book written in 1872, Nietzsche broke with the prevalent historicism of his time, which had attributed a special status to the beauty and sublimity of ancient Greek classic art. For a generation of Germans who had been preoccupied with the construction of a national culture, in the wake of the Napoleonic wars and the founding of a unified nation-state, the ancient Greeks had provided a cultural example to be emulated through a rigorous practice of education (*Bildung*), engen-dering a cornerstone for the blending of pedagogical and social reform with the construction of a cultural nationalism born out of the struggle to defeat the French invaders.[27] Whereas Baroque art was decadently overly reliant on degenerate forms drawn directly from nature, appealing to an unsophisticated audience of specta-tors, Greek art presented an example of an appeal to ideal forms of beauty with an invocation to the mind as opposed to the senses. This choice can be seen in terms of both the political imperative to achieve national sovereignty and to redefine a national culture in contradistinction to French cultural hegemony in German-speaking lands, as well as with pietistic protestant notions privileging inwardness, individual self-discipline coupled with a disdain for material comforts, and senti-mental emotionality. German intellectuals discovered in the classical world of the Athenian empire, which had also been politically fragmented and conquered, but united by a single tongue and spirit, a powerful source of inspiration.

Johann Winckelmann holds a key place in this German humanistic construc-tion of Greece. In his *Reflections on the Imitation of Greek Masterpieces in Painting and Sculpture* (1755), he saw the Greeks as

> [Living] in a world without confining clothes or disfiguring diseases, where children were raised to be beautiful and nature revealed its beauties

unabashedly before all . . . A return to the Greeks in Winckelmann was the equivalent of Rousseau's "return to nature."' Here essential humanness was to be found, without consideration of status or role. The noble and beautiful in each person was recognized and cultivated.[28]

Whereas the modern world was overspecialized, unnatural, and tyrannical, the Greeks were seen as an example of a people who had built a culture based on the cultivation of beauty – an idea that occupied a central position in an age of German aesthetics. Through a notion of *Bildung* emphasizing hermeneutical self-understanding, intellectuals like Schiller, Wolf, Humboldt, and Schleiermacher approached classical Greek antiquity as a world into which one ought to step in order to understand one's own. Through a new form of pedagogy, the Germans of the time projected themselves into a mission of recovering a lost Arcadia. It is worth considering here this redemptive attempt to recover the origins of human-kind, whose source was projected into Ancient Greece, in terms of an attempt to ground a German national cultural identity.[29] From such a vantage point, the enormous energy invested at the time into archaeological expeditions in Greece and the Orient was, of course, not delinked from such cultural and political objec-tives. It is striking to read the words of Ernst Curtius, the director of the excavation at the ancient site of Olympia: "What lies in those dark depths is life of our life."[30]

The quote is particularly striking to someone trained in depth psychology, as it points to how notions of depth, along such an imaginary, intertwine literal and metaphorical references, potentially highlighting how those two registers inform one another. Perhaps it is not too premature to pose a question that carries a certain vertiginous quality: is psychological depth here predicated on an anterior view of humankind conceived in terms of an implicit belief in the congruence between cul-ture and national territory? While Olympia – "Greece" – lies beyond the German national territory, is it too much to say that a cultural appropriation in an imaginary way is operative here to the extent that the locus of a "German life" is postulated in the depths of an ancient Greek territory? Or in another iteration of the same ques-tion: how does the principle of self-determination founded on imagined notions of collective lineage and historical origins, a cornerstone principle for an age of nation-states, condition the metaphysics of individual subjects seeking the founda-tion of their own psychological truth in the depths of their own interiority? How do national statehood and individual selfhood inform and condition one another?

And finally, in another variation of the same question: if, indeed, there is a correlation between cultivated (hermeneutically invented) notions of depth and origin at the level of a national culture, on the one hand, and individual notions of depth and interiority, on the other, how can we assess the depths of individual despair in terms of degrees of backwardness – as in Dutch disease – on the part of a nationally sponsored state culture conflating the literal (Greece as geographi-cal topos) with the metaphorical ("[Ancient] Greece" as an imaginary source of inner life)? Who could really postulate that the sources of a German life *actually* lie buried in the depths of Greek antiquity (Olympia)? Can "Greek (Dutch) disease" then be rethought as an ailment of the imagination? Is "Greek psychic debt" an imaginary deficit, a certain malaise associated with a predicament whereby one is perpetually stuck in literal and self-identical references, leaving no room for the proper invention/discovery of an individual self? How do I begin the painful process of separating the territory of (an imagined and projected) Greece from the body of my individual psyche? Would anything be left after such a painful procedure of decathexis? Would the nothingness of such individual destitution, as here envisaged, be any different from the nihilistic existence of a collective literalism lived and experienced perpetually as an individual destiny?

Nietzsche's *Birth of Tragedy*: Apollo and Dionysos

But I have jumped ahead of myself. It was such aforementioned humanistic notions about beauty and form that Nietzsche boldly contested with his *Birth of Tragedy*. In a heroic articulation, which is a lasting emblem of the individual task of the modern subject to be in a process of constant inventiveness, he asserted that "Only as an aesthetic phenomenon is existence and the world justified."[31]

In the humanistic world of Schiller and his contemporaries, the Greeks had represented an example of living in harmony and in beauty. They had comprised an example that Schiller had undertook to rearticulate in his *Aesthetic Education of Man*, where he posited two inimical demands confronting man and corresponding to his double nature. The sensuous impulse proceeding from his physical existence, concerned with setting man within the bounds of time, turning him into matter, and the formal impulse striving to set man free, derived from his rational nature. In a Jungian prefiguration, Schiller describes liberty in terms of "bring(ing) harmony in to the diversity of his manifestation and to maintain his person throughout every change of circumstance."[32]

Indeed, Schiller understood this in terms of the absolute indivisibility of the person. He posited personality as the unchanging ground that engenders the condition for the possibility of time and alteration. Personality, he claimed, "annuls time and change: it wishes the actual to be necessary and eternal, and the eternal and necessary to be actual; in other words, it aims at truth and right."[33]

Schiller also articulated the clash between reason and feeling in a historical trajectory. He saw a progression from the Greek living harmoniously with nature to his time exemplified by the disintegration of personality and further extending to a future of a perfect-whole-man-to-arrive.

Nietzsche would attack both the aforementioned notions of humanism regarding beauty, harmony, and form, and with them the traditional accounts of fifth-century Greece. Nietzsche undertook to respond to Schopenhauer's pessimism in the *World as Will and Representation*, which had taken Kant's Copernican revolution to its natural conclusion by using the notion of an inaccessible thing-in-itself – the unmediated object lying beyond our realm of possible experience always conditioned by the *a priori* categorical apparatus of (transcendental) subjectivity – to suggest that we live in a world of deceptive appearances.

At this point, we are not too far from Jung who, in his "*Structure of the Psyche*," specifies "the psyche is the only phenomenon that is given to us immediately and, therefore, is the *sine qua non* of all experience."[34] Jung would recognize that the ego rests on two distinct bases, both a somatic and a psychic one. A key notion/ criterion that separates these two realms is the presence of a *"will capable of modifying reflex or instinctual processes."*[35]

Both the allusion to the "will" and to immediacy carry overtones reminiscent of Schopenhauer's philosophy and the implications about our access to the world beyond our own apparatus of representation. We are, as such, forever doomed to live in a mediated, represented world, of whose nature the only direct recourse that we have is the apperception of a Will acting on us impersonally, blindly. For the pessimism of Schopenhauer, the denial of the Will offers the sole possibility for free individual action. In our deceptive subjective existence, music for Schopenhauer presents the closest we can ever come to directly apperceiving the Universal Will.

Similarly, for Nietzsche, music – especially as he encountered it in Wagner – constituted our primordial home. In a masterly stroke, an example of fashioning the world as an aesthetic phenomenon with literary inventiveness, as opposed to the scientific historicism of his predecessors, Nietzsche would posit two primordial impulses, drives of the will that shaped human culture across the ages. On the one side stood the drive for reason, order, and individuation represented by Apollo and evidenced in the plastic arts of the Greeks, which the humanists had so much idealized for their form, harmony, and intelligibility. On the other side stood the primordial and undifferentiated chaotic flux of the realm of flesh (*Leib*), Nietzsche's equivalent of the Schopenhauerian Will and arguably Jung's collective uncon- scious, which Nietzsche identified with Dionysos and which in Jung's archetypal soul would include a polyvalence of mythic images. The Greeks, according to Nietzsche, had managed to strike a balance between the two elements during the era of the tragic theater before Euripides. Henceforth, when the Apollonian spirit, associated with the world of appearance, predominated, they became gradually alienated from the primordial world of flux – the primal Oneness – beyond appear- ances leading to a degeneration of (Greek) culture. But,

> The divine power of Heracles cannot lie eternally dormant in the prodigal ser- vice of Omphale. From the Dionysian spirit a power has arisen that has nothing in common with the original conditions of Socratic culture: that culture can neither explain nor excuse it, but instead finds it terrifying and inexplicable, powerful and hostile-German music, as we know it pre-eminently in its mighty sun-cycle from Bach to Beethoven, from Beethoven to Wagner. Even under the most favorable conditions, what can the knowledge-hungry Socratism of our own times do with this daemon rising from the bottomless depths?[36]

"Greek decadence" and the search for cultural and individual regeneration

For Nietzsche, then, a humanistic return to the Greeks of the fifth-century Golden Age would not be sufficient to do justice to the German spirit. The Apollonian

Age, Greek Socratism with its optimistic belief in human reason and knowledge, exemplified the beginnings of degeneration, which Roman and French culture had perpetuated, and which the founding of the German Reich would have to now undo by going even deeper into the source of (Greek) history (and will).

> Whither does the mystery of the union of German music and German phi-
> losophy point, if not to a new mode of existence of which we can only gain
> an inkling through Greek analogies? For the Greek model is of inestimable
> value to us as we stand at the boundary between two different modes of exist-
> ence; all transitions and struggles assume classical and instructive form in that
> model. Only we seem to be experiencing the great epochs of Hellenism in
> reverse order, and seem now, for example, to be moving backwards from the
> Alexandrian age to the tragic period. And as we do so we have a sense that
> the birth of a tragic age for the German spirit would mean only a return to
> itself, a blissful self-discovery. For a long time terrible external invading pow-
> ers had forced it, living as it did in a helpless barbarism of form, into slavery
> under their own form. Now at least, having returned to the original source
> of its being, it can dare to stride bold and free before all peoples, free from
> the apron-strings of Romance civilization; if it can only learn constantly from
> one nation; the Greeks.[37]

With this *coup de force* Nietzsche essentially inserted the German spirit right at the very source out of which the Greeks – past their best moment in Aeschylean tragedy – had faltered, ostensibly into decadence and metaphysical nihilism.

When the Apollonian principle becomes the predominant one, the schemes of rational perception – which in Kantian-speak represent the subject's mental appara-tus, the categories through which she is able to render intelligibility to an otherwise chaotic flux of sensory data – are elevated to the thing-in-itself; appearance is held for the true unmediated object. The primordial excess, the Dionysian animality, which belongs to the realm of the flesh, is held hostage to the artifice of Apollonian individuation and rational schematization. The overriding of the fictitious over the flux creates an époque where nothing circulates any more, where life is held immobile, and where destitution replaces plenitude and nothingness is inserted in the place of the excess.[38] "The epoch of Nihilism is one where the poorest human flesh dominates; a time when the human flesh has become impoverished and nar-row. Instead of excess, it is the void that predominates in the flesh."[39]

In language coming strikingly close to Jung, Nietzsche speaks about myth as the vehicle of Dionysian wisdom and of music manifested in tragedy as able to inter-pret myth with new and more profound eloquence.[40] Furthermore,

> For this is how religions tend to die: the mythic premises of a religion are
> systematized, beneath the stern and intelligent eyes of an orthodox dogma-
> tism, into a fixed sum of historical events; one begins nervously defending the
> veracity of myths, at the same time resisting their continuing life and growth.

The feeling for myth dies and is replaced by religious claims to foundations in history.[41]

In a Jungian transcription one could say that if the decadence of contemporary culture could be attributed to the mass collective consciousness, evidenced in dogmatic ideologies (isms) and ossified religiosity, an active relationship with the collective unconscious could provide a source of revitalization and irrigation, not merely for individual neurotic souls, but also for an ailing society as a whole. In this regard the work of Jungian individuation involves the work of psychological differentiation from collective consciousness and, concurrently, the confrontation of the individual with the perennial psychic images (archetypes) spontaneously erupting in her dream (unconscious) life. This confrontation with the archetypal images, an epitome of which is Jung's own *Answer to Job*, does not merely point to individual psychic growth and integration, but also holds the prospect of transforming culture itself. As such, the human unconscious psyche – as repository of a psychological heritage not merely of her culture, but moreover of humanity as a whole – becomes a site of momentous potential for individual, social, and cultural transformation. It is in such a context, arguably, that Jung's insights into the nature of the Trinitarian god through his own confrontation with his own God-Image were posited as assertions about the evolution of the West's collective God-Image from Christianity's incomplete Trinitarian form to a more wholesome Quaternity.

This is another moment to register a certain feeling of vertigo. Jung's import is momentous. We have come a long way from the origins of the modern subject linked with Descartes's postulate: "I think, therefore I exist." The hiatus between this self-referential and immediate knowledge of consciousness and the epistemological doubt that it inaugurated – how can I ever know the validity of any other statement mediated through my senses? – was radically addressed by Kant. The latter's Copernican revolution consisted in conceiving this insoluble problem upside-down. The question for Kant was no longer how empirical facts could be validated, but rather how certain truths could be possible in the first place. The condition for their possibility was to be found in the preexistence of a transcendental subject – other than our empirical self (ego/cogito) – positing the very categories through which our experience was possible. Time, space, causality could not be proven in the empirical world; they were rather the *a priori* categories through which reason could apprehend such a world in the first place. We never perceive the thing-in-itself, but merely its phenomenological manifestation mediated though our mental apparatus – is Kant's point. To this Schopenhauer would attempt to bring more consistency by pointing out that if we, indeed, always deal with a mediated experience of the world, how can we ever even postulate any correspondence between our phenomenological objects and the thing-in-itself? How can we even meaningfully assert such a paradoxical object as a thing-in-itself subsisting outside of the categories conditioning the phenomenal world?

This is not much different from asking this question: if, as Jung suggests, we can only have access to psychic images of archetypes and not to archetypes *per se*, how can we even postulate a correspondence between images existing in a phenomenal world and structures subsisting in a noumenal realm outside of time and space? How can we even think of a plurality of archetypes in a noumenal world anterior to space and time, preconditions for any meaningful understanding of plurality? Yet, this is exactly what Jung would boldly assert, that there is indeed such a realm deep in our interiority. Kant's transcendental subject is here radically reconceived as a realm of the psyche. Schopenhauer's blind Will is reposited so it is no longer blind at all, but rather a repository of rich imagery, which informs and conditions our experience of the phenomenal world. Even more boldly, there is a differential correspondence between archetypal imagery (phenomenal world) and archetypal structure (noumenal world):

> *The collective unconscious contains the whole spiritual heritage of mankind's evolution, born anew in the brain structure of every individual.* His conscious mind is an ephemeral phenomenon that accomplishes all provisional adaptations and orientations, for which reason one can best compare its function to orientation in space. *The unconscious, on the other hand, is the source of the instinctual forces of the psyche and of the forms or categories that regulate them, namely the archetypes . . . This is particularly true of religious ideas, but the central concepts of science, philosophy, and ethics are no exception to this rule.* In their present form they are variants of archetypal ideas, created by consciously applying and adapting these ideas to reality. For it is the function of consciousness not only to recognize and assimilate the external world through the gateway of the senses, but to translate into visible reality the world within us.[42]

Depth psychology here discovers a depth that is both deeper and more ecumenical than the one we have examined so far in past cursory references. If the enlightenment humanists and the nineteenth-century archaeologists imagined/ invented the life source of their national culture in terms of ancient Greek antiquity, what we encounter here is a postulation of psychic depth that encompasses the "totality of the spiritual heritage of humanity subsisting in the brain of each individual."[43] If Nietzsche boldly would posit the existence of two functions conditioning culture and existence, Dionysian and Apollonian principles, Jung would up the ante and posit a whole mythology (Greek and beyond) as an archaeological site of archetypal psychic images. From this remarkable point of view, mythological motifs acquire tremendous significance as gateways into the primordial texture of human psyche.

Arguably, this fertile epistemological premise also has ontological implications. The functioning of a Jungian phenomenology requires, it seems, implicit faith – not necessarily in God. Yet, to assume the existence of unrepresentable (noumenal) reality, or that there is a correspondence between such reality and the images manifest in our unconscious, or the conjunction of opposites as a principle reflecting both the nature of this meta-reality and the capacity of psyche to individuate, already amounts, I submit, to inhabiting the realm of the sacred.

> In archetypal conceptions and instinctual perceptions, spirit and matter con-
> front one another on the psychic plane. Matter and spirit both appear in the
> psychic realm as distinctive qualities of conscious contents. The ultimate
> nature of both is transcendental, that is, irrepresentable, since the psyche and
> its contents are the only reality which is given to us *without a medium*.[44]

The epistemological impetus that seems to engender Jung's hermeneutics of faith,
despite the references to ancient mythology and religion, rests firmly on a bold
proclivity for innovation that runs throughout Western modernity: an unforgiving will for power as a desire to know. As old as the objects that lie in an
archaeological museum might be, the actual institution of the museum – as a space
where a certain relationship between objects, knowledge, and historical time is
postulated – is in itself a quite recent one. As old as ancient (Greek) myths might
be, their rediscovery as archetypal motifs of a collective unconscious is a bold
modern construction requiring the willingness, readiness, or ability to inhabit
a certain "science" – that to this writer's sensibilities seems to be reminiscent
of Bavarian-inspired neoclassical architectural edifices in the midst of a muddy
nineteenth-century Athenian town.

Indeed, I remember visiting a few years ago the museum of the ancient site
of Delphi. Together with ancient objects curated so as to tell a certain story, one
compliant with our collective notion of Delphi as an important archaeological site,
there were also pictures of the early twentieth century where one could clearly see
how the local inhabitants had, until recently, used the very same object-matter,
now curated in the museum, as building materials for their rudimentary homes.

These rudimentary homes – long foregone – arguably still inform a certain
sensibility that I might call Greek. From the point of view of Greek rudimentary homes, all this boldness and innovation, which in a plenitude of references I
have been trying to broadly sketch, is intimidating. The epistemological questions
informing a Western tradition extending from a Cartesian era to a contemporary depth-psychological one, the desire for regeneration, the search for origins
and foundations, the bold search for depth, the (re)discovery of the sacred within
individual interiority, all dazzle leaving one/me in agony – as long unprepared, in
search for words. I am anxiously back to Santorini.

Contemporary perspectives on Greek nihilism

There is a certain way of looking at the West of which Christos Yannaras, eminent
contemporary theologian in Greece, is an emblematic figure. Yannaras associ-
ates the estrangement from Being with the West, which he sees as a civilization
founded on ontic materialist, epistemological positivism, individualism, and cogni-
tivism. In turn, Yannaras traces the above in terms of a scholastic inheritance in the
West oriented toward providing logical proof for religious dogma conjoined by a
reductive legalistic tradition, which codified the (erotic/ecstatic/personal) religious
event by the rigid institution of the Catholic Church. In Western modernity,

Yannaras sees the civilization of the antichrist. Arguably what is here professed extends beyond the theological domain to castigate not solely Western late modernity but, as boldly, a decadent Greek nation, which has allowed itself to be pulled into a defeatist and alienated form of forgetful existence. This is evidenced by its servitude to Euro-Atlantic institutions and by the persevering crisis that plagues its economy, society, politics, and culture. Greece's westernization/modernization constitutes for Yannaras an affront to the Greek Orthodox tradition and the Byzantine heritage of personhood as a form of ecstatic union (*theosis*) and love in God's community/church.[45] In a text addressing the nature of nihilism characteristic of the present moment, Yannaras writes the following:

> In other words, nothingness is a mode of existence which is defined by insistence on natural individuality. A possibility of free personal choice, it is the distantiality (apostasis) of atomic individuality as against the ecstasy (ekstasis) which recapitulates the total unity of existence in personal otherness. Nothingness is the existential reality of being outside-of-Being as the fullness of personal existence, that is to say, outside the relation and communion of humanity with god, the only relation which recapitulates nature in its totality in a personal ecstatic reference outside-of-nature.[46]

Another contemporary Greek thinker, philosopher Stelios Ramfos, provides a point of view to the problem of nihilism, which in many ways represents an antithesis to what Yannaras seems to be suggesting. Ramfos deplores the absence of a developed teaching associated with the notion of the individual in the Greek Orthodox tradition.[47] As an advocate for the reformation of Greek thought, Ramfos underlines how until the beginnings of the eleventh century the Eastern Church was closely affiliated with the West. The Schism of 1054, however, marked a point of growing cultural and religious diversion between East and West. Whereas in the West a practice of hermeneutics was able to take root (Schleiermacher), enabling the individual's relationship with religious texts, in the East religious texts and references were kept hostage to the rigid form of ecclesiastic authority. Locked in a foregone time, a Byzantine theocentricism is still operative today in Greece, according to Ramfos, keeping Greek tradition statically fossilized outside of the dynamism of modernity. In Ramfos's eyes, Yannaras's Orthodox invocation of a theology of personal, ecstatic, erotic union with God is, in essence, a regressive gesture covering up for the fact that in the Greek East there is no adequately developed notion of individual subjective interiority. In terms deployed in a different section of this narrative, this could be rearticulated as suggesting that the ekstasis of the person, as envisaged by Yannaras in theological terms, is another version of what has been described in historical terms as a national proclivity toward escape from reality.

According to the same thinker, Yannaras's notion of the "person," together with the injunction to overcome notions of subjectivity associated with the West, carries all the backward baggage of a theological tradition, one which was unable to follow the West in its evolution toward the definition of a subject possessing an individual identity, consciousness, and interiority. In a philosophically provoking stroke, Ramfos suggests that the nature of Greek backwardness can be traced in terms of Trinitarian theology. Whereas in the Western notion of the Trinity, God's substance holds primary place, in the East the person is placed above substance. The implication is that henceforth it was practically impossible in the East to progress into a notion of the person that was not secondary to that of God, whereas in the West it became possible to forge a road to individual salvation by means of following a moral paradigm of an *imitatio Christi*.[48] In contrast to the West, where the Holy Spirit emanates from the Father and the Son, in the East the Father retains exclusive primacy according to the fourth-century ce articulation of the Cappadocian Church Fathers. In this theological patriarchy, Ramfos recognizes, in a twofold manner, first, the nonparticipation of the other two persons of the Trinity in the substance of God and, second, as a direct consequence, a proclivity toward a definition of salvation by means of a mystical personal union with God (*Theosis*) in the Orthodox East.

> The trinitarian personhood of the Cappadocian Fathers of the 4th century AD imbues a person only to God making it thus exceedingly difficult to subsequently establish a link of communication with the autonomous person of modernity . . . Thus, in the Byzantine society from the 4th to the 14th century the notion of the person (πρόσωπο) stood indistinguishable to that of the image or the mask. There was no notion of interior development since man found root in God, rather than inside of himself.[49]

It seems that we are back to "Greek (Dutch) disease" by an alternative route. The point is the same: there is a deeply ingrained structural backwardness that conditions cultural and individual existence in Modern Greece. The measure of this backwardness lies outside in a bigger world, which has progressed into a future that remains perpetually out of reach for those residing here in a deprived present. The Greek modern lifeworld is a wasteland of individual nihilism. Modern Greek interiority is a narcissistic self-same mirroring. The life of the subject is embedded within the life of the group.

In lieu of an endnote: holding firm to the no-man's land

Who are we and where are we going? I sometimes murmur to myself. My analyst, while recently accompanying me in the distress of yet another descent to my wasteland, asked me in her gentle and caring way: where is the progressive function? This was an allusion to the Jungian notion that the psyche has a teleological progressive momentum. In moments of extreme tension, if the opposites can be held, the notion goes, a transcendent third in the form of a symbol emerges to point to a progressive move of the psyche, which represents an individual solution to a hitherto intractable problem. A comforting idea surely, but from a certain point of view, that of rudimentary homes, it carries too much metaphysical baggage separated by a thousand-year-old schism of divergent sensibilities. As such, it is too reminiscent of foreign-imposed notions and dialectical ambitions to provide a meaningful response to what plagues the heart. "What if there is no progressive function?" I answer back with some nihilistic irony.

And (yet) a dream:[50]

> *I am sitting in my analyst's practice. She is lying on a couch ahead of me listening to my endless chattering. My speech had the quality of a continuous stream of thoughts. There is a streak of complaint in my voice. Something that one would associate with the description of a problem or a riddle that was insoluble. At one point, my analyst interrupts me to share a moment of insight: "Evangelos, this is* limb love,*" she says and I know immediately that she is right. The point, as I took it, is that this is never going to be solved in thought or in speech. Whatever I am trying to address is deeper and it is part of who I am; and this is a moment to pause and to accept. Then at 12:15 my analyst has to interrupt our session to help the analyst who is working next door, Liz* [our guide at a recent visit at the Vatican museum], *bring over a new analysand. Oddly, this would happen from the window with a contraption that looked like a winch* [associated in my thoughts with the contraption that brings a *deus ex machina* on stage in Greek tragedy]. *I remember waiting for her to return and recognizing from the window of her practice the view from a different window. It is the one I could see from the house of a close friend of my father, Dimitris T.* [whom I loved and admired for his intellect, humor, and compassion when I was a child], *at the island where we spent our summers in Greece.*

How I would like to return to a simpler era before this commercial one of commodified scenic views, where everything seems to be up for sale or, alternatively, an opportunity for profitable investment. This is how Greece is nowadays mostly imagined, both from outside and inside. Admittedly, we have come a long way from the search for the lost Arcadia to the search for the perfect selfie. How I would run to go back to the island before the tourists came. I would go back to the beach before the asphalt road was built to walk in bare feet on the pristine sand, marvel at the lilies growing in this barren soil, and then plunge into the sea. How I yearn to revisit the old (lost) house overlooking the youthful summer horizon under the blazing sun. To sit there on the terrace in late afternoon before two sublime white arches, I can never forget, losing myself gazing in a careless contemplation of the shapes carved by the northern wind on the boundless surface of the sea.

But there is nowhere to return to. Who we are, who I have become, past sediments of (historical) construction, by outside conditioning, by force, and by time, cannot be undone. A return to a simpler world or to a more authentic and pristine existence is no longer possible in an unmediated way. Limpingly I might learn to make small steps toward remembering and toward loving. No, this is not some *Amor Fati*, some reiteration of a Nietzschean bold concept about some great return, about fate, freedom, and heroic selfhood somehow leading to a more complete-man-to-arrive-in-the-future. Neither does it have anything to do with moving to more quaternal wholeness by developing a more complete (personal) God-Image. No, this is small, very small and perhaps not deep in that sense at all, as it firmly belongs to the realm of the devalued, the trivial, and the long forgotten. As importantly, this is as secular and as mundane as the forgotten mud of a nineteenth-century town called Athens.

This is about stepping down from all this artifice, all this artillery of words and concepts aiming to serve some insatiable, alas, desire for sovereignty, security, and power as knowledge or science or nation/selfhood, which is long overdue and, frankly, only an impediment to living. It is about learning how to inhabit rudimentary homes; about how to learn to live with Dutch disease, in permanent psychic debt, in a state of homelessness. It is about learning to be in the company of those who do not have access to coherent and intelligible narratives: the defeated, the forgotten, the aggressed, the overexposed, and the overpowered. This is about self-forgiveness and acceptance; it is about welcoming vulnerability, as my analysands – my people, as I hope to be theirs – teach me all the time. This is about self-mocking laughter finally bringing relief to a pompous and unsustainable somber existence. Perhaps, here at my wasteland, in a world or a self, left behind in permanent underdevelopment, hanging in limbo in a no-man's land – separating two epochs and two ways of being that seem impossible to ever reconcile – there might be something worthwhile to discover. Perhaps out of this nothingness something might grow: who knows what I might learn, if I could only hold firm to the un-knowing?

Notes

1 European Civil Protection and Humanitarian Aid Operations, European Commission, June 14, 2018. Available: http://ec.europa.eu/echo/files/aid/countries/factsheets/turkey_syrian_crisis_en.pdf.
2 *Ulysses' Gaze*, directed by Theo Angelopoulos, screenplay by Theo Angelopoulos, released on May 24, 1995. By permission of Theo Angelopoulos Heirs Association.
3 Nikos Kazantzakis, *Zorba the Greek*, New York: Simon and Schuster, 1952. The film of the same name was directed by Michael Cacoyannis who also wrote the screenplay. The film was released on December 17, 1964.
4 *Shirley Valentine*, directed by Lewis Gilbert, screenplay by Willy Russell, released on August 30, 1989.
5 See my chapter "The inner riddle of 'Greek Psychic Debt,'" in *Europe's Many Souls: Exploring Cultural Complexes and Identities*, ed. Joerg Rasche and Thomas Singer, New Orleans, LA: Spring Journal Books, 2016.
6 David Roessel, *In Byron's Shadow: Modern Greece in the English and American Imagination*, Oxford: Oxford University Press, 2002, p. 65.
7 Ibid., p. 74.
8 Ibid., p. 7.
9 Ibid.
10 Ibid., 15.

11 Ibid.

12 Benedict Anderson, *Imagined Communities*, London: Verso, 1991.

13 Ernest Gellner, *Nations and Nationalism*, New York: Cornell University Press, 1983, p. 34.

14 Ibid., p. 111.

15 Ibid., p. 57.

16 Roessel, *In Byron's Shadow*, p. 31.

17 Richard Clogg, *A Concise History of Greece*, Cambridge, UK: Cambridge University Press, 2013, p. 49.

18 *Habitus* is a term associated with the work of sociologist Pierre Bourdieu and is described by L. Wacquant in the *International Encyclopedia of Economic Sociology* (eds. J. Becket and Z. Milan, London: Routledge, 2005) as "the way society becomes deposited in persons in the form of lasting dispositions, or trained capacities and structured propensities to think, feel and act in determinant ways, which then guide them." See also www.powercube.net/other-forms-of-power/bourdieu-and-habitus.

19 Βερέμης Θ., Κολιόπουλος Γ., Η Σύγχρονη Συνέχεια, Αθήνα: Εκδόσεις Καστανιώτη, 2006, p. 135.

20 Ibid., p. 239.

21 Roessel, *In Byron's Shadow*, p. 218.

22 Ibid., pp. 221, 233.

23 Ibid., p. 234.

24 Quote from Rex Warner's *Views of Attica*; cited in Roessel, *In Byron's Shadow*, p. 254.

25 Quote from Henry Miller's *Colossus of Marousi*; cited in Roessel, *In Byron's Shadow*, p. 254.

26 Ibid.

27 Suzanne L. Marchand, *Down from Olympus: Archaeology and Philhellenism in Germany, 1750–1970*, Princeton, NJ: Princeton University Press, 1996.

28 Ibid., p. 9.

29 "[Bildung engendered] blending the rigorous individualism of Rousseau pedagogy with the republican aspirations of the humanist tradition. Sound formation of social morals dependent on individual self-transformative progress from natural immaturity to self-willed citizenship. Bildung celebrated the diverse talents and characters of individual humans; it promised the intellectual overcoming of anomie and the liberation of the individual for a mechanical and compartmentalized external world. One sided-ness in men was a terrible debility. Bildung sought to bind male graduates together in civic harmony and loyalty to the state." Ibid., pp. 28, 37.

30 Ibid., p. 81.

31 Friedrich Nietzsche, *The Birth of Tragedy Out of the Spirit of Music*, New York: Penguin Classics, 1994, Kindle Edition, Loc. 149.

32 Friedrich Schiller, *On the Aesthetic Education of Man*, New York: Dover Publications, 2004, p. 66.

33 Ibid.

34 C. G. Jung, "The structure of the psyche," *The Structure and Dynamics of the Psyche*, in *The Collected Works of C. G. Jung*, Vol. 8, London: Routledge & Kegan Paul Ltd, 1960, ¶283. Hereafter references to Jung's *Collected Works* will be reference by CW followed by volume number and paragraph number.

35 Ibid., ¶3.

36 Nietzsche, *The Birth of Tragedy out of the Spirit of Music*, Loc. 1979.

37 Ibid., Loc. 1996.

38 Barbara Stiegler, *Nietzsche et la critique de la Chair: Dionysos, Ariane, le Christ*, Paris: Presses Universitaires de France, 2011, Kindle Edition, Loc. 4878.

39 Ibid., Loc. 5087. Translation mine.

40 Nietzsche, *The Birth of Tragedy Out of the Spirit of Music*, Loc. 1280.

41 Ibid., Loc. 1284.

42 C. G. Jung, *The Structure and Dynamics of the Psyche*, CW 8, ¶342.

43 Ibid.

44 Ibid., ¶420.

45 I am reminded of Jacques Derrida: "After all, communio is a word for a military formation and a kissing cousin of the word 'munitions'; to have a communio is to be fortified
on all sides, to build a 'common' (com) 'defense' (munis), as when a wall is put up around
the city to keep the stranger or the foreigner out." John D. Caputo, *Deconstruction in a
Nutshell: A Conversation with Jacques Derrida*, New York: Fordham University Press, 1997,
pp. 107–108.
46 Χρήστος Γιανναράς, *Person and Eros*, Brookline, MA: Holy Cross Orthodox Press, 1987,
p. 273.
47 Ράμφος, Στέλιος, *Ο Καημός του Ενός*, Εκδόσεις Αρμός, Αθήνα, 2000.
48 Ibid., p. 143.
49 Ibid., p. 154. Translation mine.
50 Segments from the essay are drawn from Evangelos Tsempelis, "Evil, nothingness and
negativity in C. G. Jung's phenomenology: A comparative cross-disciplinary exploration,"
ISAPZurich Thesis, Spring 2017.

CLOSING

"The God Abandons Antony," C. P. Cavafy (1863–1933)

At midnight, when suddenly you hear
an invisible procession going by
with exquisite music, voices,
don't mourn your luck that's failing now,
work gone wrong, your plans
all proving deceptive – don't mourn them uselessly:
as one long prepared, and full of courage,
say goodbye to her, to Alexandria who is leaving.
Above all, don't fool yourself, don't say
it was a dream, your ears deceived you:
don't degrade yourself with empty hopes like these.
As one long prepared, and full of courage,
as is right for you who were given this kind of city,
go firmly to the window
and listen with deep emotion,
but not with the whining, the pleas of a coward:
listen – your final pleasure – to the voices,
to the exquisite music of that strange procession,
to say goodbye to her, to the Alexandria you are losing.[1]

Note

1 *Collected Poems* by Constantine Cavafy. Reproduced with permission of Princeton University Press in the format book via Copyright Clearance Center.

INDEX

Page numbers: figures given in *italics*; notes as: [page number] n [note number].

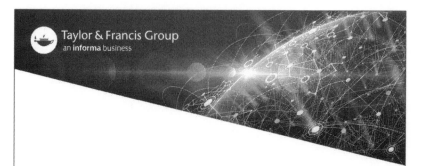

Printed in Great Britain
by Amazon

87056770R00140